Women, Religion and Feminism in Britain, 1750–1900

Women, Religion and Feminism in Britain, 1750–1900

Edited by
Sue Morgan
Head of the School of History
University College Chichester

First published 2002 by
PALGRAVE MACMILLAN
Houndmills, Basingstoke, Hampshire RG21 6XS and
175 Fifth Avenue, New York, N.Y. 10010
Companies and representatives throughout the world

PALGRAVE MACMILLAN is the global academic imprint of
the Palgrave Macmillan division of St. Martin's Press,
LLC and of Palgrave Macmillan Ltd.
Macmillan® is a registered trademark in the United States, United
Kingdom and other countries. Palgrave is a registered trademark in the
European Union and other countries.

ISBN 0–333–99307–1

This book is printed on paper suitable for recycling and made from fully
managed and sustained forest sources.

A catalogue record for this book is available from the British Library.

Library of Congress Cataloging-in-Publication Data

Women, religion, and feminism in Britain, 1750–1900 / edited by
Sue Morgan.
    p. cm.
Includes bibliographical references and index.
ISBN 0–333–99307–1
    1. Women and religion—England—History. 2. Women in
Christianity—England—History. 3. England—Church history—18th
century. 4. England—Church history—19th century. 5. England—
Religion. 6. Feminism—England—History. I. Morgan, Sue, 1957–
BR755 W65 2002
200′.82′0941—dc21   2002066329

10   9   8   7   6   5   4   3   2   1
11   10   09   08   07   06   05   04   03   02

Printed and bound in Great Britain by
Antony Rowe Ltd, Chippenham and Eastbourne

Contents

Acknowledgements

I would like to thank Carole Farnfield for her invaluable help and patience in the preparation of this typescript and the generous, constructive comments made by the external reader which did much to enhance the final text. I would also like to thank Keith Jenkins who, despite his own 'disobedient disposition' towards the historicization of the past, provided support and encouragement throughout. This book is for him with much love.

An earlier version of Chapter 4 appeared in *Nineteenth-Century Contexts*, 2001, Vol. 23, 241–64; the editor of that journal has kindly given permission to revise and reprint.

Notes on the Contributors

Kristin G. Doern completed her DPhil in History at the University of Sussex. Her thesis explored the relationship between feminism and leading temperance women in nineteenth-century England. She is Lecturer in Historical Studies at Bath Spa University College where she teaches modern British history from the late seventeenth century through to the beginning of the twentieth century. She is a contributor to the *New Dictionary of National Biography* and to *Alcohol and Temperance in Modern History: an International Encyclopedia* (both forthcoming).

Gulnar (Guli) Francis-Dehqani lived in Iran for the first 13 years of her life. After the Islamic Revolution she moved to England with her family and has, to date, been unable to return to Iran. Between 1989 and 1994 she worked for the BBC as Studio Manager at World Service Radio and Producer in the Religious Department of domestic radio. She was ordained in 1998 and completed her PhD at the University of Bristol in 1999. She currently lives and works in Richmond, Surrey with her husband Lee, two-year-old son Gabriel and pet labrador Comfort.

Joyce Goodman is Reader in the History of Education at King Alfred's College, Winchester. Her research interests include women, education and authority, professional identities, education and empire and the history of disability and education. She has published *Women, Educational Policy-Making and Administration in England: Authoritative Women Since 1800* (2000) and has two books forthcoming.

Camilla Leach is a postgraduate student at King Alfred's College, Winchester. She is researching Quaker women and education, 1790–1850. Her articles have appeared in *Faith and Freedom, Quaker Studies*, and the *History of Education Society Bulletin*.

Laura Lauer completed her PhD on Nonconformist churchwomen's organizations in England, *c*.1880–1920 in 1998 and is presently co-authoring a book on women's spirituality in the nineteenth century. She has taught at St Hilda's College, Oxford and at the University of Liverpool. Dr Lauer is currently taking a career break to look after her young son.

Helen Mathers is a Research Fellow of the History Department at Sheffield University. She has co-authored a history of the women's health services in Sheffield, *Born in Sheffield*, (2000) and is currently working on a history of Sheffield University. She has a longstanding ongoing research interest in Josephine Butler, particularly her religion and ideology, and has published and lectured widely on this theme.

Sue Morgan is Head of History at University College Chichester where she teaches modern cultural and gender history. She has published widely on women's history, religious history and feminist theology. Publications include *A Passion for Purity: Ellice Hopkins and the Politics of Gender in the late-Victorian Church* (1999), *Masculinity and Spirituality in Victorian Culture* (2000), co-edited with A. Bradstock, S. Gill and A. Hogan, and the forthcoming *Feminist and Postfeminist Histories: a Reader*, with Keith Jenkins.

Suzanne Rickard's doctoral research focused on women, writing, publishing and philanthropy in mid-nineteenth-century England. She is contributor to a number of scholarly reference works, including the *New Dictionary of National Biography* and the *Australian Dictionary of Biography*. In 1999–2000 she was C.H. Currey Memorial Fellow at the State Library of New South Wales in Sydney. Her most recent work is *George Barrington's Voyage to Botany Bay: Retelling a Convict's Travel Narrative of the 1790s* (2001).

Judith Rowbotham is Senior Lecturer in History at Nottingham Trent University. Recent publications include ' "Hear an Indian Sister's Plea": Reporting the Work of Brtish Women Missionaries *c.*1870–1914', *Women's Studies International Forum* Summer (1998); ' "Soldiers of Christ"? Images of Female Missionaries in the Late Nineteenth Century: Issues of Heroism and Martyrdom', *Gender and History* 12:1 (2000) and 'All Our Past Proclaims our Future: Popular Biography and Masculine Identity during the Golden Age 1850–1870', in I. Inkster *et* *al.* (eds) *The Golden Age: Essays in British Social and Economic History 1850–1870* (2000).

Anne Stott is an Associate Lecturer with the Open University and a sessional Lecturer at Birkbeck College, University of London. Since completing a PhD on Hannah More, she has written several articles about her. Her biography of More is to be published in 2002–03.

Martha Vicinus is the Eliza M. Mosher Distinguished University Professor of English, History and Women's Studies at the University of Michigan, Ann Arbor, USA. She has written extensively on Victorian women and the history of sexuality. She is the author of *Independent Women: Work and Community for Single Women, 1850–1920* (1985, reprinted 1994) and the forthcoming *Intimate Friends: Women Who Loved Women.*

Ruth Watts is Reader in the History of Education at the University of Birmingham. Her many publications on the history of gender and education include *Gender, Power and the Unitarians in England, 1760– 1860* (1998). Her most recent work has dealt with gender and imperialism, the cultural history of women and science and the effects of class, ethnicity and gender on students in twentieth-century British education.

Linda Wilson is a part-time lecturer in the School of Theology and Religious Studies at the University of Gloucestershire. She also tutors various correspondence courses in church history. Her published works include 'Nonconformist Obituaries: How Stereotyped was their View of Women?' in A. Hogan and A. Bradstock (eds) *Women of Faith in Victorian Culture* (1998) and *Constrained by Zeal: Female Spirituality amongst Nonconformists* (2000).

Sheila Wright teaches in the Centre for Continuing Education at the University of York. Her publications include *Friends in York: the Dynamics of Quaker Revival, 1780–1860* (1995). Her current research interests include women in York in the late nineteenth century. She is a member of the international review panel for the journal *Quaker Studies.*

Introduction. Women, Religion and Feminism: Past, Present and Future Perspectives

Sue Morgan

This collection of essays deals with the interaction between religious belief and feminist consciousness, two of the most formative intellectual and discursive influences upon nineteenth-century women. Taking as its central concern the impact of Christianity upon the lives and strategies of women activists, this book addresses a general historiographical lacuna on the relationship between religion and gender and asks in particular how religious faith vindicated both private and public forms of selfhood for women.

Given the highly gendered understanding of religiosity during this period, the absence of any sustained historical analysis of women's religious and feminist convictions is striking. Just as church historians have shown little interest in gender issues until comparatively recently, so the feminist historical challenge has not yet extended to a serious evaluation of the role and dimension of religion in women's lives.[1] Yet nineteenth-century religious teaching exercised considerable authority in defining the ideological parameters of femininity and masculinity through the mass reception of sermons, educational tracts and prescriptive literature, and much ecclesiastical ink was poured forth on delineating modes of behaviour appropriate to either sex, of which William Wilberforce's classic manifesto, *A Practical View of the Prevailing System of Professed Christians* (1797) was but just one. The 'feminization of piety' was, arguably, another significant numerical and conceptual feature of Victorian devotion in which women constituted the majority of church and chapel congregations and the

1

association of the female sphere with all things moral and spiritual emerged as axiomatic in dominant evangelical constructions of middle-class domesticity.[2]

Bearing in mind the strategic relationship posited by contemporaries between religion and gender, then, and mindful of Gail Malmgreen's caution that 'if feminist historians ignore religion . . . we will have forfeited our understanding of the mental universe of the no doubt substantial majority of women who were believers',[3] this volume explores how, in a variety of cultural and denominational contexts, women negotiated the boundaries between personal religious beliefs, moral attitudes and social action. Relative to the extant scholarship, this is an important text, which offers a pioneering set of perspectives in a crucial yet under-researched field. By way of introduction, I first briefly explore the complexities of the historical dynamics of religion and feminism. Secondly, issues of immediate interest raised by the chapters are examined. Finally, I discuss the pertinence of key themes in the book to broader debates and approaches in women's history.

Religion and feminism: defining relations

The nineteenth century witnessed the parallel development of the organized women's movement and a massive expansion of female religious activity. The growth of voluntary female involvement in church life through educational work and organized philanthropy, and the emergence of full-time roles for women in domestic evangelism, the deaconness movement, sisterhoods and missionary work, provided an unprecedented array of opportunities, such that it has been suggested that 'evangelical religion was more important than feminism in enlarging women's sphere of action during the nineteenth century'.[4] The consequences of religious commitment for women have always proved paradoxical, however. Historically, the Christian faith has been a powerful exponent of sexual inequality while simultaneously declaring the equality of souls before God, irrespective of gender. The following essays situate the contradictory nature of the Christian message for the female subject at the heart of their analyses, fully cognizant of the tensions involved in the rehabilitation of such seemingly conservative, pious and thoroughly socialized women.

Historians of women have become increasingly aware of the diversity of political approaches and moral perspectives to be found under the banner of 'feminist consciousness', although attempts to identify the religious roots of feminism have proved somewhat equivocal. The most favourable assessments forthcoming have been that of the Quaker and Unitarian traditions, whose radical, progressive outlook on social and political issues provided an important intellectual impetus and leadership resource for British feminism. More problematic has been the attempt to establish causal links between evangelicalism and feminism. Initial analyses concluded that the effect of the evangelical movement on feminism was ultimately a conservatizing one, where the Christian exaltation of female moral superiority served to limit the radical potential of much subsequent feminist vision. Involvement in philanthropic enterprises it was argued, did not necessarily lead to the disputation of traditional gender roles and often proved diversionary from more explicitly feminist campaigns.[5]

More recently, scholars such as Olive Banks and Philippa Levine have noted the wide variety of religious beliefs – from freethinkers to Roman Catholics – that retained a high profile amongst the women's movement well into the twentieth century. Even if the institutional history of religion and the history of feminism do not connect up that closely, religious questions were still of central importance to Victorian women activists.[6] In particular, there has been greater awareness by historians of the enormous strategic significance of evangelical religion which brought into selected feminist campaigns those women who, in their orthodox espousal of sexual difference, were vociferous advocates of female moral and educational welfare.

Clearly, to include many of the women mentioned in this book under the 'name' of 'feminism' is to work with a far broader understanding of the term than that normally indicated by scholars. Indeed, it is unlikely that many of them would have endorsed the types of legal and economic reforms advocated by mainstream feminists, for it was invariably sexual difference not sexual equality, women's duties not women's rights, that formed the mainstay of religious women's visions of a new social and moral order. That said, there are a number of common gendered concerns within their writings and activism, such as an acute awareness of the subordinated condition of women, the recognition that this condition was not biologically but societally determined, the development of a sense of sisterhood and the proffering of alternative visions of the future that compels some collective or generic expression – and it is difficult to think of a more convenient shorthand term or heuristic device for this than 'feminist'.[7]

It is worth noting that in examining the historical relationship between women, religion and feminism the emphasis of this book is more about the challenges that taking religion seriously may pose to our existing historical understandings of feminism than it is about establishing a 'correct' set of feminist credentials for a diverse group of Christian women. The essays contained here press home the fluidity and expansiveness of what it meant to be 'woman-centred' in the nineteenth century. At times religious women found themselves at the centre of a feminist storm, in other moments they expressed convictions and ideas which would have located them on the very margins of the feminist enterprise. Yet it is precisely these tensions – where involvement in social action sometimes did, sometimes didn't, shade off into feminist areas – that makes them such an interesting *cadre* of women to explore, particularly if, with Denise Riley, we see the history of feminism as the systematic contestation of what it meant to be a woman and the very instability of that category.[8] Nor is there total unanimity between the authors on either the use of, or the appropriateness of, the designation 'feminist' – a lack of consensus which, despite the book's title, seemed a fitting reflection of the range of positions and differences of opinion that have invariably formed part and parcel of the history of feminism itself.

Introduction to the chapters

The essays in this book have been grouped into four general themes which constitute Parts I–IV: 'female education and moral reform', 'sexuality and female friendships', 'women writers with causes' and 'independent women missionaries'. Together they provide a multi-denominational approach, with a particularly strong coverage of Nonconformity. As discrete studies, each author draws upon a diverse range of source material, whether to provide new readings of more familiar figures such as Hannah More and Josephine Butler, or to bring to light lesser known figures such as Marianne Farningham or Emmeline Stuart, not least because use of the biographical genre to explore the interior reflection of what it might have meant to be female and religious in a given historical context has proved particularly effective in theorizing the nuances between faith and feminism.[9]

Part I then concentrates on education, a major vehicle through which nineteenth-century religious women could seek to achieve social, moral and political transformation, particularly the establishment of a sober, rational education for women that might better equip them for the vital responsibilities of motherhood and citizenship. Anne Stott examines the religious and educational views of the celebrated evangelical reformer Hannah More (1745–1833) whose political and moral conservatism engaged her in a wholesale condemnation of fashionable society with its 'cheap and indolent Christianity'. More proffered an inclusivist educational agenda which extended from the daughters of the upper middle classes to those of the working poor. Concerned to distance herself from the language of women's rights, More's antagonism towards the then current triviality of female education ironically echoed the writings of her radical contemporary, Mary Wollstonecraft. But if More is a good example of the potentially subversive implications of a conservative political and religious position, then Ruth Watts' consideration in Chapter 2 of the progressive pedagogical values of Unitarianism indicates that the reverse was also possible. A liberal milieu of social and educational egalitarianism meant that, throughout the century, Unitarian women were particularly receptive to feminist campaigns. Yet in a culture which still stigmatized the Unitarian faith as 'heretical', the desire for respectability could prove a hindrance to certain forms of female activism. Watts illustrates the dominance of class and gender proprieties in the lives of four Unitarian women, concluding that radical religious affiliation for women was both a source of individual inspiration and a social disadvantage. In the final chapter of this section on education and moral reform, Joyce Goodman and Camilla Leach analyse the international dimensions of female education through Quaker women's involvement in the British and Foreign School Society Ladies Committee. Quaker women developed extensive educational networks around the world as part of their ministerial duties and claimed for themselves an authoritative role in the education of non-western women, but as Goodman and Leach illustrate, the publications and reports of itinerant Quaker pedagogues revealed many of the ambiguities of imperial power for British Quakers in their infantilizing depictions of indigenous peoples.

Turning to 'sexuality and female friendships', John Maynard wisely commented in his *Victorian Discourses of Sexuality and Religion* (1993) that 'sexual discussion is anything but free from religious issues and traces'[10] and in Part II both Martha Vicinus and Sheila Wright demonstrate just how permeable the boundaries between spirituality and sensuality could be. Vicinus looks at how religious commitment could vindicate sexual subjectivity, focusing on the connections between homoerotic desire and spiritual fulfilment in the life of Mary Benson (1842–1916), wife of the Archbishop of Canterbury. Vicinus offers a pioneering analysis of the way in which lesbian passion could reinforce rather than undermine the stability of that most traditional of Victorian religious institutions – marriage. She argues that religious and sexual solace found in the arms of other pious women was Benson's resolution to a loss of faith in the patriarchal authority of her husband, Edward, and suggests that sexual radicalism might also produce more innovative forms of spiritual and theological expression. Sheila Wright also examines female friendships, this time in the late eighteenth and early nineteenth-century networks of travelling Quaker ministers. Wright highlights the supportive and intimate nature of these friendships in a world of unequal relations with men, public ridicule and physical hardship, but unlike Vicinus defines them in purely spiritual and non-somatic terms, taking as her model the definition of 'spiritual friendship' offered by Aelred of Rievaulx some six centuries earlier. Such friendships provided an additional emotional dimension to women's lives argues Wright, but were not necessarily born out of unsatisfactory marital relations.

In the section on 'women writers with causes', attention is initially drawn to the didactic moral literary genre, a celebrated nineteenth-century evangelical female tradition which included such luminaries as Hannah More and Elizabeth Gaskell. The group of women examined here used their pens as a platform upon which to express and 'preach' their particular causes; motivated and bolstered by religious belief, they articulated a notably female vision of a more perfect and equitable society. Linda Wilson's chapter provides the first sustained analysis of the popular evangelical journalist and poet Marianne Farningham (1834–1909), whose writings were known in thousands of Nonconformist homes. Farningham wrote at length on the roles and responsibilities of women, encouraging her female audience to emulate the lives of worthy heroines such as Elizabeth Fry and Grace

Darling. After meeting with the influential feminist campaigner Frances Power Cobbe, Farningham wrote in favour of women's property rights, tertiary education and the female franchise, but always in such a way that women's traditional domestic and maternal roles remained uncompromised. For many Victorian women writers, the production of popular religious novels was neither a genteel nor a 'handmaidenly' task. Rather, as Suzanne Rickard makes clear in her discussion of the successful but little-known authors Hesba Stretton (1832–1911) and Felicia Skene (1821–99), religiously-inspired fiction was frequently underpinned by considerable philanthropic involvement and painstaking social investigation. Like Farningham, both Stretton and Skene were single and financially independent, although Stretton was denominationally more eclectic than the High Church aristocratic Skene. Stretton was exercised by the problems of juvenile crime and prostitution. Skene, like her renowned contemporary Josephine Butler, was also committed to exposing the inequities of the sexual double standard. Butler, of course, is best known for her tireless campaigning against the Contagious Diseases Acts. Her Christian motivation, the subject of Helen Mathers' research, is less well-known, but it is evident from Butler's own writings that she was a deeply pious woman with an ardent private spiritual life. Against the reluctance of earlier feminist historical readings to attribute much credence to Butler's religious convictions, and drawing upon a wealth of source material including her *Spiritual Diaries, Autobiographical Memoir* and 'Private Thoughts' journal, Mathers explores the nature of Butler's evangelical faith and illustrates the sheer inseparability of her religion and her feminist political persuasions. In the final chapter of this Part, Kristin Doern shows how the temperance writer and reformer Clara Lucas Balfour (1808–78) championed both the causes of women and total abstinence simultaneously. Balfour's Baptist faith provided the overarching context for her pioneering activity with the British Women's Temperance Association. Doern argues that religious motivation was also critical in the evolution of Balfour's writing career and her brand of 'separate spheres feminism', which looked to the bible and other spiritual foremothers for examples of female moral heroism.

By the beginning of the twentieth century, women outnumbered men as workers in the British Foreign Missionary Movement, itself one of the most significant organizational developments in modern

British Protestant Christianity. In Part IV, Judith Rowbotham's essay poses the question as to what extent this phenomenon reflected a shift in ecclesiastical attitudes towards women's competence and their capacity for inclusion in the hierarchy of the Church of England. The establishment of a number of Ladies Societies ensured a considerable degree of practical independence in the daily routine of women workers, but, as Rowbotham points out, this principle of separatism, while gaining greater public visibility for women, ultimately served to maintain their status as auxiliary lay workers. Despite women's high profile work in foreign missions, the Anglican hierarchy regarded such labours as temporary and exceptional. Paradoxically, the successful opening-up of the mission-field to women made it more difficult for them to win parity of rights and esteem in organized religion in Britain.

Guli Francis-Dehqani considers the role of women's medical work within the Iranian missionary strategy and the tensions between religious faith and professional demands that surfaced in the career of Dr Emmeline Stuart (1866–1934). As one of the earliest women to train as a doctor at a British university, Stuart was attracted to the mission-field when domestic opportunities for women doctors were few. Her status and skill as a physician certainly afforded her greater freedom than most female missionaries, but Stuart always regarded her senior medical role as a direct extension of women's 'natural' maternal and nurturing qualities. Stuart is presented by Francis-Dehqani, then, as a woman whose attitudes demonstrated the persistence of Victorian norms of femininity well into the twentieth century, but whose own life and career in many ways belied her rhetoric of sacrifice and service.

Like Rowbotham, the historical back-drop for Laura Lauer's chapter is the emergence of the missionary career for single women – in this case, Baptist women called to the mid-Victorian Zenana Mission in India. With its sole purpose that of the conversion of Indian women to Christianity, female missionaries presented themselves through a finely honed rhetoric of separatism as the culturally privileged saviours of their 'heathen' sisters. For Baptist women, missionary work served to carve out a public space of activity within a denomination largely unwilling to recognize any form of female authority. Lauer's chapter thus provides us with a more positive reading of the woman-to-woman mission than usual: not only were female missionaries important mediators of Indian culture to a domestic audience, but the Baptist Zenana Mission provided an unparalleled opportunity for Nonconformist women to enter into high-status evangelism – which may in turn have prompted the home churches to reconsider women's abilities.

The role of religion in women's history: rethinking the separation of the spheres

Turning to the final section of this introduction, what I now want to highlight is a number of the major themes and approaches raised by the essays and locate them in a wider historiographical framework of women's history. In so doing I hope to show the way in which a greater appreciation of the significance of religion in women's lives can expand and refine our current readings of the history of women and feminism.

To begin with, then, this book demonstrates how serious consideration of religious beliefs might refine that most dominant conceptual framework of women's history – the separation of the spheres. In fact religion has always played a central part in historians' constructions of the demarcated, gendered realms of private and public activity. Many early references to religion, for example, depicted the feminization of piety as the root of women's domestic 'incarceration' and an entirely disempowering process. Barbara Welter's article 'The Cult of True Womanhood' (1966) was the first to identify the discursive propagation of a subordinated feminine stereotype whose cardinal tenets – domesticity, piety, purity and submissiveness – were sanctioned by patriarchal Christian values.[11] Twenty years later, Leonore Davidoff and Catherine Hall's seminal text, *Family Fortunes* (1987), showed how evangelical discourse converged with the formation of early-Victorian middle-class identity to produce the pious wife and mother, who as guardian of the spiritual welfare of the home found herself by definition excluded from the corruptability of worldly (male) pursuits. As Barbara Taylor was to conclude, the association of the feminine sphere with that of religion and the church flattered to deceive:

> Once God had settled into the parlour, mammon had free range in public life – and the exclusion of women from virtually all areas of

public existence guaranteed that this tidy division was main-tained. An ideal of femininity which combined holy love with social subordination served to suppress women in an elision of spiritual power with social impotence.[12]

The gendered public/private dichotomy of the separate spheres has become increasingly problematic as an interpretative tool in recent years, however, and is regarded now by many as an insufficiently nuanced framework. As evidenced by this collection of essays, treat-ments of it are now often directed towards demonstrating the per-meability and flexibility of spatial boundaries, not just for women but for men as well. As Amanda Vickery has perceptively commented, historians should never confuse prescriptive ideology with actual practice, for '[w]omen, like men were evidently capable of professing one thing and performing quite another'.[13] Religion, seen as so significant in the 'privatization' and curtailment of women's lives, is thus of critical interest in the reconsideration of the separate spheres framework. Following Vickery's argument that in the light of so much research demonstrating the spirited, capable and overtly public activity of women, it made more sense to argue not for the diminution of the female public role during this period but its expan-sion: it is now surely possible to argue for a feminization of religion in similarly positive terms? Rather than holding religion culpable for the creation of the meek and dutiful female, therefore, institutional forms of Christianity arguably offered unprecedented opportunities for the public profile of women in the burgeoning of voluntary associations and charitable campaigning.[14]

The notion of an autonomous female social space that afforded women the chance to exercise real historical agency and power, where religious affiliation was less a source of oppression and more a vehicle for female autonomy and group solidarity, was first mooted by historians of women's culture many years ago. According to Car-roll Smith-Rosenberg's celebrated article, 'The Female World of Love and Ritual' (1975), the cultural division of female and male spheres spawned a rich and supportive female world, encircled by the social institutions of family, neighbourhood and church.[15] As Ruth Watts and Sheila Wright argue in their essays here, religious affiliation offered women ample opportunities for sororial networks through lives bound by shared religious practices in close-knit communities which provided men and women with a complete life-style of emotional, spiritual and physical needs. Common religious values aided female networks not only in everyday matters such as fund-raising and charity work, but, as Wright shows, throughout more perilous events such as the constant travelling, hostility and religious persecution that were part of Quaker women's ministerial duties.

Nowhere was the homosocial bonding of women's culture more emphatically displayed perhaps than in the emergence of religious sisterhoods and the deaconness communities of the mid-nineteenth century, and historians like Martha Vicinus and Susan Mumm have paid particular attention to the formation of these congregations as evidence of the communal power of women.[16] Separatist forms of organization in varying degrees were built into most denominational structures, as the existence of numerous Ladies Committees and Women's Meetings indicates. Many Christian women were wary of mixed societies as not only improprietous but as a threat to their own autonomy and influence. Thus the late-Victorian High Church spinster and purity activist, Ellice Hopkins, viewed the discrete female culture of moral reform as the most positive and effective way for churchwomen to successfully manoeuvre for power within the wider ecclesiastical community.[17] In this book, Laura Lauer and Judith Rowbotham examine the advantages and disadvantages of a separatist religious discourse and its implications for women's religious authority. In the face of limited denominational roles, Lauer contends that the all-women Baptist Zenana Mission provided a unique moment of vindication for the female churchworker overseas, but as Rowbotham points out, the negative side effects of separatist rhetoric were that it continued to sideline women from the central power bases of ecclesiastical authority.

Whatever the complex realities of the organizational autonomy of all-female institutions, we can see in the focus on a separatist women's culture an articulation of the more radical potential of religion for women and its culturally subversive influence. According to Mumm, women-centred communities were often 'an avenue for successful revolt against male authority and conventional morality'.[18] Martha Vicinus's essay on lesbian passion illustrates in striking form the type of radical sexual morality that could arise out of a female homosocial religious culture. The cultural and emotional significance of intimate, long-term attachments between nineteenth-century women has already been well documented.[19] As Vicinus and Wright show, these relationships were characterized by the sharing of personal confidences, spiritual anxieties and secret desires. Their intensity is beyond doubt, their longevity remarkable and because of dominant constructions of passive female sexuality, such friendships constituted a source of neither cultural nor social disapproval. These two chapters exemplify the diversity of approaches and interpretations surrounding women's religious and emotional vocabulary that is highly productive for wider considerations of religion and sexuality; not least it is clear that in strengthening their friendships with each other, single and married women 'minimised their heterosexuality'.[20] But *contra* Vicinus, Wright argues that it is the spiritual, non-somatic dimension of women's friendships that rendered them so powerful a phenomenon; to define such friendships in a sexualized fashion is therefore inappropriate. If spirituality transcends sexuality for Wright, however, then for Vicinus the relationship, and therefore the discourse, is a far more interconnected one, demanding a more open and fluid understanding of women's multiple relationships with dominant heterosexual society. Intimate friendships or lesbian-like behaviour could form part of a heterosexual marriage and childbearing existence – thus Minnie Benson regarded the purity of her love for Lucy Tait as neither adulterous nor unfaithful to her husband Edward.

The separate spheres was a quintessentially nineteenth-century metaphor which emerged as much from female writings as from male texts. Closer analysis of women's religious discourse can therefore help us to unpack their negotiation of private and public identities, and examine their various strategies of subversion of the dominant ideas of the day. For Joan Scott, women's historical discourse has always been positioned paradoxically. On the one hand, women have accepted and worked within authoritative definitions of gender; on the other they have resisted them.[21] The contradictory nature of women's discourse is particularly manifest in religious feminist expression, for as Anne Stott and Linda Wilson show in their essays on Hannah More and Marianne Farningham, it derived from an evangelical theology that sought to maintain existing social hierarchies while empowering women to realize their full spiritual potential.

One of the most prevalent themes in this book is the way in which women subverted the traditional patriarchal language of religion and piety into a political arsenal for the self-advancement of themselves and their own sex. Here the hegemonic notion of women's 'natural' disposition towards religion constituted a powerful rationale for the expansion of their domestic role as spiritual custodians into more public arenas of activity. Ongoing controversy over female participation in the public sphere, however, has meant that the effective mobilization of women into philanthropy, missionary work or temperance, and so on, required a highly convincing and persuasive rhetoric. Only by appropriating dominant ideologies of femininity – female domestic sovereignty, motherhood, women's moral superiority and the greater compassion of the female sex – did women activists successfully allay their co-worker's fears as to the impropriety of public roles for women while counteracting male opposition at the same time. As Kristin Doern highlights in her account of Balfour's 'separate spheres feminism', religious language was sufficiently malleable to allow women to create meaningful forms of political and public involvement without compromising their feminine identities: thus the orthodox Christian emphasis on feminine self-sacrifice was transformed into a powerful claim for the regenerative mission of women.

Critically, women's self-designated role as saviours of humanity was sanctioned by charismatic authority and underpinned by the reconstruction of a historical tradition of feminist biblical activism. Charismatic authority, or divine calling from God, was an irrefutable and unquestionable source of power for women which enabled them to circumvent patriarchal ecclesiastical conventions in all sorts of ways. This authority could take the form of the Quaker 'inner light' doctrine, or the Christocentric evangelicalism of Josephine Butler which, as Helen Mathers shows, convicted Butler of her right as an individual and a woman to stand before God, and empowered her to trust her own judgements above those of men. A feminist theologian before the letter, Butler regarded Christ's message to women as one of radical liberation, was critical of many aspects of the churches' self-serving mechanisms to uphold male privilege and, like Clara Balfour, trawled the scriptures for emulatory models of female leadership and heroism.

One of the most powerful reworkings of a dominant religious symbol of femininity was that of motherhood which had reached cultic proportions in the nineteenth century as the most exalted symbol of femaleness. In 1839, Sarah Lewis's popular domestic hand-book, *Woman's Mission*, described maternal love as 'the only truly unselfish feeling that existed on this earth',[22] and scholarship has shown that the duties of dedicated maternity were endowed by Vic-torian writers with a range of social, cultural and political meanings far beyond its biological state. For single women, active spiritual leadership provided a successful reworking of the negative connota-tions of redundancy and, as Eileen Yeo has argued, women philan-thropists such as Mary Carpenter rationalized the rhetoric of maternity and ennobled their own celibate status by introducing a new icon: that of 'a virgin mother engaged in self-sacrificing work with the poor and needy'.[23] Suzanne Rickard's essay in this collection depicts the independent Hesba Stretton as working with just such an enlarged, redefined vision of social or spiritual motherhood. While she regarded the institution of marriage as economically exploitative of women, she expressed her maternal instincts through visiting orphanages and campaigning on behalf of legislative protection for children. Industrial schools, rescue homes and workhouses all offered single women the opportunity to create alternative families and, as Carpenter put it, be 'mothers in heart, though not by God's gift on earth'.[24]

Whether biological or social mothers, devout women clearly saw their birthing of a new moral order as an act of such profound moral and political significance that it imitated the redemptive work of Christ. Women's spiritual and theological creativity sometimes trans-lated this analogy into a vision of a female messianic figure or a feminized Christ. Probably the most celebrated example of an early nineteenth-century self-appointed female messiah was Joanna South-cott (1750–1814).[25] Later in the century, heterodox philosophical systems such as that proffered by the theosophist Frances Swiney also argued for the divine status of the female intermediary.[26] Within the mainstream Christian tradition, Florence Nightingale's *Cassandra* (1861) and the devotional prose of Christina Rossetti, compared the spiritual superiority of women with the figure of Christ.[27] In this volume, Vicinus gives us a tantalizing glimpse of Minnie Benson's vision of a gender-inclusive Godhead, but nineteenth-century women's literary and theological expression is a topic that merits far more exploration if religion is not to be reduced to a simple, social determinant.

Yeo has commented that 'however ingeniously women remade dominant discourses... they were sometimes insensitive to the way in which their very formulations... helped to sharpen social differences between women',[28] and one particular area of discursive tension in Christian feminist writings was the conviction of racial and class-based subordinations. The essays by Francis-Dehqani and Goodman and Leach, for example, highlight the way in which female missionaries and ministers overseas frequently constructed other social groupings of women as morally degenerate and childlike, in order to underscore the civilizing mantle of their own work. All three authors seek to qualify the religious imperialist sentiment of their subjects, however, arguing that prioritizing the indigenous female condition as of supreme political and national significance went some way to mitigating these colonial attitudes.[29] Nevertheless, we need only think of the resocialization of British working-class girls throughout the period via penitentiaries or industrial schools and the accompanying moral justifications, to recognize that whether through the languages of ethnicity or class there were many different meanings of 'woman' operating in tandem on the part of religious women reformers.

There is now a need to generate new theoretical concepts beyond that of the separate spheres, perhaps as Robert Shoemaker and Mary Vincent have suggested, not so much along the boundaries of public and private, but according to type of activity, where 'women were concerned at home and abroad with issues of maternity, morality, religiosity and philanthropy, while men dominated "high" politics, institutional management and most forms of paid employment which did not involve domestic skills'.[30] This type of categorization could help to prevent any mechanistic usage of the separation of the spheres, for women's religious activity certainly could and did occur in both private and public realms. Religion had the capacity to cross fixed spatial boundaries because it was experienced as a private, personal source of empowerment which might inspire women to move into public and political areas of life. Thus, any dichotomous polarization of private and public fails to explain adequately the convergence of the spiritual and the social that is so prevalent in these women's thought. As mentioned earlier, the primary force that inspired and legitimated the personal and public lifestyle of every woman in this book was charismatic authority. As a result, religious women frequently exhibited a lack of distinction between the private and the public in their occupation of what Sheila Wright has described as a third sphere, a space which was sometimes shared, sometimes not, with men. Linda Wilson shows how by depicting women's life choices, private and public, as an act of obedience to God and as all part of one mission-field, Marianne Farningham was able to suggest to her vast female audience the appropriateness of being 'singular' in mind and action. In the light of this frequent convergence of the spiritual and the social, then, any dualistic understanding of the separate spheres completely misses the mark.

Efforts are now abroad to refine what we understand by public space. Anne Summers has made a useful distinction between 'public' and 'civil' spheres in which the latter might represent the more acceptable type of religious and charitable work undertaken by women such as fund-raising or district-visiting – a sort of 'home-from-home' – but where 'public' work and activity could mean any type of secular organization or institution, including those financially supported by the state, or multi-denominational activities where 'neither welcome nor acceptance could be guaranteed'.[31] Similarly, Jane Rendall has recently commented that nowadays 'a single version of the public sphere is insufficient'.[32] No area of women's history illustrates this point better than religious activity. For what are we to make of the travelling ministries of Quaker women and missionaries and educational work carried out overseas, or women's popular religious fiction which sold to huge audiences? And how are we to 'categorize' it? If, like Marianne Farningham, religious and secular life in its entirety was regarded as part of God's kingdom, with oneself as a dutiful labourer in that kingdom, then there was no area of life from which women could be excluded. Whether through more detailed analysis of homosocial female spaces or the inter-relation between religion and sexuality; whether through closer attention to the role of Christian discourse in constructions of gender, class and ethnicity or women's own theological writings, religion has already been firmly harnessed in the service of the separate spheres ideology, and it seems now only appropriate that the religious dimension of women's lives should contribute to its dissipation.

Notes

1 See Sue Morgan, *A Passion for Purity: Ellice Hopkins and the Politics of Gender in the late-Victorian Church* (Bristol: Bristol University Press, 1999) for a fuller discussion of the historiography of religion in the writings of women's history. For a recent example of the emerging interest in gender by ecclesiastical historians see R. Swanson (ed.) *Gender and the Christian Religion. Studies in Church History*, 34 (London: Boydell and Brewer, 1998). See also the special issue of *Women's History Review*, 'Between rationality and revelation: women, faith and public roles in the nineteenth and twentieth centuries', vol. 7, no. 2 (1998) for a useful consideration of religion and gender.

2 See J.S. Reed, ' "A Female Movement": the feminization of Anglo-Catholicism', *Anglican and Episcopal History*, vol. 57 (1988), pp. 199–238. American treatments of the feminization of piety include Ann Douglas, *The Feminization of American Culture* (New York: New Avon Books, 1977) and Barbara Welter, 'The Feminization of American Religion, 1800–1860', in Mary Hartmann and Lois Banner (eds) *Clio's Consciousness Raised: New Perspectives on the History of Women* (New York: Harper and Row, 1974). For a recent and stimulating although not unproblematic treatment of the 'feminization of piety' as part of the secularization narrative, see Callum Brown, *The Death of Christian Britain* (London: Routledge, 2001).

3 Gail Malmgreen (ed.) *Religion in the Lives of Englishwomen 1760–1930* (London: Croom Helm, 1986), p. 3.

4 David Hempton and Myrtle Hill, 'Born to Serve: Women and Evangelical Religion', in Alan Hayes and Diane Urquhart (eds) *The Irish Women's History Reader* (London: Routledge, 2001), p. 119.

5 See Olive Banks, *Faces of Feminism: a Study of Feminism as a Social Movement* (Oxford: Blackwell, 1993) and Jane Rendall *The Origins of Modern Feminism: Women in Britain, France and the United States 1780–1860* (Basingstoke: Macmillan, 1985).

6 See Barbara Caine's introduction to *Victorian Feminists* (Oxford: Oxford University Press, 1992) pp. 1–17, Olive Banks, *Becoming a Feminist: the Social Origins of 'First Wave' Feminism* (Sussex: Wheatsheaf Books, 1986) and Philippa Levine, *Feminist Lives in Victorian Britain* (Oxford: Blackwell, 1990) for helpful discussions of all of these issues.

7 These particular collective concerns are among those listed by Gerda Lerner as part of her five-part definition of feminist consciousness in *The Creation of Feminist Consciousness from the Middle Ages to Eighteen Seventy* (Oxford: Oxford University Press, 1993), p. 274.

8 Denise Riley, 'Am I That Name?' *Feminism and the Category of 'Women' in History* (London: Macmillan, 1988).

9 Studies such as Barbara Caine's *Victorian Feminists* and, more recently, Anne Summers' *Female Lives, Moral States* (Newbury: Threshold Press, 2000) ably demonstrate the way in which biography can illuminate the intricacies of how women experienced their domestic and social worlds, what strategies

of self-emancipation they employed and at what cost to themselves. By studying the lives of individual women of faith it is possible to give texture to and concretize a broader account of female religious existence which avoids the generalities of institutional religious histories. See also Elaine Showalter, 'Florence Nightingale's Feminist Complaint: Women, Religion and Suggestions for Thought', *Signs*, vol. 6, no. 3 (1981), pp. 395–412 and Carol Bauer, 'The role of religion in the creation of a philosophy of feminism: the case of Frances Power Cobbe', *Anima*, vol. 10, no. 1 (1983), pp. 60–70.

10 John Maynard, *Victorian Discourses on Sexuality and Religion* (Cambridge: Cambridge University Press, 1993), p. 3.

11 Barbara Welter, 'The Cult of True Womanhood: 1820–60', *American Quarterly*, vol. 18, no. 2 (1966), pp. 151–74.

12 Barbara Taylor, *Eve and the New Jerusalem: Socialism and Feminism in the Nineteenth Century* (London: Virago, 1983), p. 127.

13 Amanda Vickery, 'Golden Age to Separate Spheres? A Review of the Categories and Chronology of English Women's History', *Historical Journal*, 36 (1993), pp. 383–414.

14 Ibid., p. 395.

15 Carroll Smith-Rosenberg, 'The Female World of Love and Ritual. Relations between Women in Nineteenth-Century America', *Signs* vol. 1, no. 1 (1975), pp. 1–29.

16 Martha Vicinus, 'Church Communities: Sisterhoods and Deaconnesses' Houses', in *Independent Women: Work and Community for Single Women 1850–1920* (London: Virago, 1985), pp. 46–84 and Susan Mumm, *Stolen Daughters, Virgin Mothers: Anglican Sisterhoods in Victorian Britain* (London: Leicester University Press, 1999).

17 Sue Morgan, 'Faith, Sex and Purity: the Religio-Feminist Theory of Ellice Hopkins', *Women's History Review*, vol. 9, no.1 (2000), pp. 13–34.

18 Mumm, *Stolen Daughters, Virgin Mothers* op. cit., p. x.

19 Key texts in British lesbian historiography include Lilian Faderman, *Surpassing the Love of Men. Romantic Friendships and Love between Women from the Renaissance to the Present* (London: Women's Press, 1985); Sheila Jeffreys, *The Spinster and Her Enemies. Feminism and Sexuality, 1880–1930* (London: Pandora Press, 1985); Lesbian History Group (eds) *Not a Passing Phase: Reclaiming Lesbians in History, 1840–1985* (London: Women's Press, 1989); Martha Vicinus (ed.) *Lesbian Subjects: a Feminist Studies Reader* (Bloomington, IN: Indiana University Press, 1995); Alison Oram and Annemarie Turnbull, *The Lesbian History Sourcebook. Love and Sex between Women in Britain from 1780–1970* (London: Routledge, 2000).

20 Vicinus, *Independent Women*, op. cit., p. 17.

21 Joan Scott, *Only Paradoxes to Offer: French Feminists and the Rights of Man* (Cambridge, MA: Harvard University Press, 1996).

22 Cited in A. James Hammerton, *Cruelty and Companionship. Conflict in Nineteenth-Century Married Life* (London: Routledge, 1992), p. 57.

23 Eileen Yeo, 'Social Motherhood and the Sexual Communion of Labour in British Social Science, 1850–1950', *Women's History Review*, vol. 1, no. 1 (1992), p. 75.
24 Ibid., pp. 75–7.
25 Taylor, *Eve and the New Jerusalem*, op. cit., pp. 161–71.
26 Jeffreys, *The Spinster and Her Enemies*, op. cit., pp. 35–9.
27 Florence Nightingale, *Cassandra* (1860, reprinted New Haven, CT: The Feminist Press, 1979). See also Anthony Harrison, 'Christina Rossetti and the Sage Discourse of High Anglicanism', in Thais E. Morgan (ed.) *Victorian Sages and Cultural Discourse: Renegotiating Gender and Power* (New Brunswick, NJ: Rutgers University Press, 1990), pp. 87–104.
28 Eileen Janes Yeo, 'Some Paradoxes of Empowerment', in E. J. Yeo (ed.) *Radical Femininity: Women's Self-Representation in the Public Sphere* (Manchester: Manchester University Press, 1998), pp. 15–16.
29 There is already a considerable body of feminist scholarship on women, feminism and imperialist discourse. See, for example, Antoinette Burton, *Burdens of History. British Feminists, Indian Women and Imperial Culture* (Chapel Hill, NC: University of North Carolina Press, 1994); L. Donaldson, *Decolonizing Feminisms: Race, Gender and Empire-Building* (London: Routledge, 1993); Sara Mills, *Discourses of Difference: an Analysis of Women's Travel-Writing and Colonialism* (London: Routledge, 1993) and N. Chaudhuri and M. Strobel (eds) *Western Women and Imperialism: Complicity and Resistance* (1992). For discussions on nineteenth-century philanthropic activity as a method of working-class resocialization, see Linda Mahood, *The Magdalenes. Prostitution in the Nineteenth-Century* (London: Routledge, 1990) and Paula Bartley, *Prostitution: Prevention and Reform in England, 1860–1914* (London: Routledge, 2000).
30 Robert Shoemaker and Mary Vincent (eds) *Gender and History in Western Europe* (London: Arnold, 1998), pp. 178–9.
31 Summers, *Female Lives, Moral States*, op. cit., p. 16.
32 Jane Rendall, 'Women and the Public Sphere', *Gender and History*, vol. 11, no. 3 (1999), p. 482.

Part I

Female Education and Moral Reform

1

'A singular injustice towards women': Hannah More, Evangelicalism and Female Education

Anne Stott

The purpose of this chapter is to set the educational views of the Evangelical philanthropist Hannah More (1745–1833) in the context of contemporary debates on the education of women and the poor. Her argument that upper- and upper-middle-class girls should be weaned away from trivial literature and showy accomplishments by being made to study more demanding subjects was given especial urgency by the moral challenges thrown up by the French Revolution and German Romanticism. She also taught reading to the plebeian women and girls who attended her Sunday schools and adult schools, and in some cases at least, provided them with the opportunity to rise socially. Her programmes for women's education were part of a wider reformation of manners agenda and paralleled her friend William Wilberforce's campaign for the abolition of the slave trade. As critical moralists, the Evangelicals worked for a fundamental refashioning of society, and they recognized the importance of women in effecting this transformation. While apparently supporting the existing social and political order, they engaged in a vigorous cultural warfare which laid the foundations of the energetic, activist Victorian religious culture in which women were to play an important role.[1]

Hannah More's whole life was dominated by education.[2] She was born in Fishponds near Bristol, the fourth of five daughters of Jacob More, the master of the local charity school and his wife, Mary Grace, a farmer's daughter. Her early education was strictly limited: 'I, a girl', she told a friend, 'was educated at random'.[3] She was taught Latin on an informal basis by a Baptist minister, the Rev. James Newton, who later said that 'for the limited period of his instruction she surpassed in her progress all the others he had known'.[4] The family's modest income meant that the daughters would have to earn their own livings, and in 1758 the eldest sisters founded a school in Bristol which became one of the most successful girls' schools in the country. The young Hannah More taught at the school. Following her visit to London in 1774, she became friendly with David Garrick and her play *Percy* had a successful run on the London stage in 1777 and 1778. In the late 1780s her life changed direction once again as, under the influence of the former slave-trader, John Newton, she converted to Evangelical religion. This brought her into contact with William Wilberforce and provided the inspiration for a series of widely read conduct books in which she urged the upper classes to adopt her own brand of rigorous Christianity. In 1789 she founded the first of what were to be nine Sunday schools in the Mendip area of Somerset where she lived from 1786 to 1828. From this time onwards her energies were devoted to supervising her schools and writing her books.

The late-Georgian period witnessed an intense debate in which radical reformers joined with conservative moralists and novelists to condemn the trivial nature of women's education and its failure to implant moral and religious values. As the preface of Hannah More's most influential conduct book, *Strictures on the Modern System of Female Education* (1799), declared,

> It is a singular injustice which is often exercised towards women, first to give them a most defective education, and then to expect from them the most undeviating purity of conduct.[5]

A political conservative, deeply hostile to the French Revolution, More was eager to distance herself from the language of women's rights. Nevertheless, there was a considerable overlap of agendas. In her *Vindication of the Rights of Woman* (1792), a book More refused on principle to read, Mary Wollstonecraft complained that 'in the education of women, the cultivation of the understanding is always subordinate to the acquirement of some corporeal accomplishment'. Using the language of orientalism, she compared British women to 'Turkish bashaws'.[6] In unconscious agreement, Hannah More too condemned the 'Mahometan education' which 'consists entirely in making woman an object of attraction'.[7] Such sentiments can be echoed in numerous writings of the period. The debate on women's education can be summed up in extracts from two novels, Jane Austen's *Mansfield Park* (1814) and Hannah More's *Coelebs in Search of a Wife* (1809):

> it had been the most direful mistake in [Sir Thomas Bertram's] plan of education. He feared that principle, active principle, had been wanting, that they had never been properly taught to govern their inclinations and tempers, by that sense of duty which alone can suffice.... To be distinguished for elegance and accomplishments – the authorized object of their youth – could have had no useful influence that way, no moral effect on the mind. He had meant them to be good, but his cares had been directed to the under-standing and manners not the disposition.[8]

> The education of the present race of females is not very favourable to domestic happiness. For my own part I call education not that which smothers a woman with accomplishments, but that which tends to consolidate a firm and regular system of character:...not that which is made up of shreds and patches of useless arts, but that which inculcates principles, polishes taste, regulates temper, cultivates reason, subdues the passions...and, more especially, that which refers all actions, feelings, sentiments, tastes and passions to the love and fear of God.[9]

Such was the consensus, that More came to fear that the whole subject was becoming hackneyed. In preparing for what she saw as her most politically important conduct book, her *Hints towards Forming the Character of a Young Princess* (1805), written for Princess Charlotte, the heiress presumptive to the throne, she told her friend, Ann Kennicott, 'I have avoided the word *Education* in the title, because we have been Educated to Death by so many books on the Subject'.[10] Nevertheless, though avoiding the word, she continued to engage with the issue.

The reasons for this intense concentration on female education lie in a set of material and intellectual factors that came together at the end of the eighteenth century. The rapid growth of the 'middling sort', improvements in education, and the expansion of printed literature fed off each other and created a culture of politeness and an avid taste for reading. The range of writings included national and provincial newspapers, periodicals, novels, sermons and travel literature. Women were very much part of this literary public sphere. Avid readers included the literary hostess, Hester Thrale, the bluestockings, Elizabeth Montagu and the youthful Hannah More, as well as relatively unknown women such as the Lancashire gentlewoman Elizabeth Shackleton and Anna Larpent, wife of the theatrical censor.[11] Women were also going into print as never before. The shy Fanny Burney astonished her family and friends by writing the bestselling novel, *Evelina* (1778). Catharine Macaulay produced political polemics and a multi-volume history of England. Hannah More's friend, Elizabeth Carter, probably the most learned woman of her day, was the renowned translator of Epictetus. More herself earned a substantial sum from the performance and the printed text of her play, *Percy*. There can be no doubt that though they remained disadvantaged compared with men, many women gained status and stimulation from the expansion of the print culture.

The intellectual developments of the period, however, were more problematic. The 'sentimental' revolution of the third quarter of the eighteenth century had constructed women as creatures of sensibility, more compassionate than men and with more delicate nerves, with faculties that were imaginative rather than analytical, and reasoning that was lively rather than solid.[12] In the eighteenth century's most influential novel of education, Jean-Jacques Rousseau's *Emile*, the heroine, Sophie, educated solely that she may be a pleasing, but undemanding companion for her husband, reads no books until her marriage. Julie, the heroine of his sensational bestseller, *La Nouvelle Héloïse*, faces a conflict between her violent love for her tutor and her duty to her family that leads to her eventual death.[13]

The gendered polarity of thinking man and feeling woman was part of the Enlightenment's ambiguous legacy to women. But many tributaries fed into that broad river, some of which gave rise to a more positive view of women's educational potential. Descartes' philosophy in particular, worked both ways. If his dualism set up woman as the 'other', his epistemology, with its insistence on the thinking self as the touchstone of all knowledge, opened the way for the French Cartesian, Jacques Du Bosc and the English feminist, Mary Astell, to argue that women should be taken seriously as rational beings.[14] In a separate intellectual development, the evolutionary theories of the

Scottish writers, Adam Ferguson, William Robertson and John Millar, showed that far from being fixed by nature, the position of women was contingent upon social developments and thus capable of improvement.[15] Above all, John Locke's theory of the *tabula rasa* gave recognition to women as the prime educators who supplied the child with its first impressions.[16] Locke's views resonated powerfully with the Evangelicals. As Hannah More's clerical friend, Thomas Gisborne observed,

> The human mind in infancy has been compared, in some respects justly, to a blank sheet of paper.... The mind is originally an unsown field, prepared for the reception of any crop; and if those to whom the culture of it belongs, neglect to fill it with good grain, it will speedily be covered with weeds.[17]

If this Lockean point was conceded, then the religious, moral and even political arguments for giving women a sound education became irrefutable.

Hannah More's *Strictures* was explicitly addressed to women of the upper and upper-middle classes, 'the ladies of the *ton*', on the grounds that they were the most influential members of society.[18] To modern feminists, her message to these women seems mixed. In language that would never have been used by Catharine Macaulay or Mary Wollstonecraft, she condemned 'the bold and independent beauty, the intrepid female, the hoyden, the huntress, and the archer; the swinging arms, the confident address'.[19] She begged women not to become 'female warriors' or 'female politicians: I hardly know which of the two is the most disgusting or unnatural character'.[20] In sharply differentiating women's education and conduct from men's, she seemed thoroughly conservative. On the other hand, believing as she did that 'education [is] a school for life, and life [is] a school for eternity',[21] and influenced as she was by Lockean psychology and Evangelicalism, her book could not fail to be a critique of current educational practice. She argued that the vital importance of education was neglected in favour of what she sardonically termed the 'phrenzy of accomplishments', the precocious 'Lilliputian coquettes', the over-emphasis on music which meant that 'a young lady now requires, not a master, but an orchestra'.[22] In spite of this negative language, More was not opposed on principle to the traditional accomplishments of the genteel female, but she believed that they had been over-emphasized. 'The wise mother', she asserted, 'knows that the superstructure of the accomplishments can be alone safely erected on the broad and solid basis of Christian morality'.[23]

The 1790s was a decade of acute cultural conflict. From 1793, Britain and France were at war, and in her popular loyalist tract, *Village Politics*, More had strongly asserted the conservative view that the French Revolution posed a threat to the morals as well as the liberties of the nation. But as she saw it, the attack was also mounted on another front, the whole literature of sensibility that had begun with Rousseau. By alluring the warm-hearted and impressionable and by giving vice 'so natural an air of virtue', he had constructed 'a net of...exquisite art and inextricable workmanship, spread to entangle innocence and ensnare experience'.[24] More recent culprits were 'the modern apostles of infidelity and immorality',[25] the German Romantics, Goethe and Schiller, and the playwright, Kotzebue, whose *Das Kind der Liebe*, translated by Elizabeth Inchbald as *Lovers' Vows* (and familiar to every reader of *Mansfield Park*) was in performance at Covent Garden in 1798 and 1799, the time *Strictures* was being written and published. The new German literature coincided with the huge increase in light literature supplied by the 'ever-multiplying authors' of John Lane's Minerva Press, who 'with unparalleled fecundity are overstocking the world with their quick-succeeding progeny'.[26] To More, both plays and novels conveyed the same pernicious message, elevating the 'softer qualities' of sympathy and feeling 'at the expense of principle'.[27] This sensibility, divorced from morality, flourished in shallow soils, nurtured on 'the streams of *Abridgements, Beauties*, and *Compendiums*, which form too considerable a part of a young lady's library...an infallible receipt for making a superficial mind'.[28] In More's view, the superficially educated woman posed the most acute threat to the moral health of the nation.

Her remedy, set out not only in *Strictures* but also in her conduct novel *Coelebs*, was 'serious study' which 'lifts the reader from sensation to intellect...and...helps to qualify her for religious pursuits....There is to woman a Christian use to be made of sober studies'.[29] It is with this principle in mind that Mr Stanley, the exemplary father in *Coelebs*, teaches Latin to his daughter, Lucilla, while her less docile sister, Phoebe, is taught mathematics in order to correct her fancy. The implications of her plea for rational education were far-reaching, and she was not always prepared to follow through her argument. In *Coelebs*, she encouraged the teaching of Latin and mathematics to girls, but, on what seem to be aesthetic rather than logical grounds, sharply condemned the scientific lady.[30] In a thoroughly conventional passage in *Strictures*, she asserted that women lacked the masculine 'faculty of comparing, combining, analyzing and separating'. However, she also asserted that

> there is much truth in the remark, that till women shall be more reasonably educated, and until the native growth of their mind shall cease to be stinted and cramped, we shall have no juster ground for pronouncing that their understanding has already reached its highest attainable perfection, than the Chinese would have for affirming that their women have attained to the greatest possible perfection in walking.[31]

The passages in *Strictures* which dealt with the education of women were well received. Criticisms of the book focused on More's Evangelical attack on the 'cheap and indolent Christianity' of fashionable society – an anticipation of Dietrich Bonhoeffer's condemnation of 'cheap grace'.[32] Richard Watson, the Whig Bishop of Llandaff, described the book as 'elegant Methodism'.[33] Horace Walpole's friend, Mary Berry, detected 'a principle radically false, which...vitiates every system built upon it and saps the foundation of morality'.[34] The high church clergyman, Charles Daubeny, accused her (unfairly) of Calvinism.[35] On the other hand, the bluestocking writers, Elizabeth Montagu, Elizabeth Carter, and Hester Mulso Chapone, loved the book, as did the daughters of George III, bored and isolated at Windsor.[36] The *Ladies Monthly Museum*, a magazine devoted to expanding women's intellectual horizons, thought that 'the tendency of the whole [work] is so exalted that we really think her labors above all praise'.[37] Another enthusiast was a young American reader, who interpreted the book's message as one of female empowerment rather than subordination.[38] Mary Berry, who read the book alongside the *Vindication of the Rights of Women*, noted wryly that 'on all the great points of the education of women', More was in agreement with the much more radical Mary Wollstonecraft.[39]

The book was a success because (on the whole) she gave her women readers the lesson they wished to hear. In the late-Georgian period writers as different as Mary Wollstonecraft, Catharine Macaulay, Marie Edgeworth, Elizabeth Hamilton, Jane West and Jane Austen all argued that women could not be companionable wives to their husbands, fit educators of their children and true citizens of their country, unless they had first developed their intellectual and moral faculties through a rational education rather the pursuit of showy and trivial 'accomplishments'.[40] As far as the education of genteel women was concerned, More was operating from within a growing consensus. It was only her Evangelicalism that set her apart. She found more difficulties, however, when she attempted to improve the education of plebeian women.

From 1789, two years or so after her Evangelical conversion, More and her equally devout sister Martha (Patty) founded Sunday schools and promoted literacy in the deprived mining and agricultural villages of the Mendips. They began this work at the instigation of William Wilberforce and the project was largely financed by the Evangelical banker and MP, Henry Thornton, but they would hardly have undertaken such expensive, time-consuming and exhausting work without strong motivation of their own. As with her conduct books, More's work was part of a wider trend; the Sunday school movement was the latest fashion in charitable endeavour, and women were prominent in it from the start. Hannah More knew and approved of Sarah Trimmer's Sunday school in Brentford, and her friend Elizabeth Montagu had founded her own school at her country house at Sandleford in Berkshire. However, More's venture was particularly ambitious. By 1795 she had founded nine schools, attended by about a thousand children. She made a greater contribution to elementary education in Somerset than any other individual, and three of the schools and the two women's benefit clubs which she founded at Shipham and Cheddar survived into the twentieth century.[41]

From the start, she relied on other women. The school at Cheddar, the first to be founded, was put in the hands of Sarah Baber, a widowed charity-school mistress of strongly Evangelical beliefs, and her daughter. She proved to be an accomplished and compassionate teacher, and the More sisters exhausted their vocabulary of praise in order to describe her. They frequently resorted to masculine language, calling her 'the bishop' and referring to Cheddar as her little 'diocese'. When she died suddenly in 1794, devastating the villagers who had come to rely on her, they borrowed from the Methodists the term 'mother in Israel' with its layered meanings of refuge, mother, leader and prophetess.[42] In a letter to Wilberforce after the funeral, More reflected on a conversation she had had with the Earl of Cornwallis, former Governor-General of India, and added 'how little in my estimation are the most brilliant of Heroes when compared with this dear woman, who has turned *many*, I almost said, has turned *hundreds* to righteousness'.[43] Though as a member of the Church of England, Sarah Baber was debarred from the preaching activities open to some Methodist women, her exceptional qualities subverted the traditional hierarchies of class and gender and undermined ideologies that attempted to confine women to the purely domestic sphere.

Like most charity-school teachers, Sarah Baber belonged socially to the lower middle class (to use an anachronistic term). It was a harder task to find teachers for the isolated and disorderly mining villages of Shipham and Rowberrow and the More sisters took a gamble when they descended the social scale and appointed a poor farmer's daughter, Patience Seward, and her half-sister, Flower Waite, as mistresses. Patience Seward was employed as a diary-maid but in her spare time,

> from the love of doing good, and a great desire of instructing the ignorant [she had] raised a little Sunday-school of her poor neighbors, and had actually collected thirty poor children, and from her little pittance brought books and provided rewards of gingerbread for those who improved most.[44]

An even more remarkable example of plebeian aspirations is found in the Banwell mistress, Nelly Spencer, a servant in an apothecary's family. 'An old mother taught her to read, and here ended her education; but her love of books was so great, she would procure them from her master's study, and rather than not read, she would amuse herself with medical books'.[45] Such intellectual curiosity was not confined to women, and the More sisters found a similar thirst for knowledge and religious commitment among some of the miners at Nailsea, three of whom became schoolmasters. But the Nailsea miners fit into an already well-documented narrative of male working-class self-improvement.[46] The evidence for women is far scantier and the experiences of the More sisters provide useful evidence for female aspiration and upward mobility. For all its stress on female subordination, Evangelical religion proved an effective means for the advancement of women as well as their spiritual awakening.

To make this point is to cut across the commonly accepted view that the Mendip schools were deeply conservative. Hannah More herself encouraged this interpretation as time and again she went out of her way to stress that she taught 'such coarse works as may fit them for servants. I allow of no writing. My object has not been to teach dogmas and opinions, but to form the lower class to habits of industry and virtue'.[47] But against this it has to be stressed that she was writing to people who were more reactionary than herself and who were deeply suspicious of any attempts to teach the poor to read. She had to guard against critics like the Oxford don, Dr Edward Tatham, who, as she told Wilberforce, 'says I am labouring to ruin this Country by enlightening the Common people, the *source of all national ruin'*.[48] While it is true that her curriculum was narrow, it is also undeniably the case that in introducing people (women and girls as well as men and boys) to the written culture, she had started a process she could not control. At the end of her life she regretted what she saw as the over-ambitious agendas of the 'ultra-educationalists' without fully recognizing her own contribution to this process.[49]

It is unrealistic either to idealize the Mendip schools or to dismiss them as mere agents of hegemony and colonization. Like most schools, they experienced a mixture of success and failure, and the pupils' responses varied according to temperament and age. In most of their parishes the More sisters offered weekday classes for girls as well as Sunday schools for the younger children. When William and Barbara Wilberforce visited the schools on their honeymoon in 1797, they were particularly struck with a '*little* Girl [who] interested us much; the animated expression of the fine eyes & Countenance, her fixed attention & intelligent answers caught our attention'. They were grieved to learn that this promising child was suffering from cancer.[50] By the time they became teenagers and were out in domestic service, however, many of the girls had become recalcitrant; they were often drawn away 'by the temptation of bad company' and had to be 'coaxed' to attend the evening classes, sometimes with the bribe of a dish of tea.[51] Now that they were earning, they considered their leisure time to be their own to spend as they wished and could choose to make use of the schools or to ignore them. Far from being instruments of social control, the Mendip schools had constantly to compete against the rival attractions that tempted children and adolescents away from their lessons. Hannah More could no more enforce her will upon the poor than she could upon the genteel readers for whom she wrote her conduct books. In all cases she was forced to negotiate and persuade.

Between 1795 and 1798, while she was busy with her schools, More also devoted some of her energies to the project of the Cheap Repository Tracts, a series of ballads and stories similar in appearance to the popular chapbook literature, designed to improve the morals of the common people, to arm them against radical propaganda, and to convert them to Evangelical religion.[52] It has been argued that the Tracts are a feminized, domesticated genre, stories of 'how an entire community can be remodeled through female enterprise and persuasive influence'.[53] In writing them, More vividly used her own experiences of the Mendip poor, and one of the stories in particular, *Hester Wilmot*, describes in some detail a working-class girl's social advancement through her Sunday school. Hester's formidable mother, Rebecca, wishes to keep her daughter at home to mind the baby and help with the household tasks, but when she is at last persuaded to allow Hester to attend the school, the girl shows 'a quick capacity'. Her teacher lends her a little book to take home, a common practice with promising pupils in the Mendip schools. By rising earlier than her family, she quickly learns to read from St John's gospel (which More astonishingly describes as 'the easiest') and in due course undergoes an Evangelical conversion.[54] In part II of the tract, *The New Gown*, Hester converts her family, and becomes an under-teacher at a school. Eventually, we are told, she may be promoted to headmistress.[55] It is difficult to believe that at some stage the fictional Hester Wilmot would not have been taught to write as well as read – how could she have kept a pupils' register without this skill? More's message for the poor, then, could be more ambitious than she was prepared to admit. While she assured conservatives that her aim was to reinforce rather than subvert the social order, in practice she gave her more promising pupils the chance to better themselves. Such an opportunity was arguably more important for the girls than the boys. The More sisters' perennial difficulty in finding good male teachers suggests that upwardly mobile men, with a wider range of occupations to choose from, had less need of the schools. Where the girls were concerned, the Mendip schools, limited though they were, provided one of their very few avenues of escape from domestic service.

Though Hannah More's conduct books and her Sunday school work might seem very different activities, she saw them as part of the same agenda. As she told Richard Beadon, Bishop of Bath and Wells, 'the morals of those of my own sex have been the constant object of my peculiar regard'.[56] In both areas, she operated as a conservative moralist, deeply critical of existing society, who struggled to remould it in accordance with her Evangelical principles. This involved her in constant internal negotiation between her desire to preserve the social order and at the same time to transform the lives of the individuals within it. Because she chose to focus on women, the paradox became even more problematic. Genteel women were important because they set the tone for social mores, and therefore had to be urged to educate their daughters for their future responsibilities. But plebeian women were important too. Their souls were no less valuable, and their role, as wives and mothers of the labouring men whose work underpinned the whole economy and society, was vital to the stability of the nation at a time of war and revolution. Hannah More sought to rescue the well-to-do from Mary Wollstonecraft and the poor from Tom Paine, but in doing so, she unavoidably sought to transform their lives. She believed that, whatever their differences in social status and economic circumstances, women in all social classes were being sold short. Denied an appropriately demanding education, women in polite society were fed on the pernicious sensibility that made them the slaves of their instincts. Plebeian women, on the other hand, were victims of what the More sisters called 'fatalism': the view expressed by a farmer's wife that the poor 'were intended to be servants and slaves, it was preordained that they should be ignorant, and it was a shame to alter the decrees of God'.[57] Though avoiding the language of rights which she so disliked, More nevertheless sought to gain women justice. Her apparently self-contradictory attitudes were the logical consequence of a paradoxical Evangelical theology that sought to uphold existing hierarchies while urging women of all classes to realize their full spiritual potential.

Notes

1 For the Evangelical agenda, see Ford K. Brown, *Fathers of the Victorians. The Age of Wilberforce* (Cambridge: Cambridge University Press, 1961); Ian Bradley, *The Call to Seriousness. The Evangelical Impact on the Victorians* (London: Jonathan Cape, 1976); Gerald Newman, *The Rise of English Nationalism. A Cultural History 1740–1830* (London: Weidenfeld and Nicolson, 1987), pp. 234–5. For the ambiguities of More's conservatism, see, for example, Kathryn Sutherland, 'Hannah More's Counter-Revolutionary Feminism', in Kelvin Everest (ed.), *Revolution in Writing. British Literary Responses to the French Revolution* (Milton Keynes and Philadelphia: PA, 1991), pp. 27–63; Charles Howard Ford, *Hannah More. A Critical Biography* (New York: Peter Lang, 1996).

2 For biographies of More, see William Roberts, *Memoirs of the Life and Correspondence of Mrs Hannah More*, 4 vols., 2nd edn (London, 1834); H. Thompson, *The Life of Hannah More with Notices of her Sisters* (London, 1838); M.A. Hopkins, *Hannah More and her Circle* (New York: Longmans, Green and Co., 1947); M.G. Jones, *Hannah More* (Cambridge: Cambridge University Press, 1952); P. Demers, *The World of Hannah More* (Lexington, KY: University Press of Kentucky, 1996).

3 UCLA, William Andrews Clark Memorial Library: Hannah More MS; More to Sir William Weller Pepys, 11 Nov. 1783 (uncatalogued).

4 Joseph Cottle, *Early Recollections: Chiefly Relating to the Late Samuel Taylor Coleridge During his Long Residence in Bristol*, 2nd edn (London, 1837), p. 53.

5 *Strictures on the Modern System of Female Education, with a View of the Principles and Conduct Prevalent among Women of Rank and Fortune*, 2 vols (London, 1799), i, p. ix.

6 Mary Wollstonecraft, *Vindication of the Rights of Woman* (Harmondsworth: Penguin, 1982), pp. 105 and 125.

7 *Coelebs in Search of a Wife*, op. cit., 2 vols (London, 1809), i, p. 195.

8 *Mansfield Park*, op. cit., (Oxford, 1990), p. 422.

9 *Coelebs in Search of a Wife*, op. cit., i, p. 14.

10 Clark: Hannah More MSS; More to Ann Kennicott, 11 Jan. 1805 (uncatalogued).

11 Olwen Hufton, *The Prospect Before Her. A History of Women in Western Europe, vol. 1, 1500–1800* (London: Fontana Press, 1997), pp. 419–20; Amanda Vickery, *The Gentleman's Daughter. Women's Lives in Georgian England* (New Haven and London: Yale University Press, 1998), pp. 258–9 and passim; John Brewer, *The Pleasures of the Imagination. English Culture in the Eighteenth Century* (London: Harper Collins, 1997), pp. 56–9, 79, 84, 120, 194–7.

12 Janet Todd, *Sensibility. An Introduction* (London, 1986); G.J. Barker-Benfield, *The Culture of Sensibility. Sex and Society in Eighteenth-Century Britain* (London, 1992).

13 For a discussion of the implications of the novel, see Susan Moller Okin, *Women in Western Political Thought* (Princeton, NJ: Princeton University

Press, 1979), pp. 174–6; Robert Darnton, 'Readers Respond to Rousseau' in his *The Great Cat Massacre and other Episodes in French Cultural History* (New York: Basic Books, 1984), pp. 215–56. Mary Wollstonecraft singled out Rousseau for especial attack as one of the writers 'who have rendered women objects of pity'. *Vindication*, pp. 173–91.

14 Anthony Fletcher, *Gender, Sex and Subordination in England 1500–1800* (London, 1995), pp. 289–90; Ruth Perry, *The Celebrated Mary Astell. An Early English Feminist* (London: University of Chicago Press, 1986), pp. 70, 171–3, 332; J.K. Kinnaird, 'Mary Astell and the conservative contribution to English feminism', *Journal of British Studies*, xix, i (Fall 1979), pp. 53–75.

15 Jane Rendall, *Origins of Modern Feminism*, pp. 23–7; Sylvana Tomaselli, 'The Enlightenment debate on Women', *History Workshop Journal*, 20 (Autumn, 1985), pp. 101–24.

16 Sheryl O'Donnell, 'Mr Locke and the Ladies: the Indelible Words on the Tabula Rasa', *Studies in Eighteenth-Century Culture*, 8 (1979), p. 151; Terry Lovell, 'Subjective Powers? Consumption, the Reading Public and Domestic Woman in Early Eighteenth-Century England', in Ann Bermingham and John Brewer (eds), *The Consumption of Culture 1600–1800. Image, Object, Text* (London: Routledge, 1995), p. 34.

17 *An Enquiry into the Duties of the Female Sex*, op. cit., (London, 1797).

18 *Strictures*, op. cit., i, p. 15.

19 *Strictures*, op. cit., i, p. 75.

20 *Strictures*, op. cit., i, p. 5.

21 *Strictures*, op. cit., i, pp. 63–4.

22 *Strictures*, op. cit., i, pp. 69, 99, 79.

23 *Strictures*, op. cit., i, p. 94.

24 *Strictures*, p. 34.

25 *Strictures*, op. cit., i, p. 42.

26 Allardyce Nicoll, *A History of English Drama*, iii, *Late Eighteenth-Century Drama* (Cambridge: Cambridge University Press, 1952), pp. 61 ff; D. Blakey, *The Minerva Press 1790–1820* (London, 1939); *Strictures*, op. cit., i, p. 188.

27 *Strictures*, op. cit., i, pp. 73–4.

28 *Strictures*, op. cit., i, p. 178.

29 *Strictures*, op. cit., i, p. 184.

30 *Coelebs*, op. cit., ii, p. 145.

31 *Strictures*, op. cit., ii, p. 30.

32 *Strictures*, op. cit., p. ii, 292; D. Bonhoeffer, *The Cost of Discipleship*: (translated R.H. Fuller, London: SCM Press, 1959)

33 Duke University, NC, Rare Book, Manuscript and Special Collections Library, William Wilberforce Papers, More to Wilberforce [1810].

34 T. Lewis, (ed.), *Extracts from the Journals and Correspondence of Miss Berry from the year 1783 to 1852*, 3 vols (London, 1866), ii, pp. 91–2.

35 For this and the subsequent Blagdon controversy, see Anne Stott, 'Hannah More and the Blagdon Controversy, 1799–1802', *Journal of Ecclesiastical History*, vol. 51, no. 2 (April, 2000), pp. 319–46.

36 Roberts, op. cit., ii, pp. 65–8.
37 *Ladies' Monthly Museum*, ii (June 1799), p. 485.
38 Rendall, *Origins of Modern Feminism*, op. cit., pp. 207–8.
39 *Journals and Correspondence*, pp. 91–2.
40 Marilyn Butler, *Jane Austen and the War of Ideas* (Oxford: Clarendon Press, 1987), pp. 219–20; Rendall, *Origins of Modern Feminism*, pp. 109–12.
41 For the history of the schools see Arthur Roberts (ed.), *Mendip Annals; or a Narrative of the Charitable Labours of Hannah and Martha More in their Neighbourhood, being the Journal of Martha More* (London, 1859); Edward Belsham, 'The origins of elementary education in Somerset, with particular reference to the work of Hannah More in the Mendips', unpublished MA thesis, University of Bristol (1953); Anne Stott, 'Hannah More: Evangelicalism, Cultural Reformation and Loyalism', unpublished PhD thesis, University of London (1998), pp. 57–88.
42 Roberts, *Life of More*, op. cit., ii, p. 441; Deborah Valenze, *Prophetic Sons and Daughters. Female Preaching and Popular Religion in Industrial England* (Princeton: Princeton University Press, 1985), pp. 35–7.
43 Duke University, NC. Wilberforce MSS, More to Wilberforce [Aug. 1794].
44 *Mendip Annals*, op. cit., pp. 28–9.
45 *Mendip Annals*, op. cit., pp. 34–5.
46 David Vincent, *Literacy and Popular Culture: England 1750–1914* (Cambridge: Cambridge University Press, 1989); R.A. Houston, *Literacy in Early Modern Europe: Culture and Education 1500–1800* (London: Longman, 1988).
47 *Mendip Annals*, op. cit., p. 6.
48 Duke University, NC. Wilberforce papers, More to Wilberforce, 3 Aug. 1796 [misdated 1799].
49 Bodleian Library, University of Oxford, MS Wilberforce, *c.* 48, fols 29–30, More to Wilberforce [1820].
50 Ibid., d.20, Barbara Wilberforce, 'Recollections of Mrs Hannah More and her sisters and the schools which Mrs H. More and her sister Miss Patty established and taught', fols 37–8
51 *Mendip Annals*, op. cit., p. 92.
52 See G.H. Spinney, "Cheap Repository Tracts: Hazard and Marshal Edition', The Library, 4th ser., 20, 3 (Dec. 1939), pp. 295–340; Susan Pedersen, 'Hannah More meets Simple Simon: tracts, chapbooks and popular culture in late eighteenth-century England', *Journal of British Studies*, 25 (1986), pp. 84–113.
53 Mitzi Myers, 'Hannah More's Tracts for the Times: Social Fiction and Female Ideology' in Mary Anne Schofield and Cecilia Macheski (eds), *Fetter'd or Free? British Women Novelists 1670–1815* (Athens, OH: University of Georgia Press, 1986), p. 275; see also Sutherland, 'Hannah More's Counter-Revolutionary Feminism'.
54 The History of Hester Wilmot; or the second part of *The Sunday School* (London and Bath, 1797); published in hard covers in *Cheap Repository Tracts, entertaining, moral and religious* (London, 1798), pp. 341–73.

55   *Cheap Repository Tracts: entertaining, moral and religious*, p. 373.
56   St John's College, Cambridge, MS K.34, Hannah More to Richard Beadon, 24 Aug. 1802. By permission of the Master and Fellows of St John's College, Cambridge.
57   *Mendip Annals*, op. cit., pp. 208–9.

2
Rational Religion and Feminism: the Challenge of Unitarianism in the Nineteenth Century[1]

Ruth Watts

This chapter will explore the powerful challenge that the rational tenets of Unitarianism posed to accepted perceptions both of women's intellect and their role in the nineteenth century. Such beliefs and the corresponding deep education they stimulated led its adherents to demonstrate both in theory and in practice that women were capable of much more than was commonly realized. Thence, despite their small numbers, Unitarians provided or influenced many of the more progressive feminists of this period.[2] At the same time both economic and social considerations and their own deferral to more conservative gender conventions of their time could limit the logic of their arguments.

The dynamic incentives of a liberating religious message and its contextual limitations will each be analysed through examining a small network of four Unitarian women, Elizabeth Rathbone, Kitty Wilkinson, Lady Byron and Mary Carpenter. Stimulated by their religion, all four wished to find ways to illumine the lot of the poor, particularly through extending the educational ideals of their sect. Through exploiting those avenues open to them, especially within a network based upon a liberal philosophy of social justice, they were able to become influential in those matters in which they so passionately engaged. Nevertheless, their opportunities to exercise their talents were limited not only by their varying class and marital status, but also by their gender. The roles they played exemplify both the interrelationship and the complexities of religion and feminism.

In this chapter a brief exploration of the significance of Unitarianism in challenging orthodox notions of femininity will be followed by a discussion of the influence of each woman's religious beliefs on their role in reform, the different means by which each came into the public arena and the significance of their work for the articulation of gender identities.

Modern Unitarianism grew chiefly out of eighteenth-century Protestant dissent and the Enlightenment. Unitarians preferred reason, thoughtful assent, to belief, and an emphasis on ethics and good works to that of emotional or blind faith (as they perceived it) and sacramental, cloistered piety. Such a religion needed education as a base, a need extended in eighteenth-century Britain by Unitarianism's association with the psychology and educational philosophy evolved by Joseph Priestley from David Hartley and John Locke. Thus the supreme importance of a careful intellectual, moral and physical education from birth was emphasized for developing fully not only mind and body but also virtue. Thus to be a good person and to be a Unitarian, people needed a good education, a phrase interpreted by Unitarians to mean a modern education, scientific in method and approach. Such beliefs injected great vitality and vigour into a group simultaneously stimulated by economic and political considerations to become a dynamic force in the new industrial England, although Unitarianism itself was generally despised as heresy.[3]

The significance of such beliefs for women was manifold. Since the rational religion of the Unitarians challenged orthodox Christianity by denying such standard tenets as the trinity and original sin, it was well placed to challenge other traditional beliefs too. Indeed, Unitarianism itself was an optimistic, open-ended, non-dogmatic religion in which women and men debated freely on theological issues. A passionate commitment to individual, civil and religious liberty and to social justice further shaped a religion able to question gendered ideology. Unitarian men and women interrogated the intellectual and moral inequalities imputed to women and subsequently were in the vanguard of attempts to win greater marital and political rights and greater formal educational opportunities for them.

Furthermore, the emphasis on knowledge and understanding led Unitarians to promote an education for females which was far wider and deeper than the contemporary norm, both for the individual's own sake and to ensure the most intelligent education of the young.

Their enthusiastic interest in education led them to value the art of teaching and to see education in all its forms as a most important plank in their extremely active concern for political and social reform. Education too was an area in which women could more easily share in public action for public welfare – an exercise Unitarians highly valued as character forming. Yet, because of their anxious quest for 'respectability' in a world which anathematized their religious beliefs, they tended to mind the proprieties which restricted the lives of middle-class women, the class to which many of them belonged. Thus Unitarian women were both enabled and stimulated by their religion and education to play an active part in social and educational initiatives, but were circumscribed by social customs and assumptions which in other ways they challenged. At the same time the small, closely-knit Unitarian world provided them with the familial and professional networks of a vibrant, liberal and reformist culture which could lend both support and encouragement.

The four Unitarian women whose lives are examined here were each stimulated by their religion to take part in social and educational reform, albeit, having different social and marital status, they found divergent ways to do this. Through working for others they found, in varying degrees, a public voice, their varied success demonstrating what women could and, perhaps should, do and so helping to forge a more rounded perception of 'woman's role'.

Elizabeth Rathbone, eldest of 12 children of the prosperous cotton spinner Samuel Greg of Styal and his wife Hannah, enjoyed the excellent liberal education which her mother ensured for all her children, boys and girls alike. With her sisters she helped in her mother's remarkable social ventures in the mill community at Quarry Bank, Styal, especially the education of the apprentices. Among Hannah's outstanding brood it was Elizabeth who most realized her ideals.[4] This she accomplished from 1812 through working with her husband, William Rathbone V of Liverpool, a later convert to Unitarianism. According to her granddaughter, the MP Eleanor Rathbone, Elizabeth was consulted by her husband in all his work, usually initiating the educational part of it although the 'custom of the day prevented her from coming forward openly'.[5] When William had helped win the Municipal Corporations Act, becoming first a Councillor and then, in 1837, Mayor of the reformed Liverpool Corporation, she did much in the background to establish the Irish National system. Through this, two rate-supported elementary schools were set up for the poor in which the children experienced secular instruction together but had religious instruction separately, taught by either an Anglican or a Roman Catholic priest. This experiment, unique for the day both in funding and religious instruction, tried to bridge the bitter problem of educating children of different faiths together. Such a 'Unitarian' solution led to acrimony and political repercussions for Rathbone and the Liberals, but the schools became models of their kind, training many excellent teachers. In 1870 the elderly Elizabeth Rathbone sent a memorandum on them to William Forster when he was introducing his Education Act.[6]

Similarly, Elizabeth Rathbone was deeply interested in various forms of schooling set up for the poor and children in trouble, especially those schools established by enterprising male members of her family. The latter included her son-in-law, John Hamilton Thom, one of the 'quaternion' of ministers who were promoting a more intuitive and imaginative form of English Unitarianism. Elizabeth, immersed in the cultural life that centred on her home at Greenbank, explored the religious and educational ideas of a wide range of thinkers from different religions, including Roman Catholics and Quakers. She preferred, however, the rational impulse of Unitarianism.[7] She pondered much on the position of women. She wondered why there were no Protestant Sisters of Charity to match their Roman Catholic counterparts, but knew that women were banned from voluntary work in the workhouses and hospitals in Liverpool because the Catholic priests feared they would try and convert the inmates. Concerned about women's neglect of the religious 'rights' of others, she was delighted when, in 1859, Anglican, Roman Catholic and dissenting women were allowed to visit the workhouse in equal numbers. In additional, as her voluminous correspondence with Lady Byron illustrates, She was certainly interested in female enterprise generally. For example, in this correspondence there are many references both to Mary Carpenter and Kitty Wilkinson. She admitted the early influence on herself of the 'extraordinary' example of the Quaker, Elizabeth Fry, and corresponded with the American reformer, Dorothea Dix.[8] Nevertheless, she herself worked through the male members of her remarkable family, especially her husband and eldest son.[9]

It is harder to detail the influence of religion on Catherine or 'Kitty' Wilkinson as she was more commonly called, since she has left no personal accounts of her life. Nevertheless, she worked by a set of principles very much in keeping with those of the rational Unitarians to whom she belonged and by whose wealthier members in Liverpool she was helped. Brought up in Liverpool, by twelve she was apprenticed at a cotton mill near Lancaster. From this, Kitty went into service, married, had two children and suffered a series of tragedies in the next 20 odd years in which she lost all her family. Through these vicissitudes, Kitty worked in a series of 'respectable' jobs for poor women, eventually becoming a washerwoman. At the same time she nursed those in need around her, including a series of orphaned and abandoned children.[10]

Kitty's remembered achievement stems from her initiatives in the cholera epidemic of 1831–32. The benefits of her generous use of her copper and yard for the necessary extra laundry work in her neighbourhood were so apparent that a benevolent society provided a common cellar for families to use for their weekly wash. Medical men tapped into this service and washers were soon hired to do the washing for cholera patients. From this service came the idea of cheap public baths and washhouses, a reform attributed to fellow Unitarians Elizabeth and William Rathbone who urged the appointment of Kitty and her second husband Thomas Wilkinson as managers of the first set built by the Liverpool Corporation. This useful provision was soon copied in London and other places.[11]

There was more to Kitty Wilkinson's achievement. She used a present of oatmeal to make porridge for breakfast for up to 60 neighbours a day and acted on behalf of the hard-pressed doctors by administering remedies to patients. Another example of her work in the cholera epidemic was when, helped by a neighbour, she looked after destitute children until the numbers grew so large an infant school was established by the managers of an elementary school to accommodate them. The neighbour became its paid mistress.[12]

Kitty Wilkinson had her own educational venture. She somehow found time to take in lodgers for whom she provided a good fire and borrowed books and newspapers to tempt them from the pub in the evenings. This grew by 1835 to what became in effect a self-improvement society providing vocational training, subscription and cheap periodicals. On the men's own request others were invited to come on the payment of 6d a week which covered supper too. Apparently all these initiatives were accomplished with remarkable economy. Another venture of this resourceful woman was lending her rent from her lodgers each week to some poor women so that they could buy goods to sell at market, returning her loan on Saturday night.[13]

This caring, albeit it appears rather hasty-tempered working-class woman, seems to have taken every opportunity throughout her life to exploit her resources and traditional feminine skills to the utmost to help those around her. Turning her initiatives into more public ventures required assistance from the more powerful, including wealthier Unitarians such as the Rathbones. It was through them that her works became known, held up, indeed, as a public example of what even the very poor could do with prudence and economy to help themselves. Thus Kitty Wilkinson features in some of the leading 'self-help' collections of the day, collections mostly devoted to men.[14] In 1839, Lady Byron had urged a rather reluctant Elizabeth Rathbone to lend materials on Kitty to a Mrs Barwell who was writing for Chambers 'a kind of biography of those women from whose example the middle and humbler classes may derive benefit'.[15] The Unitarians themselves, approving both her tolerance in religion and the intelligent application of principle that they so highly valued in both sexes, devoted several pages to her in their proud record of *Unitarian Worthies* in 1876.[16] It was not unusual for Unitarians to record outstanding women, although Kitty Wilkinson was much poorer than their other heroines. Without expounding any feminist arguments, therefore, she was able to become a model of female working-class public work.

Lady Byron, who carefully harnessed her own wealthier circumstances to aid a range of educational ventures for the poorer classes, held similar principles. Born Annabella Milbanke into a family of 'staunch Unitarians', she received an excellent education from the Unitarian scholar William Frend who became a lifelong correspondent. She shared her tutor's passion for educational experiment and became an outstanding mathematician and astronomer, talents she passed on to her daughter Ada.[17] Her talents, however, were academic in both senses of the word in nineteenth-century England: thus Lady Byron's 'voice' had to be heard chiefly through the work of those she patronized. Her unsuccessful marriage to the notorious Lord Byron left her considerably poorer but, nevertheless, with sufficient means to be benevolent and with the freedom to please herself.[18]

Like many Unitarians, Lady Byron studied the methods of the continental reformer, Johann Pestalozzi. In the 1830s, she was also a prominent publicist of the Swiss reformer, Philipp von Fellenberg. His maxim that only a life associated with nature could ensure the happiness of mankind greatly appealed to her while his stress on the need for education to be a holistic experience, not mere instruction, was a principle Unitarians like herself already accepted. Sending the book she instigated in 1839, *What de Fellenberg has done for Education*, to Elizabeth Rathbone, she was sure that both the latter and John Hamilton Thom would share her liking for such a practical exposition of Christianity. Having established close personal connections with Fellenberg at Hofwyl, she set up an agricultural school of her own at Ealing Grove in 1834. There the prominence given to moral development, and the library, like the respective ban on corporal punishment, religious discrimination and using the Bible either as a lesson book or for doctrinal teaching, very much reflected both Lady Byron's and Unitarian educational preferences. The initial practical application of Fellenberg's principles owed much to the first head teacher Edward Thomas Craig who was responsible for establishing a model of active learning within a balanced curriculum. His very appointment, however, reveals Lady Byron's knowledge of the contemporary players in radical education and her willingness to use the best for her purposes despite some differences of approach – in this case between her patrician outlook and Craig's working-class Owenism. After his somewhat arbitrary dismissal, she personally trained the succeeding head teacher, Atlee, in the same aims and principles, so effectively indeed, that the school was deemed by HMI Tremenheere to be excellent academically as well as in horticulture and craft training.[19]

Although the Ealing Grove School became somewhat of a showplace and stimulated some imitations, its model was not incorporated into the educational system, partly because its non-sectarianism did not fit the religious ideas of the day. Importantly, however, it influenced James Kay (from 1842 Kay-Shuttleworth), the dynamic first secretary of the newly established Committee of the Privy Council on Education, who adopted some of its principles, particularly those on gardening, into his schemes for workhouse education and teacher training.[20] Indeed, Lady Byron consistently enabled other educationalists to achieve ideals in which she believed. For example, she paid for the ex-Chartist and stocking weaver, John Gent Brooks, to be trained as a teacher at Ealing before he took the post of domestic missionary at the New Meeting in Birmingham in 1844. Although she did belong to that 'clearing-house for radical educational thinking', the Central Society of Education, she chose to work through patronage and networking, rather than take centre stage herself.[21]

Nevertheless, Lady Byron was not against women taking a public role. Her network of friends included Mary Somerville, a fellow Unitarian and a rare example of a prominent woman scientist, and she was visited by Harriet Beecher Stowe. She hoped that such women would raise 'the respect for Women's *Judgement* amongst men generally' and she supported higher education for women. Very concerned with educational schemes for the working classes, she worked publicly with Matthew Davenport Hill to support the ideas on the reformatory and industrial schools of their mutual friend, Mary Carpenter. Especially after moving to Bristol in 1844, she gave the latter her moral and all-important financial support.[22]

The work of Mary Carpenter has been more fully discussed by historians than that of the other three women referred to above[23] and fresh studies are being published.[24] In this chapter, therefore, only the interplay of religion with gender roles and ideas will be analysed. There is no doubt that throughout Mary Carpenter's life, religion played a key role. Her charismatic father, Lant Carpenter, was a Unitarian minister and one of their foremost educationalists. From him Mary inherited an almost evangelical type of Unitarianism that focused on the loving inspiration of Jesus towards active compassion for all conditions of humanity. Always fascinated by religious debate, her first venture into authorship was her anonymous *Morning and Evening Meditations* of 1845 on universal religious truths. Further inspired by social and educational reformers, particularly the American Unitarian, Joseph Tuckerman and the Indian reformer, Rajah Rammohun Roy, whose religious aspirations for Hinduism closely allied him to the Unitarians, she ardently longed from her twenties to work for destitute children or in India. Family exigencies, however, meant that she had to turn her excellent education and undoubted intellect into teaching, first as a governess and then as a teacher in the girls' school in Bristol run with her mother and sisters. It was only as she was able to relinquish these responsibilities that she could develop the innovative work on the education of the poorest in society and those either convicted of crime or apparently on the margins of criminality which made her one of the most well-known women of her day in liberal reforming circles.[25]

Religion was thus the springboard for Mary Carpenter's work and her Unitarian network was to provide much needed and valued support. For example, her prime collaborator on reformatory schools was first Matthew Davenport Hill, while Russell Scott of Bath and Lady Byron supplied respectively the land, building and furniture for Kingswood Reformatory School. Mary was then able to use examples from this and from Red Lodge, the separate reformatory school for girls which Lady Byron enabled her to buy, to argue the case for reformatory schools further. She was also helped in her reformatory and Indian reform work in Bristol by Frances Power Cobbe and Susannah Winkworth respectively, both Unitarian women who themselves extended professional opportunities and rights for women.[26]

Initially, despite her compelling reformist talents and cultural networks, Mary Carpenter was stifled by the conventions of female propriety to an almost crippling extent. Thus the way she both found her 'voice' and developed her own ideas were significant for gender issues. Firstly, by working through 'permitted' channels of philanthropy and social work, she extended the more usual limits of 'her sphere'. For example, as secretary of her chapel's visiting society established in 1835, she was responsible for the society's superb organization and excellent reports which she then used to compel the chapel to set up a domestic mission.[27] In 1848, she utilized the new national inspectorate to prove through her own ragged school that sympathy, respect and interesting, engaging lessons could win the attention of impoverished children in the most difficult of circumstances. When, in 1852, Parliament dragged its heels over establishing reformatory schools she went ahead and, with support from her Unitarian network, established her own.[28]

The need to persuade others of her educational ideas became a catalyst for Mary Carpenter. As she became increasingly immersed in the difficulties of reaching the many outcast and impoverished children so prevalent in the growing urban landscape of Britain, so she turned to writing in order to inform, persuade and cajole the public into action. Her vigorous, cogent studies, full of detailed statistics, not only persuaded others of the force of her reasoning, but gave Mary Carpenter herself increasing confidence in her own formidable and seemingly inexhaustible powers of intellect, research, administration and communication. Yet, at first, she remained anonymous, abiding by the custom that women did not usually write or put their names to works of scholarship.[29] Nevertheless, despite the reservations of her own family, impelled by passionate conviction, in 1851 she published *Reformatory Schools for the Children of the Perishing and Dangerous Classes and for Juvenile Offenders* in her own name. Thenceforward she became a national figure and was even invited the following year to speak before a Parliamentary Committee on criminal and destitute children, although she very nearly declined for fear of provoking male antipathies to female interference.[30]

Mary Carpenter also proved herself to be both a pioneer and an expert at a new form of reform agitation – conferences. It was she who organized the first conference on juvenile delinquency, held in Birmingham in December 1851, although her new friend, Matthew Davenport Hill, chaired it and Mary kept silent in the presence of men.[31] In the next few years she prepared papers for conferences but had them read for her. Eventually, however, she began to read her own. The catalyst for this change was the establishment of the National Association for the Promotion of Social Sciences (NAPSS) in 1857. Its regular annual conferences attracted all the 'great and the good' in liberal causes and was unusual in having women present and active from the start. In its first 20 years, however, no woman and few men spoke so often or on such a variety of topics as Mary Carpenter. From 1857 to 1876, she gave 32 papers on her own and two with others, frequently joined in the discussions after papers and by 1867 was able to speak extempore. After her death, in 1877, her services were eulogized by the President, George Hastings, yet 20 years earlier neither he nor Lord Brougham had mentioned her by name in their frequent references to the well-organized reformatory movement.[32]

The significance of the growth of Mary Carpenter's public persona was not lost upon her eldest brother, William Carpenter. His lengthy obituary to her noted that her name had been absent from the invitations to the all-important 1852 Birmingham conference despite her crucial role in it. This, he said, was because then 'there were many, alike in public and in private, who were ready to stigmatize as "unfeminine" any woman who should put herself forward in such a matter'. According to him, the obvious change that had now come about owed as much to her as anyone – 'and this, not so much by advocacy of Women's *rights*, as by practical demonstration of Women's *capabilities*'.[33]

It is certainly true that by the end of her life Mary Carpenter found an international voice. Invitations to Europe, the USA and Canada illustrated the esteem given to a woman who had become, through practice and writing, an authority in her chosen field. At the same time she consciously became an advocate of greater rights for women. Although she could be almost mysteriously 'proper' on occasion, her views had changed sufficiently for her even to speak from a pulpit in New York and to defend women's suffrage at a public meeting in Clifton in 1877. She had manipulated legislation in other ways, but, partly influenced by John Stuart Mill and partly through her growing knowledge and experience, she realized the need for women to find their voice through the ballot box. She also became an active supporter of Josephine Butler and the movement to repeal the Contagious Diseases Act.[34] In turn, other women admired her example, the *Englishwomen's Review* especially extolling her forging of an 'imperial role' for women through her activities in India.[35]

It was perhaps Mary Carpenter's four visits to India between 1866 and 1876 and her ardent commitment throughout these years to reforming female education in India, especially by establishing women's teacher training colleges, which made her more perceptive of the prevailing gender iniquities. Deeply convinced of the equality of the female and male intellect, she had always argued for all girls and boys alike to have a rigorous but lively education based on enquiry, experiment and debate, which would enable them to think for themselves. Her arguments for girls were redoubled in the Indian context where she also fought for women to have access to teaching, nursing and medicine.[36]

Mary Carpenter may have thought one of her greatest personal triumphs as a woman her invitation to speak in 1860 at Oxford to the statistical section of the British Association for the Advancement of Science, from which she had been debarred as a woman in 1836. This, indeed, marked a milestone in the acceptance of women as figures of authority.[37]

It can be seen therefore, that these four women, in different circumstances and with different talents, variously extended women's role in social and educational concerns, given that these were recognized spheres of women's influence. They did so as social reformers rather than on specific feminist agitation, even Mary Carpenter, in arguing that women were equal but different with their own God-given work limiting what women could do. Nevertheless, the three middle-class women each had an excellent education for their day and expected other females to enjoy the same. Kitty Wilkinson's education is harder to discover but she was certainly interested in adult education. Such experiences of education were typical of Unitarians and in itself both gave women greater self-esteem and enabled them more easily to take part in public concerns. It was the fact that they were in the Unitarian network which often helped them succeed in their ventures. Indeed, today their lives can be explored mostly because their own religious group eulogized them and wrote their biographies. On the other hand, being a member of a sect despised for its religious 'heresy' was not always helpful as, for example, Elizabeth Rathbone, Lady Byron and Mary Carpenter found when promoting non-sectarian educational institutions. Even so they were all motivated by their form of rational religion and their articulation of their gender identity came from within its liberal portals.

Notes

1   This chapter is based on a paper given at a *Gender and Education* conference, *Voices in Gender and Education*, held at the University of Warwick, 29–31 March 1999.
2   See Ruth Watts, *Gender, Power and the Unitarians in England 1760–1860* (1998); Kathryn Gleadle, *The Early Feminists. Radical Unitarians and the Emergence of the Women's Rights Movement, 1831–51* (1995).
3   For a more detailed discussion of the points raised in this section, see Watts, *Gender*, op. cit., especially pp. 3–8, 33–40, 99–118, 198–213.
4   Peter Spencer, *A Portrait of Hannah Greg: 1766–1828* (Styal, 1985), passim; *A Portrait of Samuel Greg 1758–1834* (Styal, 1982), passim.
5   Eleanor F. Rathbone, *William Rathbone. A Memoir* (1908), pp. 39–41.
6   Ibid., pp. 42–51.
7   'Obituary on Elizabeth Rathbone', *The Inquirer*, (4.11.1882), p. 715; J. Estlin Carpenter, *James Martineau* (1905), passim; MSS University of Liverpool, *Elizabeth Rathbone. Correspondence with Lady Byron* (1839–59), VI.1.253, passim.

8   Ibid., VI.1 pp. 227–8; 233; 236, 247; 253–4, 256, 264; 266; 277; 283; 292–333, passim.

9   'Elizabeth Rathbone', *The Inquirer*, p. 715; MSS University of Liverpool. *William Rathbone VI*, IX.2.6–4.43 passim; Eleanor Rathbone. *William Rathbone*, pp. 59, 157–75, passim.

10   *Record of Unitarian Worthies*, op. cit., pp. 181–4.

11   Ibid., p. 184; 'Elizabeth Rathbone', *The Inquirer*, p. 715; MSS University of Liverpool, *William Rathbone V*, V.3.11. William Rathbone's mother, Hannah, also had helped establish public washhouses earlier in the century – Mrs E. Greg (ed.), *Reynolds – Rathbone Diaries and Letters 1753–1839* (private circulation 1905), p. 9.

12   *Unitarian Worthies*, op. cit., pp. 184–5.

13   Ibid., p. 185.

14   See Chamber's *Miscellany* and Cassell's *Our Exemplars*.

15   *Elizabeth Rathbone*, VI.1.227–8.

16   *Unitarian Worthies*, op. cit., pp. 181–5; 340–1.

17   Frida Knight, *University Rebel. The Life of William Frend 1757–1841* (London: Victor Gollancz, 1971), pp. 238–9, 300; Benjamin Woolley, *The Bride of Science. Romance, Reason and Byron's Daughter* (London: Macmillan, 1999).

18   *Unitarian Worthies*, op. cit., p. 340.

19   W.A.C. Stewart and W.P. McCann, *The Educational Innovators 1750–1880* (London: Macmillan, 1967), pp. 154–69; Hugh M. Pollard, *Pioneers of Popular Education 1760–1850* (London: John Murray, 1956), pp. 201–8; R.G. Garnett, 'E.T. Craig: Communitarian, Educator, Phrenologist', *Voluntary Aspect of Secondary and Further Education* (1963) XV, no. 31, pp. 140–1; *Elizabeth Rathbone*, VI.1.229. Her friend Elizabeth Rathbone knew and admired Robert Owen – Ibid., VI.1.253.

20   Ibid., pp. 141–2; R.J.W. Selleck, *James Kay-Shuttleworth. Journey of an Outsider* (Ilford: The Woburn Press, 1999), pp. 131, 132, 148, 154, 160, 161, 163, 175, 194.

21   Ibid., p. 150; Emily Bushrod, *The History of Unitarianism in Birmingham from the Middle of the Eighteenth Century to 1893* (unpublished MA, University of Birmingham, 1954), pp. 9–10, 42.

22   Mary Somerville, *Personal Recollections from Early Life to Old Age: with Selections from her Correspondence*, ed. Martha Somerville (1873), p. 154; *Elizabeth Rathbone*, VI.1.235–7, 256–8, 260, 262, 264, 266, 274, 283; *Unitarian Worthies*, op. cit., p. 340; Rosamund and Florence Davenport Hill, *The Recorder of Birmingham. A Memoir of Matthew Davenport Hill* (1878), pp. 172ftn., passim.

23   For example, J. Manton, *Mary Carpenter and the Children of the Streets* (London: Heinemann, 1976); R.J.W. Selleck, 'Mary Carpenter: a Confident and Contradictory Reformer', *History of Education*, vol. 14, no. 2 (June 1985), pp. 101–16; Watts, *Gender*, pp. 101, 169–70, 174–8, passim.

24   Ruth Watts, 'Mary Carpenter: Educator of the Children of the 'perishing and dangerous classes', in Mary Hilton and Pam Hirsch (eds), *Practical*

Visionaries. Women, Education and Social Progress 1790–1930 (Harlow: Pearson Longman, 2000), pp. 39–51; forthcoming: 'Mary Carpenter and India: Enlightened Liberalism or Condescending Imperialism?', *Paedagogica Historica* vol. 37, no. 1 (2001).

25 J. Estlin Carpenter, *The Life and Work of Mary Carpenter* (1879), op. cit., pp. 1–47, 85–6, passim; William Carpenter, *Sketch of the Life and Work of Mary Carpenter* (Bristol, 1877), pp. 3–6.

26 J. Estlin Carpenter, *Mary Carpenter*, op. cit., pp 143–77, 207; Bristol Reference Library, B115 68 L98.2Car., Frances Power Cobbe, *Personal Recollections of Mary Carpenter* (no date), pp. 279–300; Norman C. Sargant, *Mary Carpenter in India* (Bristol: printed for A.J. Sergant, 1987), pp. 102, 105.

27 Bristol Central Library BL 2D B7054 *First Report of the Lewin's Mead Chapel Working and Visiting Society* (1836); *Second to Twelfth Reports* (1836–52).

28 J. Estlin Carpenter, *Mary Carpenter*, op. cit., pp. 101–13, 169–73.

29 Thus Mary Carpenter, *Morning and Evening Meditations* (1845); *Life of Tuckerman* (1849); *and Ragged Schools* (1849) were all anonymous at first.

30 Estlin Carpenter, *Mary Carpenter*, op. cit., pp. 162, 169.

31 Ibid., pp. 153–9.

32 See *Transactions of the National Association for the Promotion of Social Science (TNAPSS)* 1857–1877 and especially *TNAPSS 1857* (1858), pp. xxiii–xxvi, xxx–xxxii, 22–3; G.W. Hastings, 'Tribute to Mary Carpenter', *TNAPSS 1877* (1878), pp. 148–50; J.E. Carpenter, *Mary Carpenter*, op. cit., pp. 222, 276–7.

33 William Carpenter, *Mary Carpenter*, op. cit., pp. 20–1.

34 See above, Helen Mathers, Chapter 7 , 'Evangelicalism and feminism: Josephine Butler 1828–1906'.

35 Estlin Carpenter, *Mary Carpenter*, op. cit., pp. 399–423, 427–30; F.P. Cobbe, *Personal Recollections*, pp. 279–300; Barbara Caine, *English Feminism, 1780–1980* (Oxford: Oxford University Press, 1997), pp. 127–8.

36 Mary Carpenter, 'On Female Education' *TNAPSS 1869* (1870), pp. 351–2; 'On Female Education in India' *TNAPSS 1867* (1868), pp. 405–18, (1871) pp. 383–4, (1877), pp. 471–4. For the imperial context of this see Watts, 'Mary Carpenter and India' op. cit..

37 Estlin Carpenter, *Mary Carpenter*, pp. 266–7; Mary Carpenter, 'On the Principles of Education' *TNAPSS 1869* (1870), p. 393.

3
'At the center of a circle whose circumference spans all nations': Quaker Women and the Ladies Committee of the British and Foreign School Society, 1813–37

Joyce Goodman and Camilla Leach

Quaker women were at the forefront of both philanthropic and radical activity during the early nineteenth century.[1] They engaged with relief work during several continental wars, with prison reform, lying-in charities and non-denominational education, as well as with the anti-slavery movement, peace societies and temperance.[2] It was existing Quaker humanitarianism, overlaid with the growing influence of Evangelicalism and coupled with Quakers' rising socioeconomic status, that drew Quakers into philanthropy. In addition, the system of Women's Meetings gave Quaker women an official role and status unavailable to women more generally.[3] Such meetings also provided Quaker women with administrative experience and skills. According to Christine Trevett, in *Women and Quakerism in the Seventeenth Century*, Quakers did not acknowledge a rigid distinction between religious, social and political spheres, which, when united with their belief in the equality of women's souls, offered Quaker women both 'opportunities in the sphere of religion and a rationale for public activity'.[4]

This chapter focuses on Quaker women's philanthropic involvement in the management of non-denominational female education within the British and Foreign School Society (BFSS). Founded as the Lancasterian Society in 1810 but renamed in 1814, the BFSS aimed to extend Joseph Lancaster's monitorial methods for teaching poor children on religious but non-denominational grounds. Under Lancaster's system of 'mutual instruction', the teacher instructed older pupils at some convenient time – the monitors – who were each responsible for the instruction of a small group of pupils during normal school time, with the teacher acting as supervisor.[5] Comparatively cheap as a method, Lancasterian schools spread widely in Britain, and the method was implemented overseas.

The BFSS established its Ladies Committee in 1813, to oversee the work of the Society's girls' schools. The Ladies Committee supervised the female teacher training department at the Borough Road School, took on prospective trainee teachers, and was responsible for the brief teacher training of some of the first single women attached to English missionary societies.[6] Members envisaged their activities stretching out to 'all nations' from their base at the Borough Road School in London, noting:

> The Central Establishment may be regarded as . . . the center of a circle, whose circumference includes all nations, Christian, Heathen and Mahometan. From this point the lines of activity diverge and their termination is only to be found at the ends of the earth.[7]

Although the BFSS Ladies Committee was interdenominational, a significant proportion of members between 1813 and 1837 were Quakers.[8] In this chapter we use the example of the BFSS Ladies Committee to look at ways in which philanthropic work in education constituted part of religious ministry for some Quaker women, tracing some of the Quaker networks and identifying a number of committee members who were Quaker ministers. We then examine aspects of the religious, social and political languages used by Quaker women to represent their educational activities, to construct themselves as authoritative educators and to legitimate their educational work abroad. We focus on the overseas activities of BFSS committee member Martha Yeardley, née Savory. Although much of Yeardley's writings have been lost, we draw on material included in the memoir of Martha and her husband, John, as well as their jointly-authored letters and books, to explore an area of particular interest to the Ladies Committee and the Yeardleys: education for women and girls in the Ionian Islands.[9]

Several Ladies Committee members attended Quaker meetings that were within easy travelling distance of London, particularly in Gracechurch Street, where many leading Quakers worshipped, as well as meetings at Tottenham, Southwark, Stoke Newington and Devonshire House.[10] Elizabeth Dudley, for example, had moved with her mother and siblings from Clonmel in Ireland to England in 1810, attending the Southwark Meeting, where she was recorded as a minister in 1811. Dudley travelled extensively in ministry with her mother Mary until the latter's death in 1823, and ministering along with BFSS Ladies Committee member, Jane Harris.[11] Dudley's brother Charles married Hester Savory whose sisters Martha and Rachel were both recorded in ministry by the Southwark Meeting in 1818 and were also members of the Ladies Committee.[12]

Quaker women like these often ministered after one another in meetings for worship. Elizabeth Dudley wrote in 1817, for example:

> Martha Savory broke the silence this morning. I thought her helped, and on sitting down felt myself engaged to express what had been the subject of my reflection, which was much in accordance with her exercise. Jane Harris followed in supplication.[13]

As Sheila Wright's chapter in this collection demonstrates, such women developed spiritual friendships, often travelling together in pairs to attend meetings that were long distances from their homes.

For some Quaker members of the BFSS Ladies Committee, work in education, such as visits to prisons, formed an integral part of religious ministry. Mary Dudley's biographer noted that 'a visit to the various schools conducted by Friends in the vicinity of London, consisted part of the present service'.[14] The religious language through which Elizabeth Dudley described a visit to William Impey's school, demonstrates the genre of ministry which Quaker women used to describe their work in education. For these Quaker women, to minister was to educate:

> after the boys had had their supper, spent some time with them.... There were thirty-five scholars, mostly sweet solid-looking children. They sat with great quietude and attention whilst we were each engaged to address them, and an encouraging feeling was raised that many among them were preciously sensible of the invitations of heavenly love, and ready to yield their hearts to its tendering influence. After leaving them we had a sweet little sitting

> with W.I. and his two sisters. The former broke forth in expression of the comfort he had felt in our visit to the dear boys; and my dear mother addressed him in the most encouraging and affectionate manner, preparing him for greater discoveries of the divine will, and exciting to full resignation and faithfulness thereto.[15]

George Fox had always charged Quaker ministers to act as models in all countries, places, islands and nations and the international view of their educational activities held by the BFSS Ladies Committee was very much in line with Quaker notions of the Commonwealth of Believers.[16] In 1825, the women of the committee wrote of:

> their earnest wish that all who know the value, and importance of being themselves acquainted with the blessings of the Gospel of our Savior, will unite and assist in extending those blessings to the ignorant and neglected of every part of the habitable globe.[17]

The Ladies Committee received, reprinted and commented upon reports from women engaged in supervising girls' education in places as diverse as Madeira, Mauritius, Malacca, North America, George Town, Colombia, Italy, Spain, The Netherlands and Paris.[18] The extensive international travelling of Quaker women ministers under the leading of the Inner Light has already been illustrated by several scholars. Alison Twells, for example, has pointed to the work of Ladies Committee member Hannah Kilham who visited the Gambia and Sierra Leone in the 1820s and 30s, wrote extensively on British and African education, and whose step-daughter, Sarah Kilham, ran the Lancasterian Girls' School in St Petersburg.[19] After serving on the Ladies Committee, Martha Savory undertook ministerial journeys before and after her marriage to John Yeardley including visits to France, Switzerland, Holland, Germany and Greece.[20] But it was education in the Ionian Islands that was of particular interest to both the Yeardleys and the Ladies Committee. From 1815 the Islands formed a British protectorate,[21] important as a strategic station upon which the British informal empire in the Mediterranean was to be sustained, secured and expanded.[22] Interest in the Ionian Islands' desolation as a result of the fighting between Turkey and Greece, and the Greek Orthodox Church's struggle for ecclesiastical independence within the Eastern Orthodox communion had captured the interest of women educationalists.[23]

From 1825, the BFSS Ladies Committee reported on 'exertions' for the education of youth in Greece and the Greek Islands, liaised with the Edinburgh Ladies Society for Promoting the Education of Girls in Greece and set up a special fund to support the extension of female education in Greece and the Ionian Islands.[24] The Edinburgh Ladies Society appointed a teacher, Miss Robertson, financed her brief teacher training at the Borough Road School under the auspices of the Ladies Committee and followed with interest her progress in the Ionian Islands, where she worked with Mrs Lowndes, a local missionary's wife.[25] Subsequent reports charted the establishment of schools for girls at Corfu, Zante, Cephalonia, Santa Maura, Ithaca, Paxo and Cerigo.[26]

The interest of Martha and John Yeardley in Greece and the Ionian Islands also dated from their period after meeting 'a very interesting missionary student' on a ministerial journey abroad who introduced them to the Priest of a Greek church at Amsterdam, culminating in a religious tour of Greece and the Ionian Islands in 1833.[27]

The Yeardleys described their travels to Greece as a visit of 'gospel love'.[28] They worked closely with the family of missionary Isaac Lowndes, whose 'diligence and perseverance in laboring for the good of others' they found 'worthy of imitation'.[29] They attended a tea for 'persons of influence', which Lord Nugent, President of the Ionian Government, arranged and at which 'all conversation was on the subject of bettering the condition of the poor and destitute children'.[30] They were also guests at a state dinner given by the governor, where their plain Quaker dress among other dinner guests attired in formal dress and national costume, seemed to cause little comment. The Yeardleys worked hard together to learn modern Greek, distributing copies of Judson's *Scripture* in Greek and travelled through difficult terrain to visit various schools and prisons and finally established a girls' school at Patras.[31]

The Yeardleys' letters depicting their ministerial travels were reprinted in 1835 at the print shop set up at the school established by William Allen at Lindfield.[32] Their subsequent publication, *Eastern Customs* (1842), expanded on their views of Greek society, the education of Greek girls and the position of women in the Ionian Islands.[33]

Extracts from their letters were later incorporated into the account of their life and ministry, published in 1859.[34]

Letters from travelling ministers such as the Yeardleys were circulated to groups of Quakers and to individuals and read as important educative texts.[35] Accounts of women's work in education overseas were also reprinted in the BFSS reports and commented upon by the Ladies Committee in their annual reports, processes which built up layers of self-referential reporting. Alison Twells has argued that in their philanthropic and educational work women often drew on a range of discourses which acted to differentiate themselves from those indigenous women on the receiving end of their mission.

> Such a process was central not only to the empowerment of white, middle-class women, but was a crucial component of the languages of ... colonialism, through which the emerging middle-class asserted its difference from and superiority over ... colonized peoples overseas.[36]

Letters and reports like those of the Yeardleys held justified potential to act as literary transmitters of early and mid-nineteenth-century colonial ideas and practice. Yet, as the following discussion will show, in the process of constructing identities at 'home' and 'abroad' as British and non-British, the Yeardleys' religious and educational language, while 'Orientalist' in framing, reflected the ambivalent positioning of the Quakers in relation to dominant British Christian subject positions.[37]

While travelling widely in the Ionian Islands, speaking with many individuals and inspecting schools and prisons, the Yeardleys wrote home to the BFSS on successive occasions:

> How often our hearts are ready to sink within us in the midst of this dark and superstitious people. We have now been here nearly three months and have not had one opportunity of publicly preaching the gospel. The power of prejudice in favor of their own superstitious rites, and the overwhelming influence of moral evil, seem entirely to close our way in this line.[38]
>
> We shall be truly thankful if ever permitted to leave these dark islands and reach the other side of the Alps, where we trust the pure light of the gospel may again shine around us.[39]

The metaphors of 'darkness' and 'light' are widely used both in religious language and in the educational language of the Enlightenment. For Quakers, the language of 'light' took on a special significance in that it related to their belief in the 'Inner Light' and so to Quakerism's more mystical elements. For Quakers, the 'Inner Light' was a manifestation of the indwelling spirit of Christ, a living spirit within the individual. Those called to minister were prompted by this Light to speak under divine inspiration.[40]

The Yeardleys wrote that the Greeks needed to partake of 'vital' religion and to renounce their outward practices of 'superstition' if Greek society was to be regenerated, understanding enlightened, morals reformed and classes to conform to the social rank designed for them by Providence.[41] They were concerned about the priests of the Greek Orthodox Church, who learned by rote the church services in ancient Greek with no apparent spiritual understanding and they were exercised by rituals such as child baptism, the 'adoration of saints' and the 'system of picture worship'.[42] The public religious festivals were particularly shocking to them:

> [F]or nearly two months at this time of year, some of the worst class are seen parading the streets in masks greatly disfigured, and from what we see and hear, we are painfully made to feel that the name of Christ may be honored with the lip and with the tongue, and numerous fasts and ceremonies strictly observed, while the power of the Savior's love is not allowed to have a place in the heart, and a darkness almost worse than pagan may prevail.[43]

These 'superstitious rites' were equated by the Yeardleys with moral evil and want of energy and character:

> Their habits are not industrious; and they have but little method in conducting their affairs.... The extreme heat of the weather often occasions them to rest in the middle of the day; when we see the lower orders of the people, lying about in the shade, in various parts of the town and neighbourhood.... The generality of the people seem to prefer a life of ease and poverty, to one of industry and comparative plenty.[44]

They attributed the chief cause of this mental and physical 'indolence' to the Ionian's 'long state of slavery', and economic dependency upon the Venetians, and drew upon a language of benefaction and protection which depicted British colonial expansion as benign. As Eileen Yeo has argued, the language of constitutionality, and the notion that such a constitution guaranteed liberty to freeborn Britons, was common currency at this point, which, mingled with Christianity, presented the 'freeborn' British woman as charged with the duty and the authority to assist those in bondage.[45] As Jane Rendall illustrates, this hierarchical view of the development of different societies, in terms of reason, 'progress', 'improvement' and civilization, was built upon a view of philosophical history which assumed that human nature was uniform across the world and that the laws of development which governed the progressive history of societies could be universally identified.[46] The Yeardleys drew on just such an Enlightenment-based hierarchy of racial and social development headed up by European civilization when they wrote:

> There is a great deal to be done among a people just emerging from barbarism, and bringing with them all the fixed habits of ignorance and superstition.[47]

The depiction of the 'condition' of woman formed a central organizing theme within this construction and a key criterion in judging the 'civilized' status of different societies.[48] Mrs Kennedy, wife of the Garrison doctor at Cephalonia, wrote to the BFSS of the women in the Ionian Islands, that 'the condition of the females here is far below that which it ought to be'[49] and the BFSS Ladies Committee commented, 'No permanent and elevated status of moral improvement and civilisation can be either gained or long maintained by the men when progress of the women does not bear a just proportion'.[50] The Yeardleys similarly devoted one section of *Eastern Customs* to 'The Degraded State of Females in Greece' and, in an interesting reinforcement of the separate spheres ideology, described their 'sense of disapprobation' and shock on observing men cooking, waiting at table, washing dishes and making beds, while the wives and daughters of the peasants were 'employed in servile out-door work' [which] in more civilized countries is performed by the men'.[51] For the Yeardleys this constituted 'the right order of things thus reversed':

We had heard much of the degraded state of Females in Greece but never believed that it existed to such a lamentable extent. In some instance the women are little above the beasts of burden in view of lordly man. During our country visits on this island it was not unusual to see the Father of the family marching before his domestic circle with upright step, stately air, staff in hand...while his wife and three or four daughters followed almost bowed to the earth under a heavy burden of wood.[52]

The seclusion of women in the Ionian Islands was a particularly difficult concept for the Yeardleys to grasp and they were quick to attribute this to the previous occupation of the Islands by the Turks:

One of the Turkish customs, which the Greeks have adopted, is the seclusion of their young women. In the middle and higher classes of society they are scarcely permitted to go out during the day without being accompanied by some elderly female, to take care of them.[53]

Hinting at possibilities of sexual danger, they pointed to the moral inconsistencies between the seclusion of women and the spurious freedoms created by the wearing of masks:

A young girl who came to do needle-work at our lodgings, always had her mother to come with her; and she returned to fetch her home, even in the broad daylight: yet so inconsistent is their conduct toward their children, that these same girls are permitted to go out in an evening to places of diversion, – not infrequently disguised in masks etc.[54]

The Yeardleys were also critical of the child marriage, the 'custom of betrothing children...without consulting the affections or inclinations of the young people'. This, they thought, led to the most unhappy consequences: 'the dissolution of the tenderest family ties – divorce and misery', concluding that: 'We may invariably observe, the more uncultivated any nation is, the more the females are kept in a state of oppression'.[55]

Martha Yeardley was not impervious to the 'dissipation' of the greater part of the English, and particularly the military, however.

To her dismay, the Senate granted leave for a ball to be held in the new school-rooms. As well as dancing, which was inimical to strict Quaker practice, the partition between the two rooms was to be broken down, delaying the opening of the school for a month.[56] Martha's critique of the English illustrates how Occidentalist and Orientalist divisions were far from absolute. This instability interwove with the boundaries between denominational groupings of Christians, which the Yeardleys constructed as they contrasted the 'superstitions' of Greek Orthodox and Quaker 'vital' religion.[57]

At the same time, much of their writing was framed within notions of British superiority and responsibility, and they urged benevolent individuals at home or abroad to promote the education of the Greeks 'to induce them to abandon all those habits, which tend to moral degradation'. Mrs Kennedy similarly wrote: 'It well becomes [women] to unite in rescuing other women from the degraded consequences of ignorance'.[58] Such representations depicted the British woman as the cultural superior of their charges, and as the female moral and educational 'rescuer' of non-western woman and girls.

As Antoinette Burton has argued, the promotion of British women's moral and cultural agency, while simultaneously denying agency for indigenous women by signifying them as the 'helpless, degraded victim of religious custom and uncivilized cultural practices', constructed the non-western woman as a 'burden' to be cared for by the white woman.[59] The familial language of 'care' used by the BFSS Ladies Committee was compatible with the maternal language used by many other British women to legitimate their educational work in both British and colonial contexts. As Eileen Yeo demonstrates, in order to legitimize their activities, women invoked a range of socially acceptable meanings and practices of maternalism, which drew on discourses that were simultaneously biological and social.[60] This enabled them to represent the extension of female authority as non-threatening and compatible with woman's sphere, while infantilizing the 'objects' of their care. The BFSS Ladies Committee typically characterized British women in terms of their maternal intelligence, moral purity and piety.

Like other early nineteenth-century women writers on education they drew on maternalist constructions to argue that the progress of society and national regeneration depended on the extension of the domestic affections into wider society through the educative activities of the preceptress.[61]

To what extent this represented a feminization of the public sphere, requires further research. Within Quakerism, however, maternalist discourse constituted a spiritual language of authority and a spiritual motherhood which supported Quaker women's public role as preachers and their activities in the public sphere.[62] Maternalist discourse drew on the term 'Mothers in Israel' to describe Quaker women who integrated ministerial and domestic roles, thereby denoting the spiritual aspects of educational work.[63] The term 'Mothers in Israel' also drew on notions of biological and domestic motherhood to point up an important educative role for women in the wider public sphere. In such rhetoric, maternalist education could be read as political discourse or patriotic duty.

Much of the educational language of the BFSS Ladies Committee invoked the Hartlean theory of association which built on Locke's view that 'all mental phenomena arise from the association of ideas and that these ideas are originally formed from sensations caused by the impression of external objects on the senses'.[64] Women writers and educationalists argued that this gave a central role to women – for it was mothers, responsible for the child's early moral and intellectual developments, who were the most likely to set up proper or improper associations between sensations and feelings upon which both the ability to reason and moral virtue depended.[65] Association theory also provided a theoretical underpinning for the Quaker notion of a 'guarded' education, in which the environment was manipulated to leave the child open to a favourable reception to the workings of the Inner Light.[66] Quaker women's education was to be 'useful' and to eschew all 'accomplishments', particularly singing and dancing, which Quakers saw as inimical to 'vital' religion. The result was a more thorough education for female Quakers than was generally the norm for early nineteenth-century women. Yet, for Quakers, the adoption of associationism did not denote an education simply geared to the honing of reason. Indeed, while the Yeardleys saw education as the key to reversing the 'superstitions' they found in the Ionian Islands, Martha, in particular, viewed rational metaphysical study as frequently opposed to 'vital' religion:

I was led to a love of metaphysical studies ... that human vice and consequently human misery, sprang from ignorance of the nature of virtue ... and that it was only necessary to behold virtue in its native beauty, to love it and to practice it. O how fallacious was this reasoning! The world by wisdom knows not God; the natural man receives not the things of the Spirit of God, for they are foolishness to him, neither can he know them, because they are spiritually discerned.[67]

In the Yeardleys' eyes, those from the Ionian Islands who sought to escape religious superstition by reading 'sceptical publications' in French and Italian and 'metaphysical works in the English tongue', were in danger of becoming unbelievers: 'It is a mournful fact, that superstition often leads to infidelity, when its deformity is discovered, before vital religion has taken root in the hearts'.[68]

Building on the view of Britain as 'superior' in the scale of societies, therefore, the BFSS Ladies Committee legitimated their educational activities by pointing to their 'superiority' as maternal educators.[69] The task of the British woman educationalist was to transmit her 'superior' knowledge of the educative process.

For Quaker Ladies Committee members, the extension of 'vital' religion though female education held the potential to provide an environment in which spiritual receptivity could be fostered. For some Quaker members of the Ladies Committee, visits to schools constituted religious ministry. For these women, the language of light stood for the Quaker spiritual 'Inner Light'. Their educational authority was underpinned by the spiritual ministry 'to the ends of the earth' undertaken by Quaker women ministers as 'Mothers in Israel'. Some, like Martha Yeardley, left a legacy of educational and devotional writings attesting to a Quaker female tradition of religious and educational authority. The metaphor of 'Light' was a powerful Christian metaphor; it underpinned the evangelical mission of diverse Christian groups. 'Light' resonated, too, through Enlightenment notions of reason and progress. As a result, Quaker understandings of 'Light' ran alongside missionary and Enlightenment discourses, all of which provided rationales for women's action in the public sphere, and so facilitated the collaboration of various groups in the cause of female education.

As their concern for the women and girls of the Ionian Islands illustrates, Quaker women interwove language that was religious, social, political and educational. They brought the language of one into the arena of the other. In religious terms, the Quaker view of the Commonwealth of Believers posited a spiritual equality that was compatible with an Enlightenment philosophical view of a uniform human nature. This, in turn, provided the epistemological underpinning for associationist educational language and the maternalist language of care which the women of the BFSS deployed. Associationist theories of education could, however, link with the view of a uniform human nature in ways which shaded into hierarchical, constitutional and stadial Enlightenment frames, as degrees of 'civilization' were measured in terms of the status and treatment of women and societies judged. As concerns for the status of Ionian women and their education illustrate, this could lead to a rationale for public action and constructions of authority based on notions of British women's cultural superiority, which denied agency to non-western women, while positing them as prospective rational mothers. Yet, as Martha Yeardley's comments about the dissipation of the English demonstrate, Quaker religious belief and practice could undermine dominant Orientalist representations. Furthermore, the struggle to construct boundaries between Christians held the potential to blur the boundaries of national and religious self and other.[70]

Quaker women brought to the women's movement a history of female spiritual ministry and built on a legacy of female action legitimated by religious, social and political rhetoric, both of which informed their civic consciousness and fostered their participation in the public sphere. The Quaker legacy was empowering for Quaker women and encouraged a public philanthropic role that was expressed at times in the political rhetoric of the day. While Quaker rhetoric and practice could undermine dominant Orientalist representations, as their concern for the status of Ionian women and their education illustrates, it also invoked contradictions of colonialism which would continue to resound.

Notes

1 J.O. Greenwood, *Quaker Encounters*, 3 Vols (London: Sessions Book Trust, 1975, 1977, 1978). Many studies point to important Quaker networks when discussing women's political activity. Holton notes the importance of the Bright circle, 'comprising a kinship and friendship circle of radical Quaker women'. Holton, S.S. *Suffrage Days: Stories from the Women's Suffrage Movement* (London: Routledge, 1996), p. 2.

2 Braithwaite, W.C. *The Second Period of Quakerism* (London: Macmillan and Co. Ltd., 1919); Brayshaw, A.N. *The Quakers, Their Story and Message* (London: George Allen and Unwin, 1953 edition); Punchon, J. *Portrait in Grey: a Short History of the Quakers* (London: Quaker Home Service, 1984). For Quaker involvement in non-denominational education in York, see: Wright, S. *Friends in York: the Dynamics of Quaker Revival 1780–1860* (Keele: Keele University Press, 1995), Chapter 5.

3 Wright, S. *Friends in York*, op. cit., p. 69. Larson, R. *Daughters of Light: Quaker Women Preaching and Prophesying in the Colonies and Abroad, 1700–1775* (New York: Knopf, 1999), p. 33. Sheila Wright illustrates that this might be restricted in practice, a situation which came to be mirrored later in the BFSS. Wright, S. *Friends in York*, op. cit. pp. 32–9.

4 Trevett, C. *Women and Quakerism in the Seventeenth Century* (London: Sessions Book Trust, 1991, 1991 edition), p. 14.

5 Wardle, D. *English Popular Education 1780–1975* (Cambridge: Cambridge University Press, 1970, 1976 edition), p. 86.

6 Bartle, G. 'The Role of the Ladies Committee in the Affairs of the British and Foreign School Society', *Journal of Educational Administration and History*, vol. 27, no. 1, 1995, pp. 51–61. Maria Newall (Malacca) and Mark Anne Cooke (India) both trained briefly at the Borough Road School. Bartle, G. 'The Role of the BFSS in Elementary Education in India and the East Indies, 1813–1875', *History of Education*, vol. 23, no. 1, pp. 17–33.

7 British and Foreign School Society (BFSS), *Annual Report*, 1824.

8 Separate reports of the BFSS Ladies Committee cease to be printed in the Annual Reports after 1837 and the minutes of the Ladies Committee were destroyed by bomb damage in the Second World War.

9 Tylor, C. *Memoir and Diary of John Yeardley* (A.W. Bennett, 1859); Yeardley, J. and Yeardley, M. *Extracts from the Letters of John and Martha Yeardley, Whilst on a Religious Visit to some Parts of the Continent of Europe, the Ionian Isles, etc.* (W. Eade, 1835); Yeardley, J. and Yeardley, M. *Eastern Customs: Illustrative of Scripture Passages: with some Observations on the Character, Manners, etc. of the Greeks* (Harvey and Darton, C. Gilpin, John Linney, the Authors, 1842). Martha and John wrote a range of devotional and educational books, some individually and some jointly authored.

10 For the development and fortunes of these meetings see: Becker, W. and Ball, T.F. *The London Friends Meetings, Showing the Rise of the Society of Friends in London* (F. B. Kitto, 1869).

11 Tylor, C. *Memoirs of Elizabeth Dudley, consisting chiefly of Selections from her Journal and Correspondence* (A. W. Bennett, 1861), pp. 5, 20, 39, 331.

12 Friend's House Biographical Register.

13 Tylor, C. *Memoirs of Elizabeth Dudley*, op. cit., p. 41.

14 *The Life of Mary Dudley, Including an Account of her Religious Engagements and Extracts from her Letters* (J. and J. Arch, 1825), p. 284.

15 Tylor, C. *Memoirs of Elizabeth Dudley*, op. cit., p. 87.

16 Kashutus, G. 'The Inner Light and Popular Enlightenment: Philadelphia Quakers and Charity Schools, 1790–1820', *The Pennsylvanian Magazine of History and Biography*, vol. CXVIII, nos. 1–2, January/April, (1994), p. 96.

17 BFSS, *Annual Report*, 1825, pp. 42, 43.

18 BFSS, *Annual Reports*, 1818–1831.

19 Biller, S. *Memoir of Hannah Kilham* (Darton & Harvey, 1827); Dickson, M. *The Powerful Bond, Hannah Kilham, 1774–1832* (Denis Dobson, 1980); Twells, A. '"So Distant and Wild a Scene": Hannah Kilham's Writing from West Africa, 1822–1832', *Women's History Review*, vol. 4, no. 3, (1995), pp. 301–18; Twells, A. '"Let us Begin Well at Home": Class, Ethnicity and Christian Motherhood in the Writing of Hannah Kilham, 1774–1832', in Yeo, E.J. (ed.) *Radical Femininity: Women's Self-representation in the Public Sphere* (Manchester: Manchester University Press, 1998).

20 Tylor, C. *Memoir and Diary of John Yeardley*, op. cit., Martha Yeardley returned home from her last journey in 1850 exhausted and 'debilitated with disease' from which she was to die.

21 Palmer, A. *An Encyclopaedia of Napoleon's Europe* (London: Constable, 1984), p. 156. The Ionian Islands were united with Greece in 1864.

22 Chircop, J. 'The British Imperial Network in the Mediterranean 1800–1870: a Study of Regional Fragmentation and Imperial Integration,' unpublished PhD thesis, University of Essex, 1997, abstract.

23 The Greek Orthodox Church was declared autocephalous (ecclesiastically independent) in 1833 and recognized as independent by the ecumenical patriarch of Constantinople in 1850, cf. *The New Encyclopaedia Britannica*, vol. 5 (Encyclopaedia Britannica, 15th edition, 1995), p. 456. For Hannah More's interest in the conflagration between Turkey and Greece see: Stott, A. 'Patriotism and Providence: the Politics of Hannah More', in Gleadle, K. and Richardson, S. (eds) *Women in British Politics, 1760–1860: the Power of the Petticoat* (London: Macmillan, 2000), p. 49.

24 BFSS, *Annual Report*, 1825, p. 41.

25 BFSS, *Annual Reports*, 1825–1830.

26 BFSS, *Annual Report*, 1833, pp. 22, 23.

27 Yeardley, J and Yeardley, M. *Letters of John and Martha Yeardley*, op. cit., p.118

28 Ibid., p. 19; Tylor, C. *Memoir and Diary of John Yeardley*, op. cit., p. 118.

29 Yeardley, J. and Yeardley, M. *Eastern Customs*, op. cit., p. 42.

30 Tylor, C. *Memoir and Diary of John Yeardley*, op. cit., p. 245.

31 Tylor, C. *Memoir and Diary of John Yeardley*, Chapter XII; Yeardley, J. and Yeardley, M. *Letters of John and Martha Yeardley*, op. cit., pp. 23, 24. By

1842, places in the girls' school they established had increased to 450, Yeardley, J. and Yeardley, M. *Eastern Customs*, op. cit., p. 101.

32 Yeardley, J. and Yeardley, M. *Letters of John and Martha Yeardley*, op. cit., frontispiece.

33 Yeardley, J. and Yeardley, M. *Eastern Customs*, op. cit., p. i.

34 Tylor, C. *Memoir and Diary of John Yeardley* op. cit.,.

35 Leach, C. '"Mothers of Israel" and the Battle of Evangelicalism 1790–1830', unpublished paper, Women's History Network (Southern) Conference (University College Chichester, 1999).

36 Twells, A. 'Let us Begin Well at Home', op. cit., p. 27.

37 See Said, E. *Orientalism* (Harmondsworth: Penguin, 1985); For a more detailed account of the self-referential reporting of the Ladies Committee see: Goodman, J. 'Languages of Female Colonial Authority: the Educational Network of the Ladies Committee of the British and Foreign School Society, 1813–1837', *Compare*, vol. 30, no. 1 (2000), pp. 7–19; see also Baker, N. '"Men of our own Nation": Gender, Race and Other in Early Modern Quaker Writing', *Literature and History*, vol. 10, no. 2 (2001), p. 3.

38 Tylor, C. *Memoir and Diary of John Yeardley*, op. cit., p. 249.

39 Yeardley, J. and Yeardley, M. *Letters of John and Martha Yeardley*, op. cit., p. 32.

40 See Kashutus, 'The Inner Light', op. cit., p. 92.

41 Yeardley, J. and Yeardley, M. *Eastern Customs*, op. cit., pp. 120, 121.

42 Tylor, C. *Memoir and Diary of John Yeardley*, op. cit., pp. 246, 250, 258.

43 Yeardley, J. and Yeardley, M. *Letters of John and Martha Yeardley*, op. cit., p. 22.

44 Yeardley, J. and Yeardley, M. *Eastern Customs*, op. cit., p. 106.

45 See a useful discussion of constitutional and patriotic language in Yeo, E.J. 'Some Paradoxes of Empowerment', pp. 1–24; Larrabeiti, M. 'Conspicuous before the world: the political rhetoric of the Chartist women', in E.J. Yeo (ed.) *Radical Femininity: Women's Self-representation in the Public Sphere* (Manchester: Manchester University Press, 1998), pp. 106–26.

46 Rendall, J. 'Writing History for British Women: Elizabeth Hamilton and the Memoirs of Agrippina' in Campbell Orr, C. (ed.), *Wollstonecraft's Daughters: Womanhood in England and France, 1780–1920* (Manchester: Manchester University Press, 1996).

47 Tylor, C. *Memoir and Diary of John Yeardley*, op. cit., pp. 249, 250.

48 Bowles, P. 'John Millar, the Four-stages Theory, and Women's Position in Society', *History of Political Economy*, vol. 16, no. 4, (1984), pp. 619–38; Tomaselli, S. 'The Enlightenment Debate on Women', *History Workshop Journal*, Autumn (1985), pp. 101–24.

49 BFSS, *Annual Report*, 1826, p. 95.

50 Ibid., p. 91.

51 Yeardley, J. and Yeardley, M. *Eastern Customs*, op. cit., pp. 120ff.

52 Yeardley, J. and Yeardley, M. *Letters of John and Martha Yeardley*, op. cit., p. 27

53 Yeardley, J. and Yeardley, M. *Eastern Customs*, op. cit., p. 124

54 Ibid.

55 Ibid.

56 Tylor, C. *Memoir and Diary of John Yeardley,* op. cit., p. 248.

57 For a nuanced analysis of the intersection of Quaker identity, Englishness and gender in the early modern period, see Baker, 'Men of our own Nation' op. cit.

58 BFSS, Annual Report, 1825, p. 14.

59 Burton, A. *Burdens of History: British Feminists: Indian Women and Imperial Culture, 1865–1915* (Chapel Hill: University of North Carolina Press, 1994), p. 8.

60 Yeo, E. J. *The Contest for Social Science: Relations and Representations of Gender and Class* (London: Rivers Oram Press, 1996), pp. 9–14 and Chapter 5; Yeo, E. J. 'The Creation of "motherhood" and Women's Responses in Britain and France, 1750–1914' *Women's History Review,* vol. 8, no. 2, (1999), pp. 201–18.

61 Goodman, J. 'Undermining or Building up the Nation? Elizabeth Hamilton (1758–1816), National Identities and an Authoritative Role for Women Educationists', *History of Education, Special Edition, Education and National Identity,* vol. 28, no. 3, pp. 279–97. See BFSS, *Annual Report,* 1829, p. 39.

62 Leach, C. 'Mothers of Israel', op. cit.

63 Mack, P. *Visionary Women* (Berkeley, CA: University of California Press, 1994), pp. 215–19.

64 Watts, R. Gender, *Power and the Unitarians in England, 1760–1860* (Harlow: Longman, 1998), p. ix.

65 Hilton, M. ' "Child of Reason": Anna Barbauld and the Origins of Progressive Pedagogy', in Hilton, M and Hirsch, P. (eds) *Practical Visionaries. Women, Education and Social Progress, 1790–1930,* (Harlow: Longman, 2000), p. 26.

66 Jones, S.V. 'Quakers and Education in the Eighteenth Century', *Quaker History,* 1992, vol. 52, no. 2, p. 91.

67 Yeardley, J. and Yeardley, M. *Letters of John and Martha Yeardley,* op. cit., p. 151.

68 Yeardley, J. and Yeardley, M. *Eastern Customs,* op. cit., p.131.

69 BFSS, *Annual Report,* 1928, p. 39.

70 See Baker, N. 'Men of our own Nation' op. cit.

Part II

Sexuality and Female Friendships

4
'The Gift of Love': Nineteenth-Century Religion and Lesbian Passion[1]

Martha Vicinus

The Victorians lived with, in, for, and against religion. Religion was both a personal force and a social organization. Their famous 'crises of faith' can still move us. No period outside the Reformation saw such active, widespread public debate about the role of religion in private life, political governance and social order. These discussions about religion and religious belief ran parallel with the nascent women's movement of the second half of the century. Religion was (and remains) both the single most important exponent of gender inequality – and of the equality of souls before God. Feminist historians have begun to document the important role of women in formal church organizations, as well as their often highly effective alternative religions and theologies, including spiritualism, theosophy, the Quakers, Christian Science and other lesser known denominations.[2] Dinah in *Adam Bede* (1859) no longer represents the sum total of women's position in organized religion.[3] Both religious and agnostic women of the nineteenth century repeatedly turned to the bible and to Church traditions to legitimate a wide range of social claims.

In this chapter I look at how religion can vindicate not public feminism, but rather private needs. Although I focus on the connections between homoerotic desire and religious fulfilment, it is within the context of Victorian marriage. Part of my argument will be that all sexual desire is a tangled skein that encompasses different needs, priorities and responsibilities in different times and circumstances. The personal claims made for religion are, obviously, difficult to

73

unravel, especially in regard to the largely unspoken world of women's sexuality. Nevertheless, through a close look at the life of one woman, Mary Benson (1842–1916), I offer an introductory analysis of the uses of religion for understanding and justifying homoerotic desire. In addition, I will examine how homoerotic friendships could contribute to the stability of an increasingly un-stable religious institution, namely marriage. Lesbian history is so new a field that it is hardly surprising that we have no studies of the impact of religion on nineteenth-century women's homosexual desires.[4] A single case history can hardly speak for the widely differing ways in which nineteenth-century believing women recon-ciled religion and their homoerotic desires and loves. But the atypical can also illuminate the typical. Since Mary Benson spent her entire life within a highly respected and respectable marriage, her spiritual and sexual negotiations offer complicated and contradictory – and inevitably partial – insights into women's religious beliefs, Victorian marital life and women's bonds with each other.

As the wife of the Archbishop of Canterbury, Mary Benson was a well-known figure in late nineteenth-century religious circles. Unhap-pily married, she was forced to consider both how she could answer the demands of her husband, while still maintaining faith in herself and in God. Benson grappled with such questions as 'What, & how far, is the union of two souls in matrimony, and what is the individuality?'[5] 'What does a woman owe to her husband and family?' 'To herself?' 'Would God accept her as a sinner?' She found the answers to these questions through her love of a series of women. A deeply religious woman, her intense Evangelical belief in a personal saviour began in earthly love. Her experience of erotic desire – and emotional support – became a divine gift. In doing so, of course, she participated in a centuries-old tradition of combining religious ardour with erotic desire. Benson's spiritual autobiography reveals some of the most profound difficulties and resolutions of a devout life.

European literature from at least the Middle Ages has found one language for love, whether divine or earthly. Nineteenth-century women naturally turned to the language of religious love in order to explain the combination of erotic and spiritual feeling that swept through them in the presence of a beloved. The boundaries between spiritual and sexual love must have seemed naturally permeable to women who found religious meaning in their lives through the love of a spiritually wise, mothering woman. The agnostic Eliza Lynn Linton wrote, 'when I thought of God, she stood ever foremost at His hand'.[6] George Eliot and her work in particular attracted numerous younger women who had lost their faith, and hoped to find spiritual sustenance in her religion of duty.[7] Edith Simcox, a devout atheist, called George Eliot 'Madonna'. The comparison of a beloved with the Madonna did not imply an acceptance of the thick aggregation of meanings around this figure in Catholicism. 'Madonna' was a kind of shorthand reference for the purity of a lover's motives and the infinite spiritual superiority of the beloved to other women. It also carried a faintly illicit anti-Protestant or anti-Jewish (with their privileging of a male God) aura to the relation.

Tracing the course of Mary Benson's life, we can see how she evolved from an unhappy mother and wife to a powerful mother-confessor who drew women to her. The Reverend Edward White Benson, 12 years her senior, fell in love with Minnie, as he called her, when she was 11. In collusion with her widowed mother, he educated her for marriage to him. When she married at 18 she had already had several crushes on women. In her poignant retrospective self-evaluation, she stated that during their engagement, 'I was happiest when I knew E. happy and yet wasn't with him'. She appears to have been raped on their wedding night:

> danced & sung into matrimony, with a loving, but exacting, a believing & therefore expecting spirit, 12 years older, much stronger, much more passionate, & whom I didn't really love – I wonder I didn't go more wrong ...

> I have learnt what love is through friendship – how I cried in Paris! Poor lonely child, having lived in the present only – living in the present still – The nights! I can't think how I lived – I cldn't have thought so much abt myself as I do now – we prayed, but didn't come near to God. I mean I didn't.[8]

For the first ten years of their marriage, the young Minnie tried to suppress her own needs and to obey her husband in all things. During the very years when George Eliot was writing about Dorothea Brooke's disastrous marriage to the Rev. Casaubon, Mary was attempting to reconcile herself to an energetic husband who shared with Casaubon an expectation of absolute obedience. Edward was a priggish bully and manic-depressive. With maddening rationalism, he supervised his wife's accounts, her expenditures and her behaviour toward him. He was not above wounding personal comments; on one occasion he told her, 'that some people shrank from things of an unpleasant nature, especially if they had fat chins'.[9] But the 'bickering' and 'jarring' Mary describes indicate that she was no Dorothea, trusting in God to help her control her temper. Indeed, Mary excoriated herself for failing to rest her faith in God, so angry was she that 'E. don't forgive as Thou forgivest – couldn't trust, though he tried. I remember how hopeless I felt – he couldn't believe in me'.[10] In spite of her overwhelming distaste for her husband's intimacies and emotional demands, it was unthinkable that she leave an ambitious clergyman.

Today, professionals are more likely to conceal a spiritual crisis, defining it in terms of the more socially acceptable job crisis. Victorians concealed a sexual crisis in the more acceptable terms of a spiritual crisis; but the two were often inextricably mixed. After the birth of their sixth child in 1871, Mary collapsed, and went to Wiesbaden to recuperate. She stayed there longer than expected, wrestling with a crisis of faith – in God, Edward and herself. Mary evaded confronting her demons by falling in love with a fellow boarder:

> Then I began to love Miss Hall – no wrong surely there – it was a complete fascination – partly my physical state, perhaps – partly the continuous seeing of her – our exquisite walks. If I had loved God then *would it* have been so – could it be so now? I trust in God, NOT – Yet not one whit the less sweet need it be – I have learnt the consecration of friendship – gradually the bonds drew round – fascination possessed me . . . then – the other fault – Thou knowest – I will not even write it – but, O God, forgive – *how* near we were to that![11]

Mary finally returned home and Miss Hall briefly joined her. About these events Mary could only say in her retrospective diary, 'I haven't gone, and I cant, fully, into the way I worryed [sic] my dear ones here – I lost my head – and, blessed by Thy name, O Lord, I came to grief – The letter – ah! My husband's pain – what he bore, & how lovingly, how gently – *our talk*. My awful misery – my letter to her'.[12] Presumably Mary told her husband that she did not love him, and would not live with him, but with Miss Hall. In the end, she did not desert her husband, and Miss Hall faded away, but Edward was forced to accept his wife's primary emotional and erotic loyalty to women. They had no more children.

While the Bensons were never to have a happy marriage, their relationship improved with Mary's clarification of her own emotional and religious needs. She ran Edward's household, softened his relations with others, and successfully helped him to make his way up the Church ladder, from headmaster to the first Bishop of Truro (in Cornwall) and then Primate of the Church of England. When divorce was impossible or too socially disgraceful to contemplate, sensible men and women had to adapt to failure. As long as neither the husband, nor more usually, the wife, spoke publicly, life could go on. For some men this meant a quiet affair on the side, for others a whirlwind of work that we now label peculiarly Victorian. This latter state certainly characterized Edward White Benson, who thought nothing of 14- and 18-hour working days.

I want to argue that for women, to an extent that we are only now recognizing, a special woman friend might give life fresh meaning. Schooled in a culture that approved of adolescent crushes, many mature women turned to old or new women friends when their marriages were unsatisfactory. Documentation is necessarily scarce; even today, overt criticism of one's spouse is seen as evidence of an impending break-up. Virtually every Victorian novel keeps marital misery within the family, forcing the unhappy heroine to turn either to God or to a relative for advice and sustenance. Virginia Woolf, in *To the Lighthouse* (1927), however, portrays a family reminiscent of the Bensons. In her dissection of that monster of Victorian patriarchal egotism, Mr Ramsey, she provides Mrs Ramsey with the adoring, albeit ineffectual, Lily Briscoe. In a scene reminiscent of Edith Simcox at George Eliot's feet, Lily Briscoe imagines flinging herself 'at Mrs Ramsey's knee' to declare her love.[13] Even in this novel, however, marital misery remains unspoken; but love gives Lily insight. If Mary Benson gave an unusual amount of time to her friends, friendship was widely regarded as an important component in the lives of professional families who often lived far from family and kin. Her choice of religious and sexual solace in the arms of pious women was simply a more extreme resolution to the loss of faith in husband and God than that taken by other unhappily married women.

Edward had to accept Mary's women friends. If she felt trapped in her marriage, he desperately needed her, both for his career and his emotional well being. But their reconciliation was slow and never complete. After giving up Miss Hall, Mary was saved from depression by the love of 'Tan' Mylne, the wife of an older theology student. We know little about this spiritual advisor outside Mary's diaries. Tan suggested that Mary write an account of her life, of her marriage, in order to review how she failed to love God. She confirmed Mary's sense of sin – of her lack of a consistent, unwavering faith in God – but she also showed how recognition of one's sinful nature could be the first step back to an all-loving God. Mary found her path to God arduous and exhilarating:

> I, having fallen away from good through the entire absence of personal religion, begin to seek God again by finding my growing weakness & poverty of soul; I am brought into close relations with one who tells me she finds her only strength, her fullest hope, her most ardent love in direct personal communion with this Xt – She says 'love', and she knows, I find, what it means, for she pours out to me what I acknowledge as sweetest & fullest human love – I begin to read the Bible....[14]

The married Tan, unlike the poor and unmarried Miss Hall, counselled Mary how best to cope with her husband. She both supported Mary's 'rebellion' against the demands of Edward and prayed with her until her heart 'was softened & turned to Thee'.[15]

Tan called Mary 'Ben', a name that all her close women friends called her, while Edward used the diminutive 'Minnie'. Even a casual acquaintance with lesbian historiography indicates an extraordinary attachment to male or androgynous nicknames. Such nicknames not only implied woman-to-woman intimacy, but also the creation of a self-sufficient world where masculinity could be assumed with the ease of a change in clothing and naming. 'Ben' was an evident shortening of Benson, without drawing too much attention to its implicit masculinity. But it could well have carried additional implications, such as 'benison', or God's blessing. 'Tan' is more difficult to decipher but may have referred to the Greek letter T (Tau), a Christian symbol for the crucifix and for life – an appropriate name for a mother-enabler. In her diary, Ben calls Mrs Mylne 'my beloved helper', 'beloved Tan, my Mother in Christ'. Alternatively, it could refer to her unfashionable skin colour or it might imply the slang 'to thrash soundly', because Ben brought her sinful nature to Tan to be scourged. But given the religious symbolism of Ben, it is more likely that Tan symbolized a Christ-given gift. Ben confidently wrote, 'Thou of thine abundant, rich goodness gavest me hours with my darling Tan – hours in the fullness of the beauties of Thy creation – and she spoke of Thee – and as she spoke, the Love of Thee – I know it – filled her heart to the brim – and its peace was shed on me'.[16]

Mary ruefully admitted that when she could at last claim Christ as her Saviour, she had expected 'all joy & no cross', but found instead that she needed constantly to suit her ways to those of her needy husband.[17] Mary's sins all circled around Edward; she could not conquer her impatience and anger. Thus, ironically, Mary needed Edward as a kind of chastisement, just as she needed her beloved Tan as a reminder that human love would bring her to God. A woman's supportive love taught her to know God's love, whereas Edward's love consumed her and destroyed her relation with God. In Mary's struggle to find a sustaining faith, she pictured her own, human obduracy, her 'hardness' as a problem, but God's obduracy was pictured as a source of strength and sustenance. Her heart is like a rocky surface, but His strength is a rock upon which to cling. She admonished herself, 'Break up your fallow ground: first is time to seek the Lord until he come & rain righteousness upon us'.[18]

In contrast to her husband's Establishment authority, Mary's faith centred on a forgiving Father. As her son Fred said, she 'looked on God as a Father, he as an omnipotent King'.[19] Edward's life-long ambition was to make the public, whether it be schoolboys, Cornish miners or discouraged clergy, acknowledge the authority of God. He bitterly regretted that the Established Church no longer wielded the kind of secular influence it once had; as Archbishop he expected unquestioning obedience and manifest deference. He was shrewd enough, however, to recognize that increasingly the appeal of the Church lay in its ceremonies and moral influence, rather than its doctrines. His theology remained a non-doctrinal amalgam of High, Low and Broad Anglicanism. Throughout his career he worked to make the Church theologically comprehensive and publicly power-ful. Yet he was fiercely anti-ecumenical, for he always feared the loss of authority.[20]

In 1876 Benson was appointed to Cornwall as the first Bishop of Truro. In this stronghold of Methodist dissent, he threw himself into improving the Church of England. He was frequently away visiting ministers in his diocese, and the children were older, leaving Mary freer. She fell in love with Mrs Charlotte Mary Bassett, who was unhappily married to an elderly invalid. Their correspondence, from 1879 to 1888, provides us with insight into how Mary came to see her relations with women as spiritual opportunities. Early in their relationship she wrote, 'The divine thing in the world would be to be able to heal a spirit one loved, wouldn't it?'[21] Just as Tan had brought her to see God through human love, Mary now instructed 'Chat' to have faith in their love for each other as part of God's plan. Mary passionately argued, 'it is all of God . . . not one whit less than *all you* will I have, in that mysterious, sacramental union where one can have all, and yet wrong no other love'.[22] Male possessiveness had crushed Chat, as it had Mary at an earlier juncture, but now Mary could promise a union that paradoxically freed one: her love would liberate Chat from spiritual doubt and earthly lovelessness. We catch a glimpse of the beginning stages of their relationship in a letter in which Mary forthrightly declares:

> Does it frighten you I wonder to find yourself beginning to *care* for anyone? It seems to me more wonderful & solemn as the years go by, and all ones inadequacies & sins – 'negligences & ignorances' – stand out in fuller relief, and one scarcely dares to put out ones hand for so great a gift – only there is really no room for shame where there is none for pride, and one knows every day more that it is all of God.[23]

As their relationship grew, they exchanged secret gifts, photos and nicknames (Chat called Mary 'Robin'). In both her retrospective diary and in her letters to Chat, Mary writes of moments of 'fusing', in which they achieved a very earthly spiritual union: 'Did you *possess* me, or I you, my Heart's Beloved, as we sat there together on Thursday & Friday, as we held each other close, as we kissed?'[24]

Mary exhorted Chat that their love was like the Resurrection, bringing forgiveness for past sins, a rebirth in faith, and a new future.[25] For Evangelicals the great mystery of Christianity was Christ dying for mankind. Since all men were sinners, the atonement – the crucifixion – was the cornerstone of belief. The incarnation – that God had become human – was less important.[26] The greatest Church holy day was Easter, not Christmas, for it represented an annual cleansing of human sin, just as baptism washed away original sin. One Easter eve Mary wrote Chat a letter that brings together all the main images and themes of her religion:

> Oh, God forgive me, my Treasure, for daring with such sinful & mean lips to speak to you so – but it seems to me He tells me – & He can use any instruments He will – This blessed time! . . . Live for gladness & love & hope – My dearest, I want you tomorrow to live in the thought . . . that the past is *forgiven* – as God forgives. [T]hat all that you sorrow over – the wrong, the inadequacy, the bitterness, the anger, the rebellion, the mistakes – that it is all *washed away* – that your flesh has come to you like the flesh of a little child, and you are clean – and not clean only – but filled with life . . . *Close* to the heart of the Father, & clasped, now as ever in His everlasting, loving, mighty arms – Do not fear.[27]

God was an accessible, loving father, ever ready to embrace a sinner and to let her begin again as a child, free from sin. But Chat did not find the same religious peace as Mary and their relationship gradually cooled.

Mary met Lucy Tait around 1883, when Edward was appointed Archbishop; she came to replace Chat as the most important person in her life. According to her son Arthur, Edward asked Lucy to live with them sometime in the late 1880s; she stayed until Mary's death in 1918.[28] Edward's invitation was an overt acknowledgement of his dependence upon his wife, but Lucy also sweetened his path by giving unfeigned homage to her father's successor. But the price was high: as Fred, her son, delicately explained, Lucy Tait 'slept with my mother in the vast Victorian bed where her six children had been born'.[29]

Ben won her sexual subjectivity within a socially sanctioned marriage; she never considered her love of women to be adultery. Marriage was not a cover, as it became for many early twentieth-century lesbians. While educated Victorians were certainly familiar with female homosexuality, they still accepted intimate friendships as a normal part of women's lives. Mary Benson was well known as someone markedly sympathetic to women, but contemporaries were careful not to pry into her married life. Moreover, the Victorians prized heterosexual fidelity more than emotional fidelity. John Stuart Mill's chaste love for the married Helen Taylor is the most famous example. For over 20 years the older John Taylor accepted Mill's frequent visits to his wife as long as he did not consummate his love of Helen. Given Mary Benson's loyalty to her husband, she had no reason to feel that she was unfaithful. Indeed, she studied hard how she might 'not think of *being at my ease*, but of suiting my ways of saying things to his feelings' because Edward 'thinks more of little remarks, is more sensitive, more easily wounded than I am'.[30]

By the mid-1890s, as Edward's health weakened from overwork, Mary leaned more and more heavily on Lucy for support. The sexual – and spiritual – base of their love is irrefutable. Just before Edward's death she wrote in her diary an analysis of her growing dependency upon Lucy; her comments focused on Lucy's superior spirituality. On the opposite page she wrote this revealing prayer:

> Once more, & with shame O Lord grant that all carnal affections may die in me, and that all things belonging to the spirit may live & grow in me – Lord look down on Lucy and me, and bring to pass the union we have both so entirely & so blindly, each in our own region of mistake, continually desired – The Desire has been fading lately, through despair of each, in our own way – & despair is very near me still as I wait & pray. I ask from thee O Lord strong & unconquerable love of the spirit, a flame of fusing, an eternal fire that the desire which came from thee may be accomplished for thee in us, forever.[31]

The diary laments, 'It still remains as it ever did for her to be strong and continuous in spirit, for me to be yielding & dependent – not with the dependence of *fear*, which I seem to have far too much, but of love, inspires my living spirit as well as hers. Unselfish love taking, her *all* in, and loving & embracing & considering all'.[32]

Mary/Minnie/Ben/Robin mingled God's love and early love throughout her life, but we do her wrong to think that these loves were wholly without their erotic component. For too long the gushing affection of Victorian letters between members of the same sex has been labelled wholly asexual and without the sexual meaning that we would impute to such florid language. Indeed, there seems to

ɔe a refusal to accept sexual sophistication on the part of the Victor-
ans because modern words are not used.[33] But Christians must re-
ɔeatedly wrestle with the contradictions between privileging the
ɔiritual, and the fact that we experience love most intensely through
he physical. Mary fully recognized this dilemma, concluding at the
ɔnd of her life,

> I believe and really I know from experience that there is a class of
> persons (of whom I am one) who DO learn God through Man. I
> remember so well when I first discovered that in really loving, one
> loved through man to God, that the only thing to avoid was to
> stop short – that selfish love always did this – but that love that
> gave never need and took one straight there.[34]

She knew and accepted same-sex love, but also recognized its potential for sin. She appears to have had a wavering boundary between
what might be an acceptable form of fusing and what might be dangerous.

Ben, as all her friends now called her, never considered giving up
Lucy or same-sex love. Nevertheless, as a Christian, she could not
wholly accept the desires of the flesh. Fire, a symbol of purification,
meant a spiritual conflagration that would take their earthly love and
purify it for God. It was a goal she did not always achieve, and
probably did not want to achieve, in spite of bouts of guilt. Years
before she had recognized the dangers of carnality. In her retrospective diary, Mary noted that she had refused to return home for Christmas in 1872 because of her infatuation with Miss Hall. She had
written uneasily about this love, 'then – the other fault – Thou kno-
west – I will not even write it – but, O God, forgive – *how* near we were
to that!'[35] 'The other fault' remains unnameable, in spite of numerous letters and diary descriptions of perfect 'fusing' with women. Yet,
given other comments, we must recognize that she is speaking of
carnal intimacies that surpassed the spiritual mergings that were her
ideal. Mary never explored in writing whether this too-close relationship with Miss Hall was itself sinful, or whether it was sinful because
it had led her to abandon her husband. But Edward approved of Lucy.
Sexual relations with her were not so much an act of adultery or
disloyalty to her husband as a falling away from a spiritual ideal, in
which Desire rather than God dominated their love.

Over a lifetime together, sexual relations can take on very different meanings for heterosexual couples. Why should the same not be true of homosexuals? Virginia Blain has warned against assuming either an unknowing asexuality or an unproblematic sexuality in lesbian couples of the past. As she documents, the aunt and niece who wrote under the pseudonym 'Michael Field' were often ambivalent about their sexual relationship. At first they glossed their satisfying physical connection in the language of classicism, but then the niece converted to Roman Catholicism. She confessed her past sins to her priest, who urged continence, and in time the women proudly confirmed that they had ceased all 'fleshly sins'.[36] Clearly, religious belief could and did alter the nature of women's friendships. Did the loss of Edward free her to think differently about having ousted him from their large Victorian bed years earlier? We cannot completely know, but all evidence points to her wholehearted acceptance of Lucy's love as God-given. Sexual sameness had brought her to God at a time when sexual difference had plunged her into the sin of despair. For Mary, who had found an acceptance of herself as a sinner to be the very means by which she had come to God's love and forgiveness, carnal affections with her beloved friend could never be an entirely bad thing. Mary was never wholly comfortable with a bodiless affection, and after Edward's death, even as she wrestled with their carnal fusing, Lucy stayed in her bed.

Ben was to know little happiness aside from her women friends. Edward never overcame either his depression or his domineering ways, and overwork brought an untimely death at 63. His favourite son, Martin (1860–78), died at 17. Arthur (1862–1925), the next son, was subject to severe, disabling bouts of depression, and crafted his life so as to avoid all emotional entanglements. Their youngest son, Hugh (1871–1914), converted to Roman Catholicism; he too evaded human relations as much as possible, and loved only his old nurse, Beth. Their daughter Nellie (1863–90) died at 27 of diphtheria, caught caring for the poor around Addington. Maggie (1865–1916), the remaining daughter, also suffered from depression and eventually had to be incarcerated. Only E.F. (Fred) Benson (1867–1940), the popular and prolific novelist, seems to have been free from the taint of Edward's melancholia, but he too avoided intimacy by constructing a life of homosocial bonhomie.[37]

As she aged, both friends and sons united in their praise of Ben's loving, accepting religion. Arthur, the teacher of Greek, noted in his diary after her death, 'Mama was an instinctive *pagan* – hence her charm – with the most beautiful perceptions and ways. Papa was an instinctive Puritan, with a rebellious love of art. Papa on the whole hated and mistrusted the people he didn't wholly approve of. Mamma saw their faults and loved them'.[38] Ben was not a pagan, of course, and would have been horrified to be labelled one, but perhaps her wholehearted acceptance of people made her seem free from the taint of Edward's debilitating religion. Towards the end of her long years as a confidante of women, she wrote a friend 'especially to say how strongly I feel that Motherhood must be, and is, as absolutely contained in God as Fatherhood . . . surely it must be so, for all to take exactly what they need – from the Deep Well of Eternal Quality'.[39] In her seventies, still living with her beloved Lucy Tait, Ben could take her religion one step further, and define God as both female and male. She came to see mothering not as an expression of spirituality, but rather as intrinsic to it. An all-forgiving God must, therefore, by definition contain both the father and the mother. It is a position that only now has gained serious inroads in theological debate. Within the confines of a traditional marriage, Mary Benson found room for homosexual love, and a radical reconceptualization of God.

Notes

1 An early version of this chapter was read at the conference 'Gendered Communities: the Challenge of Religion, Nation and Race', held at Tel Aviv University, March 16–19, 1998. I am indebted to Billie Melman for her support and enthusiasm for my project. Thanks also to Michael Schoenfeldt for sharing ideas about the relationship between religion and earthly love.
2 See the pioneering collection, *Religion in the Lives of English Women, 1760–1930*, ed. Gail Malmgreen (Bloomington, IN: Indiana University Press, 1986), as well as such recent studies as *Women of Faith in Victorian Culture: Reassessing 'The Angel in the House'*, eds Anne Hogan and Andrew Bradstock (London: Macmillan, 1998) and *Women's Theology in Nineteenth-Century Britain: Transfiguring the Faith of Their Fathers*, ed. Julie Melnyk (New York: Garland, 1998). Quotations from the Benson Deposit [hereafter abbreviated as BD] are courtesy of the Bodleian Library, Oxford.

3   For literary studies of women and faith, see Christine Krueger, *The Reader's Repentance: Women Preachers, Women Writers, and Nineteenth-Century Social Discourse* (Chicago, IL: University of Chicago Press, 1993) and Ruth Y. Jenkins, *Reclaiming Myths of Power: Women Writers and the Victorian Spiritual Crisis* (Lewisburg, PA: Bucknell University Press, 1995).

4   In contrast, see the pioneering essay by Joanne Glasgow, 'What's a Nice Lesbian Like You Doing in the Church of Torquemada? Radclyffe Hall and Other Catholic Converts', *Lesbian Texts and Contexts: Radical Revisions*, eds Karla Jay and Joanne Glasgow (New York: New York University Press, 1990), pp. 241–54. Religious homosexuals have vigorously claimed their place in today's churches. See, for example, Kathy Rudy, *Sex and the Church: Gender, Homosexuality, and the Transformation of Christian Ethics* (Boston, MA: Beacon Press, 1997) and *The Lesbian and Gay Christian Movement: Campaigning for Justice, Truth and Love*, ed. Sean Gill (London: Cassell, 1998).

5   Undated [retrospective] diary entry, BD 1/79.

6   Eliza Lynn Linton, *The Autobiography of Christopher Kirkland* (London: Richard Bentley, 1885), I, p. 203.

7   Gordon S. Haight, *George Eliot: a Biography* (New York: Oxford University Press, 1968), pp. 450–5. There are 14 references to Eliot as 'Madonna' in *A Monument to the Memory of George Eliot: Edith Simcox's Autobiography of a Shirtmaker*, eds Constance M. Fulmer and Margaret E. Barfield (New York: Garland Press, 1998). Men were more apt to call older women 'teacher', instead of mother.

8   BD 1/79. Italics in the original. In addition to this spiritual history, written at the suggestion of 'Tan' Mylne, Mary kept a diary intermittently during her long life when under special personal stress.

9   Quoted in Mary Benson's diary, January 16, 1864, BD 1/73.

10 BD 1/79. She is describing 1865. Following the birth of Maggie, but similar comments about their vexed relationship are found throughout the diary.

11 1872, BD 1/79. Emphasis in the original. Mary was staying with her brother-in-law and his wife, who took in English boarders and taught English. Edward had disapproved of his crippled brother's marriage, and had refused to attend the wedding, but relations had since been patched up. An early letter (September 26, 1872) to Edward comments 'Miss Hall, the lady boarder is a *very* pleasant person – clever & bright & merry.... - Says she has digestive problems and hints that she hopes it isn't pregnancy', BD 3/3.

12 1874, BD 3/3. Italics in the original.

13 Virginia Woolf, *To the Lighthouse* (London: Hogarth Press, 1960), p. 35.

14 Monday [1875], BD 1/79.

15 She describes an incident that occurred June 12 [1875], BD 1/79.

16 June 12 [1875], BD 1/79.

17 May 17 [1876], BD 1/79.

18 'Begun Friday, March 17, 1876', BD 1/79.

19 *Mother*, p. 26.

20 Arthur Christopher Benson, *The Life of Edward White Benson, Sometime Archbishop of Canterbury* (London: Macmillan, 1899), I, pp. 594–5, II, pp. 764–5.
21 Undated fragment, *c.* mid November 1879, BD 3/28.
22 Feb 17 [1879], BD 3/28. Italics in the original.
23 Undated fragment, *c.* Early November 1879, BD 3/28. Italics in the original.
24 January 4 [1881], BD 3/28. Italics in the original.
25 See, for example, the Easter eve letter, March 27, 1880, BD 3/28, in which Mary exhorts Chat, 'Do not fear. Do not doubt. Put away, for tomorrow all thoughts such as "how can I, at my age, love again so?" "how shall I, who have failed so often, succeed now"'.
26 The fundamental beliefs of Evangelicalism are discussed in D.W. Bebbington, *Evangelicalism in Modern Britain: a History from the 1730s to the 1980s* (London: Unwin Hyman, 1989), pp. 2–19. See also Boyd Hilton, *The Age of Atonement: the Influence of Evangelicalism on Social and Economic Thought, 1795–1865* (Oxford: Clarendon Press, 1988).
27 March 27, 1880, BD 3/28. The letter begins with a comment in brackets 'I have had to forsake my little sheets you see – I did not feel as if I had *space* enough – it was crampy'. Ethel Smyth called Mary's little notes 'prescription paper'. See *As Time Went On* (London: Longmans Green, 1936), p. 15. This letter and others hint that Chat may have loved another man; her invalid husband was notoriously ill tempered and difficult.
28 Quoted from Archbishop Benson's diary, Askwith, p. 188.
29 E.F. Benson, *Final Edition* (New York: D. Appleton Century, 1940), p. 23.
30 May 17 [1876], BD 1/79.
31 Ibid. The following prayer appears on August 17, 1896, BD 1/78, following her reading of Ethel Smyth's letters to the now deceased Nellie:

> O Merciful God, grant that the old Adam in me may be so buried that the new man may be raised up to me.
>
> Grant that all carnal affections may die in me & that all things belonging to the Spirit may live and grow in me.
>
> Grant that I may have power & struggle to have victory & to triumph against the devil, the world & the flesh. Amen.

Several entries also speak cryptically of 'when I went to bed the fall came', and of excessive carnality. 'Carnal affections' and 'carnal stains' appear again in her 1898 diary. See May 6 and St Peter's Day 1898, BD 1/78.
32 October 1, 1896, BD 1/77. Italics in the original.
33 Williams, for example, denies the sexual foundation of her friendships. Brian Masters, *The Life of E.F. Benson* (London: Chatto and Windus, 1991), agrees with him, but concludes (with Arthur) that her friendships helped to destroy the family after Edward's death. Betty Askwith, *Two Victorian Families* (London: Chatto and Windus, 1971), admits that Mary's relation-

ships 'certainly transcended mere friendship' (p. 192), but also insists 'It is not likely that Mrs Benson ever had physical relations with any of these beloveds. She probably did not even know that such a thing was possible' (p. 134). For a discussion of this attitude, see my essay 'Lesbian History: All Facts and No Theory or All Theory and No Facts?' *Radical History Review*, 60 (1994), 57–75.

34   April 30, 1907, BD 3/38. This is among the edited and typed letters in the Benson collection.

35   Undated, BD 1/79. Written in regard to her stay in Wiesbaden in 1872–73.

36   Virginia Blain, ' "Michael Field: the Two-headed Nightingale": Lesbian Text as Palimpsest', *Women's History Review*, 5/2 (1996), pp. 246, 251. Blain speculates that Edith's conversion may have been a means of gaining more solitude in a relationship that extended back to her childhood. Katherine soon followed Edith into the Roman Catholic Church for fear of losing her.

37   The details of the children's lives are discussed in Williams, op. cit. See also Masters and David Newsome's selection of Arthur's voluminous diary, *On the Edge of Paradise: A.C. Benson: the Diarist* (London: John Murray, 1980), as well as the numerous biographical memoirs published by A.C. and E.F. Benson.

38   Masters, p. 226. Quoted from a letter to Fred, undated and unattributed. Arthur also called Maggie, who resembled her father temperamentally, a Puritan. See A.C. Benson, *The Life and Letters of Maggie Benson* (London: Longmans, Green, 1917), p. 423.

39   December 27, 1916, BD Additional Box 14. This is a typed excerpt from a letter, presumably selected by E.F. Benson after her death.

5

'Every Good Woman Needs a Companion of Her Own Sex': Quaker Women and Spiritual Friendship, 1750–1850

Sheila Wright

Friendship between women, especially women who live within a religious community, has recently been awarded more attention by historians. Caroll Smith-Rosenberg's original paper on female friendship in America, Lillian Faderman's *Surpassing the Love of Men* and Janet Raymond's *A Passion for Friends*,[1] are just three of the works which have been published on an integral aspect of feminine life. In 1853, Georgina Bruce Kirkby wrote in her journal, 'Every good woman needs a companion of her own sex. No matter how numerous or valuable her male acquaintances, no matter how close the union between herself and husband, ... the want of a female friend is felt as a sad void', and it is indeed an unusual woman who does not have deep, long lasting and loving friendships with other women.[2] Indeed, friendships extend into the whole range of relationships that women have with other women. Caroll Smith-Rosenberg has commented that friendships in the late eighteenth century and early nineteenth century formed a 'world in which men made but a shadowy appearance'.[3] And these friendships, it has been argued, were the very thing which supported women in their unequal relationships with men, providing a sense of worth which was denied them in the wider world. 'Women who had little status or power in the larger world of male concerns, possessed status and power in the lives and worlds of other women'.[4]

The nineteenth century saw an increasingly clear delineation between a man's world and a woman's world and women became increasingly separated from men in their daily occupations. Although Quaker women lived in this same world, they enjoyed an additional sphere to their lives, that is the 'spiritual sphere'. This was a spiritual sphere that was occasionally shared with Quaker men, sometimes travelling together in the ministry and sometimes working alongside each other within the monthly meeting; thus theirs was not a world of clearly defined, gendered separate spheres.

In this chapter, I want to concentrate on a particular type of friendship. This was termed 'spiritual friendship' by Aelred of Rievaulx in his classic twelfth-century work *Spiritual Friendship*. For Aelred, friendship was a part of a good and sacred life and a relationship between equals within which both parties find one to whom 'you dare to speak on terms of equality as to another self; one to whom you can unblushingly make known what progress you have made in the spiritual life; one to whom you can entrust all the secrets of your heart. . . . What, therefore, is more pleasant than so to unite to oneself to the spirit of another and of two to form one'.[5] He also considered 'spiritual friendship' to be non-carnal; to be pure and raised above the lusts and demands of the flesh and so long as it '. . . possesses purity of intention, the direction of reason and the restraint of moderation . . . it will never cease to be properly ordered'.[6] Aelred's definitions of friendship establish a framework within which I shall suggest Quaker women's friendships were conducted. It is especially apposite when applied to women living within a religious community, which in the case of Quaker women, although not shut away from the 'world', was a community which did not distinguish between the spiritual and the temporal and where spiritual friendship was a friendship between women or men who held a common belief in God and had a shared belief system.[7] I shall suggest that the unique nature of Quaker organization and society encouraged Quaker women to form particularly close friendships which were influenced by their shared religious and social expectations and the nature of their ministerial work and that these friendships were carried out within the framework of a shared, spiritual world. I shall also suggest that despite the spiritual nature of the world which Quaker women shared with Quaker men, and while women often had friendships with their male companions, the nature of these friendships differed considerably in tone, and that gender differences and patriarchal mores placed constraints on the friendships which were not apparent in the relationships which developed between Quaker female friends.

Historically it has frequently been claimed that Quakerism was imbued with egalitarian principles. The founder of Quakerism, George Fox, decreed that women should have an equal and specific role within the Society of Friends and function within their own separate but equal sphere of the Women's Monthly Meeting.[8] Significantly, Quaker women were thought to be equal receptacles for the 'Inner Light' and, consequently, equal in the eyes of God. Women, as well as men, could minister if called so to do and, importantly for women, Quakers did not believe in the Fall, directly challenging nineteenth-century ideas of domestic order.[9]

Within communities of religious women it has been argued, there have always been special friendships.[10] Quaker women were members of a highly organized, tight-knit, nationwide religious community with complex friendship and kinship networks and they conducted both their private, public and spiritual lives in accordance with the rules of the Society of Friends. Women who left the Society, for whatever reason, lost not only membership of their religious community but also their personal friendships. Mary Wright Sewell of Suffolk, for example, commented when she left the Society that she was lonely because 'almost all my friends and acquaintances were Friends'.[11]

In considering these relationships between women, it is important to emphasize that eighteenth- and nineteenth-century women generally, ' . . . did not consider themselves (nor were they considered by others) "abnormal" because they loved other women'.[12] Men found such friendships neither unacceptable nor unusual and husbands regarded these friendships as a fact of life; their wives formed attachments with other women from whom they drew support and succour and this was not a source of social or cultural disapproval.[13] Female friendships were perceived to be free from the 'demon sexuality' and the 'shield of passionlessness that a woman was trained to raise before a man could be lowered with another woman without fear of losing her chastity, and reputation and health'.[14] For Quaker women, close female friendship comprised an additional spiritual dimension born out of their commitment to a particular religious and communitarian lifestyle. They cannot simply be explained, therefore, as an expression of their craving for a romantic, intimate relationship born of the lack of such a relationship with their husbands.

The concept of spiritual friendship itself has 'unique genre in the history of ideas about friendship', a genre with a 'language and style of its own' characterized by the numerous journals, letters and diaries of Quaker women which contain many of these features.[15] Quaker women developed a distinctive language for expressing both their own spiritual emotions and their relationship with God. It was a language full of spiritual metaphors and symbolism, a code understood and shared by fellow Quaker friends and replete with popular metaphors such as 'digging deep'; 'the hedge about us'; and 'in a stripping state'. These indicated to the reader the depth of their spiritual tribulations and travails, and combined with a liberal use of biblical metaphors, collectively provided a common discourse of purpose and experience which helped bind Quaker women together.

In the seventeenth century, Quaker women had been encouraged to prophesy and promulgate their beliefs and many found themselves imprisoned for their actions and activities, sharing harsh conditions, deprived of their liberty, family and friends. The bonds of friendship forged by women under these circumstances were, of necessity, powerful, supportive and unbreakable. Katherine Evans and Sarah Cheevers, for example, were imprisoned in Malta for three years, having set off to follow in the footsteps of Paul the Apostle, distributing leaflets and preaching as they went. Their tract, written in prison between 1659 and 1662, illustrates the way in which they saw the love of their friendship as sustaining them, 'with tenderness, practical help and spiritual support' and how 'their mutuality... confirmed and generated the emotional and spiritual strength which, along with their belief, allowed them to endure physical suffering and spiritual attack'.[16]

By the end of the eighteenth century, Quaker ministers came mainly from the upper echelons of Quaker society and generally no longer suffered this type of imprisonment. But they encountered other hardships, more subtle and enduring in nature. For women who ministered, supportive friendships again provided them with the strength to endure the hostility of a male world which wished to deny them influence and presence. Women's travels in the ministry brought them into contact with mixed audiences which in many cases were unfriendly to female preachers.[17] Sarah Tuke Grubb, preaching in public in 1789, wrote that she could not get silence and was jeered by a group of youths, and Mary Alexander, preaching in Douglas, Isle of Man in 1805, wrote that the men in her audience were 'large and noisy'.[18]

Quaker women ministers travelled within their own monthly meetings, throughout their own country, and often overseas. Travel was full of dangers and hardship, and these women faced long, arduous journeys by sea and road. When Anne Moore of Maryland travelled to England in 1760, her ship was captured by a French privateer and she was taken to Spain.[19] Mary Prior sailed from England to America in 1798 and endured a voyage of 13 weeks, suffering a drunken captain, a leaking ship and a shipwreck. She eventually arrived in America having lost all her possessions; dirty, stinking of fish but thankful to be alive.[20] Female Quakers faced many personal dangers and risks to their health, and for journeys by sea, seasickness was a constant problem. Rebecca Jones, travelling to England for the first time in 1784, was sick for most of the voyage and wrote in her journal soon after embarkation that she was 'Extremely sick' and the next day 'Had a poor night: high wind kept us rolling about'.[21] The loving support of companions and friends during these voyages helped these women survive the traumas of sea travel. Sarah Dillwyn, travelling with Rebecca Jones and others, who did not suffer from seasickness, was Rebecca's 'mutual friend, nurse, and help' and was especially 'attentive to our wants', also caring for two who fell and injured their legs. Despite the close confines of a ship and the stressful conditions which could often be the cause of friction, Rebecca commented that, 'Hitherto all the company in the cabin have conducted in great harmony, each being willing to assist the other in little kindnesses'.[22] These women were away from family and friends for months and, if travelling overseas, for years at a time. Rebecca Jones left America in 1784 and did not return until 1788. Ann Alexander, a minister in the York monthly meeting, travelled throughout America from August 1803 until December 1805, leaving her husband and two small sons at home and Hannah Backhouse was in America for five years between 1830 and 1835. Generally, Quaker women ministers chose to travel with a close friend, thus ensuring a compatibility and companionship which provided the women with shared and treasured experiences, deepening the bonds of friendship, enhancing mutual closeness and confidences and allowing them to spend precious time away from the demands of husbands, home and family. Writing to a friend in September 1840 who was away ministering, Elizabeth Dudley emphasized that this was a time not only of domestic freedom but also a time which allowed a woman to 'surrender of thyself unto Him who hath chosen and ordained thee.... May this surrender be so fully made...[that] the effects of dedication being freedom from every yoke of bondage'.[23] This time away from home enabled women to experience a time when they could be entirely submissive to the will of God and because their absence was legitimized as doing God's work, it was left inviolate and free from challenge by the Society, husbands or families.[24]

Quaker women, whether ministers or not, shared the female rituals of marriage, childbirth and death and the associated problems surrounding the education of children, domestic chores, overseeing servants and organizing social functions. There was also the shared experience of their life within the Society of Friends. The endless round of visiting families, the sick and the poor; attending the women's meeting, acting as overseers and clerks to the meeting and regulating the Society, all contributed to a spiritual bonding and sense of community within which there were increased opportunities for female friendships to flourish.[25] Added to their responsibilities within the meeting, for many women there was also the chance to work with other women in the many Quaker schools and of course, in the philanthropic organizations; for example, for Elizabeth Dudley, there was her work with Elizabeth Fry at Newgate Prison.[26] In York, Sarah and Esther Tuke worked together in the Quaker girl's school they had founded in Trinity Lane and in the pioneering, Quaker-owned mental institution, The Retreat. In the nineteenth century, as the number of philanthropic organizations expanded in the city, opportunities for female involvement increased. Quaker women became increasingly involved in these non-Quaker organizations and as a consequence were further integrated into York's female society.[27] All these duties were shared primarily with other women and gave Quaker women access to a distinctively female culture within which women could form and reinforce both existing and new attachments. They lived within a female world in which 'women could share sorrows, anxieties and joys confident that other women had experienced similar emotions'.[28]

I want to turn now to the specific friendships of several different Quaker women in this period. Sarah Tuke was a member of York meeting and was appointed a minister in 1778.[29] In her early years, her closest friend was her cousin, Tabitha Hoyland of Sheffield.[30] Their letters are extant for a ten-year period from 1772 to 1782 and begin when Sarah was 16. They cover an important period of Sarah's life, during which she experienced the self-doubt and conflict of her emerging convictions, while wrestling with her natural adolescent exuberance. Several early letters include admissions to playing truant from meeting and finding it irksome to have to look after her younger siblings when her step-mother was away ministering – thus she wrote in April 1774, 'I see my own insufficiency, how unable I am to act the part of elder sister'.[31] The girls swap gossip about friends and family, commenting on local events, such as the funeral of a friend during which the sister of the deceased was inconsolable, the 'poor girl she seems to think the loss irreparable and refuseth to be comforted'.[32] They exchange gifts: Tabitha gives her George Fox's comb and in return Sarah sends her a lock of John Woolman's hair 'inclosed [sic] in a pincushion cover'.[33] Tabitha was Sarah's trusted confidante and revealed to her 'beloved friend and cousin' concerns about her spiritual growth, especially the fear she experienced when first called upon by God to stand-up in meeting in 1778; 'After such a conflict as I have cause ever to remember, I ventured onto my knees and in a manner I believe scarcely intelligible poured out a few petitions that appeared and now I feel in such a state of humiliation and fear as I never before experienced'.[34] Tabitha's comforting remarks give her a 'state of properly attained peace' which arises 'from thy good wishes to me as an individual'.[35] Friendships between Quaker women were often based on commonly held spiritual anxieties and experiences and reinforced by a shared linguistic phraseology which allowed, as Sarah wrote, 'a holy intercourse and communion experienced by those whose language is similar'.[36] Marriage could affect friendships, causing divided loyalties and emotional distractions and although Sarah's correspondence apparently ends when she marries Robert Grubb in 1782, it is likely that their kinship ties would have ensured that the friendship continued.

Two years later Sarah met Rebecca Jones at the yearly meeting in London. Rebecca was 45 and Sarah 28, and their subsequent friendship was to support her until her early death in 1790.[37] It became a close, loving friendship built on mutual respect, admiration and a deep spiritual bond, reinforced by their travels together in the ministry and sustained by their weekly and often daily letters to each other.[38] In June 1785, Rebecca went to Dublin and travelled with Sarah throughout Southern Ireland until March of the following year.[39] Although their letters detail their spiritual searching and concern for their work as ministers, they are also personal, feminine, warm and loving. Letters were eagerly awaited, 'Last night I was comforted, nay more than that, rejoiced to receive a letter from my beloved R.J'.[40] Salutations included 'Dear friend', 'My dearest friend', 'My beloved friend' and 'My precious friend', with the intensity of the greeting tracing the development of the friendship. Over the years, Sarah often declared her love for Rebecca, 'Ah my precious friend, my heart does indeed salute thee' and later, 'My heart so clearly salutes thee that tho' I undertake thus to converse with thee, the medium seems quite insufficient to convey my feelings of love and sympathy... the bond of unchangeable fellowship, in which my heart has been inclosed [sic] with thine, still comfortably awaits me, and attaches my spirit to thee'.[41] And on another occasion, faced with separation, 'For did you know the full feelings of my heart towards you, you would be completely convinced, as I trust you are in a good degree, that was it in my power I should dread to move a finger to bring about too early a separation of companions united in the holy covenant.... Whom God hath joined, let no man (as man) put asunder'.[42] The symbolic use of the marriage covenant implied indissoluble ties between not only Sarah and her friend, ties which man (or men) could not destroy but importantly between the two women and their God. Although Rebecca was hers, heart, body and soul, and their friendship was the earthly expression of their love of God, their obedience was primarily to God and His directing. By October 1788, Sarah Tuke Grubb was back at her home in Clonmel, Southern Ireland and Rebecca Jones had returned to America. Their trans-Atlantic correspondence continued unbroken until Sarah's death but was tinged with the sadness of separation. 'My heart was so almost continually with thee and so affected sometimes to amount to painful conflict that I could hardly conclude it originated merely in those natural affectionate feelings which a separation from one so beloved occasioned'.[43]

Other Quaker women had similarly intense, long-standing 'spiritual friendships'. Mary Capper and Hannah Evans of Warwick monthly meeting were close friends for over 15 years and frequently travelled together in the ministry, as did Hannah Backhouse and

Elizabeth Kirkbride, and Lucy Alexander and Elizabeth Dudley.[44] Lucy and Elizabeth's intensely emotional and loving relationship lasted for over 50 years. Like Rebecca and Sarah, they too rejoiced in receiving letters from each other; Elizabeth wrote to Lucy, that 'Thy correspondence, my endeared Lucy, has been one of my chief solaces for many months back. Thy last is a precious token of that love and sympathy which is one of the sweetest fruits of friendship'.[45] They were close confidantes, exchanging such gossip and news as Lucy's hopes to be married and Elizabeth regarded it as proof of Lucy's 'affection and confidence, thus to let me partake in what so intimately concerns thyself, and allow me an opportunity of knowing a little respecting the person with whom thou art likely to be so closely connected' and will be 'glad to know more of thy Friend, T.M., for thou rightly judgest I feel an interest in all that concerns thee'.[46] Lucy married Thomas Maw in 1803, but unlike some friendships, marriage did not lessen their closeness and affection. For both Elizabeth Dudley and Sarah Tuke, long-distance friendships were frustrating and they frequently complained that letter writing was an unsatisfactory substitute for time together. They consoled themselves by envisaging a time of physical closeness. Elizabeth 'sometimes indulge[d] in the pleasing idea that an opportunity for intercourse unshackled by pen, ink and paper, may one day be afforded' them.[47] In bereavement, women drew comfort from each other, writing of their despair and distress when a close friend or family member died. In 1807, Elizabeth's brother and father died within a few days of each other and she wrote to Lucy that 'the sensations of an orphan, which, are my beloved Lucy, new and exquisitely painful, are now known by thy bereaved friend'.[48] A distraught Hannah Backhouse wrote to 'My dearly beloved friend' (Eliza Kirkbride) – 'How often hast thou been in my mind in this day of affliction, when we have had to pass through the very deep trial of parting with our beloved eldest son, just as we were hoping, that, in a few months' time we should take him from school to live with us at home!'[49] The death of a friend was also distressing and in 1835, Mary Ann Gilpin poured out her grief to her journal, firstly over the illness and subsequently the death, of her beloved friend 'S'. 'My dear heart was deeply bowed in contemplation of resigning for ever, in this world, my much loved S'.[50] And when S dies, 'Dearly loved one! Thou who hast for years entered with the tenderest sympathy into my every trial, thou who hast partaken my every joy, art *forever* removed from my eyes in this world'.[51] When Sarah Tuke Grubb died aged 34 in 1790, Rebecca wrote to another close friend, Christina Hustler of her despair admitting that 'My loss is unbearable. I travel through the vale of tears'.[52]

It has been argued that their 'language and behaviour are incredible to-day'[53] and that the letters possess an intensity and physical lucidity to which, because we live in age which denies such outpourings of depth of feelings towards others excepting our partners, we may ascribe inappropriate sexual interpretations. While it is apparent that these women did not suppress their emotions in any way and felt able to express their physical and emotional needs for their women friends, there is a lack of evidence of any physical contact which could be read as being quasi-sexual or homoerotic.[54] In a post-Freudian age, care has to be taken to ensure that we do not read into these writings sexual meanings which may not be there. It is likely that for some women these friendships did fill an emotional void left by the lack of a loving relationship with their husbands and that for single women there was a need for intense, loving personal friendships but surpassing all these earthly needs, was the fulfilment of their spiritual requirements in which their love for each other was bound by a deeper union, their union with God.[55]

As mentioned earlier, because of the shared nature of the work of the meeting, Quaker society was not rigidly separated and Quaker women's friendships were not limited to their own sex. Friendships with Quaker men also existed and many letters were written by women and men to each other without the apparent disapproval of their respective husbands or wives.[56] However, while female/male friendships are important and supportive, they do not exhibit the same intensity or intimacy as those between Quaker women. In February 1786, Rebecca Jones, writing to Henry Drinker, was pleased to have received his 'cordial brotherly salutation . . . which met me here under an exercise of both faith and patience', and in March of the same year to Joseph Williams – 'We finished on Fifth day last having visited about eighty families. From thence we came here, attended Monthly Meeting, which was large . . . and to have a public meeting in the evening with the town's people'.[57] Generally, there is a distance and a formality of tone which I believe was accentuated by gender differences and patriarchal mores. At the same time, the somewhat nebulous quality of Quakerism's equalitarianism becomes evident in these letters as the self-confidence the women exhibit between themselves evaporates and humility and self-denigration creep in. Rebecca Jones writes to John Pemberton as 'thy poor little friend' who knows her own 'littleness and unworthiness', phrases of self-doubt she never used to her women friends.[58] Her salutations to him are more inhibited and formal, 'Dear Friend James'; 'Esteemed Friend'.[59] Rebecca closes to John Pemberton – 'I am with endeared sisterly affection and sympathy', and Thomas Ross to Rebecca – 'Farewell, I remain thy brother in tribulation'.[60] Within the Quaker ministry there existed a covert patronage which enabled older, experienced ministers to take young ministers under their wing, especially when travelling (John Pemberton was both friend and mentor to Rebecca Jones), but although this may explain the tone of some of these relationships, it does not explain the difference in subject matter. Letters between Quaker men and women describe the work the women are undertaking, news of fellow ministers and the state of the meetings but they lack the outpourings of spiritual self-doubt and religious fervour. In other words, the women do not open their hearts or bare their souls, but confine their comments to ministerial and organizational issues. Despite this, these letters are often personal and contain expressions of intense affection, as for example, letters between Rebecca Jones and John Pemberton illustrate: 'May the Lord, dear John, be with thee. ...My heart again salutes thee and bids farewell' and 'Thou has been of late brought up in my mind in great nearness of affection, in that love which distance doth not rase out'.[61]

Quaker male and female ministers lived their lives, especially when ministering, within a separate sphere, a 'spiritual sphere', which although bound by traditional gender norms, allowed friendships between Quaker men and women to operate within a unique spiritual context enabling them to cross gender boundaries. In addition, despite this intensely spiritual environment, there are underlying sexual tensions and unfulfilled or clandestine emotions which found an outlet under the guise of Godly encouragement. These were young men and women writing to each other; Sarah Lynes was unmarried and 30 in 1802 and Joseph Bevan, married and 48. Although this was a period when letters were more commonly used to convey free expression of love, both spiritual and temporal, it is difficult to remove the sexual orientation from these friendships and to modern eyes these letters would appear somewhat provocative. But again it would not be appropriate to attribute present-day sexualized meanings to these expressions of love. They need to be understood within the context of the highly charged, intensely spiritual experience and environment of the Quaker travelling ministry, where expressions of love were closely linked to a love of God and letters were routinely used as a source of spiritual encouragement to men and women undertaking difficult, arduous and often unrewarding ministerial work a long way from family, friends and home.

Quaker women needed and sought the same support and love from their female friends as did women in other religious communities and their life experiences and beliefs formed a common bond upon which to found their friendships, as well as a mutual admiration for women who considered each other as equals. The love between Quaker women was both tender, spiritually uplifting and supportive. These powerful emotions, when linked to a love of God, became a *ménage à trois* of powerful symbolism. Quaker female friendships manifested a particular quality created by the spiritual nature of their world, enhancing the intensity of these women's relationships while simultaneously sanctioning and giving respectability to, close friendships with men.

Notes

1   Smith-Rosenberg, C. 'The Female World of Love and Ritual: Relations between Women in Nineteenth-Century America' *Signs*, vol. 1, no. 1 (1975), pp. 1–29; Faderman, L. *Surpassing the Love of Men: Romantic Friendship and Love between Women from the Renaissance to the Present* (London: Women's Press, 1985); Raymond, J. *A Passion for Friends: Towards a Philosophy of Female Affection* (London: Women's Press, 1986); Rendall, J, 'Friendship & Politics: Barbara Leigh Smith Bodichon (1827–91) and Bessie Rayner Parkes (1829–1925)' in S. Mendus and Jane Rendall (eds) *Sexuality and Subordination* (London: Routledge, 1989), pp. 136–70. For a discussion on the issues relating to problems of interpretation of women's friendships see Liz Stanley, 'Romantic Friendship? Some Issues in Researching Lesbian History and Biography', *Women's History Review*, vol. 1, no. 2, (1992), pp. 5–28.
2   Journal of Georgina Bruce Kirby, in E. O. Hellerstein, L. P. Hume, and K. Offen, (eds) *Victorian Women: A Documentary Account of Women's Lives in 19th Century England, France and The United States* Stanford, CA: (Stanford University Press, 1981), p. 213

3 Smith-Rosenberg, C. 'The Female World of Love and Ritual', p. 2.
4 Ibid., p.14.
5 Raymond, J. *A Passion for Friends*, op. cit., p. 87. Stoneburner, C. and J. *The Influence of Quaker Women on American History* (Lewiston NY: Edwin Mellen Press, 1986) p. 137.
6 Raymond, J. *A Passion for Friends*, op. cit., p.88.
7 Quakers extended this spiritualization of love and relationships into the choice of a marriage partner, believing that obedience was to the 'Light Within' and thus to God and that therefore their choice of a partner was 'directed' by His will. For a discussion of these concepts see: Helen Plant, 'Gender and The Aristocracy of Dissent: a Comparative Study of the Beliefs, Status and Roles of Women in Quaker & Unitarian Communities 1770–1830 with Particular Reference to Yorkshire', unpublished D.Phil. thesis. (York: University of York, 2000), pp.63–65.
8 Egalitarianism and the forms it took within Quakerism has been considered by several historians. The form it took in the early years of the sect's development had changed by the mid eighteenth and nineteenth centuries. For a discussion of women's position in the very beginnings of Quakerism see Moore, R. *The Light on their Consciences: The Early Quakers in Britain 1646–1660* (University Park, PA: Penn State Press, 2000). For the seventeenth century see Christine Trevett, *Women and Quakerism in the Seventeenth Century* (York: Sessions Trust, 1991). For the later periods see Sheila Wright, *Friends in York: The Dynamics of Quaker Revival 1780–1860* (Keele: Keele University Press, 1995) pp. 31–49 and 55–60. More recently Helen Plant, 'Gender and The Aristocracy of Dissent' op. cit., pp. 61–3.
9 George Fox believed that men and women were created equal and it was the Fall which subordinated women to men but through 'rebirth' and knowledge of Christ, essential to all true Friends, men and women could be restored to their original state of equality. Ideas of inequality between the sexes was an aberration to Quakers and this is exemplified in their marriage ceremony which places no gendered rights or duties on either party.
10 Raymond, J. *A Passion for Friends*, op. cit., p. 86. See also Gooden R.D., in *Women in Spiritual & Communitarian Societies in the U.S.* Chimielewski, W. E. *et al.* (eds) (New York, NY: Syracuse University Press, 1993).
11 Leonore Davidoff and Catherine Hall, *Family Fortunes: Men & Women of the English Middle-Class 1780–1850* (London: Routledge, 1987), p. 87.
12 Faderman, *Surpassing the Love of Men*, op. cit., p. 120.
13 Throughout the eighteenth and nineteenth centuries, women were involved in single-sex, exclusively female enterprises through the church or philanthropic activities which were undertaken with male approval.
14 Faderman, *Surpassing the Love of Men*, op. cit., p. 159. Nancy Cott, 'Passionlessness: An Interpretation of Victorian Sexual Ideology, 1790–1850', *Signs*, 4 (1978), pp. 219–36.
15 Raymond, J. *A Passion for Friends*, op. cit., p. 86. Using journals has inherent problems of 'authenticity' of voice which accompanies selection and editing by publishers of the subject's material.

16   The Tract was written during their imprisonment by the Inquisition i
     Malta from 1659 to 1662. It was first published in London in 1662 befo
     they were released later that year. 'This is a Short Relation of some of th
     Cruel Sufferings of Katherine Evans and Sarah Cheevers', in Graham, E
     Hinds, H., Hobby E., and Wilcox H., (eds) *Her own Life: Autobiographic*
     Writings by 17th Century Englishwomen (London: Routledge, 1989), p. 8.
17   For male reactions to female preachers of different sects speaking in publi
     see: Wright, S. 'Quakerism and its Implications for Quaker Women: Th
     Women Itinerant Ministers of York Meeting 1780–1840', *Studies in Churc*
     History vol. 27 (1990), pp. 405–7. Although Quaker women were held, wit
     men, to be equal recipients of the Inner Light, during the eighteent
     century, there is evidence that there was a growing tension within th
     Society of Friends caused by the 'success' of women's preaching and thei
     perceived innate spirituality and the position of men as the regulators c
     the Society. Women were concerned that Quaker men were not fulfillin
     their role as the disciplinarians of the Society to the full and were als
     failing in their spiritual obligations.
18   Elizabeth Tuke to Henry Tuke, 4.11.1789, Tuke Papers, box 15.
19   Hope Bacon, M. 'Quaker Women in Overseas Ministry'. *Quaker History*
     The Bulletin of the Friends Historical Association, vol. 77, Fall, 1988, no. 2, p
     98. For a more detailed description of these events see Allinson, W. J
     Memorials of Rebecca Jones (London, undated), pp. 246–7.
20   Letter from S. Fothergill to unknown correspondent, 16.3.1798. Tuk
     Papers, box 75.
21   Allinson, W. J. *Memorials*, op. cit., p. 56. Hannah Backhouse sailing t
     America in 1830 wrote in her journal, "Surely if a few days voyage ha
     been appointed for a punishment, some humane people would thin
     themselves bound to get it abolished! To be at sea with a very guilt
     conscience must be terrible". *Extracts from the Journal and Letters of Hanna*
     Chapman Backhouse (London, 1858) p. 79.
22   Allinson, W.J. *Memorials*, op. cit., p. 56.
23   Tylor, C. *Memoirs of Elizabeth Dudley*, op. cit., pp. 282–3.
24   Both male and female Quaker ministers had to have a certificate issued b
     the Meeting of Elders and ministers before they were able to embark on
     journey as a minister. At this stage husbands/wives could object to th
     minister going away, however, this was very rare. The request to trave
     had to be a 'true calling' and since it was a 'calling from God' it was elevate
     to a higher, spiritual level and above the needs of a husband, wife or family
     For a discussion as to how Quaker ministers negotiated and reconciled th
     demands of family and work see: Plant, H. *Gender and The Aristocracy o*
     Dissent, op. cit., pp. 67–8.
25   Although both male and female ministers undertook the task of visitin
     families, because of the nature of the work and the greater preponderanc
     of female ministers, the work fell more heavily on women. Rebecca Jone
     had 59 sittings in 16 days with Friends in Leeds in March 1786.
26   Tylor, C. *Memoirs of Elizabeth Dudley* (London, 1861).

27 S. Wright, *Friends in York*, op. cit., pp. 69–83.

28 Smith-Rosenberg, 'The Female World of Love and Ritual', op. cit., p.14.

29 Sarah Tuke was the daughter of William Tuke and Elizabeth Tuke of York monthly meeting. Her mother died in 1760 and William remarried Esther Maud of Bradford monthly meeting in 1765. See S. Wright, *Friends in York*, op. cit., pp. 46–8.

30 Tabitha Hoyland was a minister. She was Sarah Tuke's cousin, her aunt had been William Tuke's first wife, Elizabeth Hoyland. She married Benjamin Middleton of Wellingborough in 1783 and died 18.10.1809.

31 Sarah Tuke to Tabitha Hoyland, 18.4.1774, Tuke Papers, box 14.

32 Sarah Tuke to Tabitha Hoyland, 17.10.1772, Tuke Papers, ibid.

33 These gifts illustrate how intensely their lives were bound by the Society of Friends. Sarah Tuke to Tabitha Hoyland, 1773, Tuke Papers, ibid.

34 Sarah Tuke to Tabitha Hoyland, 1778, Tuke Papers, ibid.

35 Sarah Tuke to Tabitha Hoyland, 18.10.1780, Tuke Papers, ibid.

36 *Some Account of the Life and Religious Labours of Sarah Grubb* (London, 1776), p. 9.

37 Rebecca Jones was one of the four American Women Friends who supported English Quaker women, including Esther Tuke, in their efforts to be allowed to hold their own Yearly Meeting. She was born in Philadelphia in July 1739 and brought up in the Church of England. She became a Friend after her mother's death in July 1758. During this visit to England she travelled in the first instance with Christina Hustler and became a life long friend with Christina's daughter, Sarah.

38 After Sarah Tuke's death, Rebecca Jones copied Sarah's letters into a book which is now amongst the Tuke Papers held at the Borthwick Institute for Historical Research.

39 Allinson, W.J. *Memorials*, op. cit., pp. 107–6.

40 Sarah Tuke to Rebecca Jones, 2.10.1786, Tuke Papers, box 14.

41 Sarah Tuke to Rebecca Jones, 28.10.1788; 8.3.1789 and 10. 1786, Tuke Papers, ibid.

42 Sarah Tuke to Rebecca Jones. Letter dated 11.1.1785, Tuke Papers, *ibid*.

43 Sarah Tuke to Rebecca Jones. Letter dated 28.10.1788, Tuke Papers, ibid.

44 *A Memoir of Mary Capper* (London, 1847). Mary Capper, a member of Birmingham monthly meeting, was brought up an Episcopalian and became a member of the Society of Friends in 1788. She was appointed a minister in 1794. *Extracts from the Journal and Letters of Hannah Chapman Backhouse*, (London, 1858). Hannah Backhouse was born Hannah Chapman Gurney in Norwich in 1787, a daughter of Joseph and Jane Gurney, a cousin of Elizabeth Fry. In 1811 she married Jonathan Backhouse of Darlington. She and Eliza Kirkbride were friends for most of their adult lives, travelling together in the ministry, both at home and for five years in America. Lucy Alexander was a member and minister of Needham market meeting and married Thomas Maw. Her sister Mary was also a minister; her brother William married Anne Tuke , a minister in York

monthly meeting. Elizabeth Dudley was a member of Clonmel monthly meeting, Ireland; she never married.

45 Tylor, C. *Memoirs of Elizabeth Dudley*, op. cit., p. 8.
46 Ibid., pp. 7 and 8.
47 Ibid., p. 13.
48 Ibid., p. 11.
49 *Extracts from the Journal and Letters of Hannah Chapman Backhouse*, op. cit., p. 196.
50 *Memoir of Mary Ann Gilpin of Bristol* (London, 1842) p. 99. Mary Ann, a member of Bristol monthly meeting, was born in June 1813 and her journal begins when she is 16. 'S' is not identified.
51 Ibid., p. 100.
52 Rebecca Jones to Christina Hustler May 1791, Tuke Papers, box 14.
53 Faderman, L. *Surpassing the Love of Men*, op. cit., p. 120.
54 In the many Quaker women's journals and private papers I have studied, I have found no evidence of a homoerotic nature. There are no instances of the Society of Friends warning women about their friendships with other women, although they were concerned about the conduct of female ministers when travelling with male ministers.
55 Claire Brandt has suggested that twentieth-century critics of women's letters have read them in terms of subjectivity or sexuality but that these tropes can block out a third, the soul. Many eighteenth-century women writers insisted that 'The Soul, and its Faculties, are not of any Sex'. This located epistolary writing in a discursive realm both androgynous and 'higher'. Brandt, C. *Varieties of Women's Writing*, in Jones, V. (ed.) *Women & Literature in Britain 1700–1800* (Cambridge: Cambridge University Press, 2000), pp. 285–305.
56 These letters were written for a wider public. Ministers' journals and letters were usually published and approved by the Society of Friends which apparently saw nothing amiss in the nature of the letters.
57 Allinson, W.J. *Memorials*, op. cit., pp. 119 and 125.
58 Allinson, W.J. *Memorials*, op. cit., pp. 71 and 143.
59 The word 'Friend' with a capital was the formal way to address another member of the Society of Friends.
60 Allinson, W.J. *Memorials*, op. cit., Rebecca to John Pemberton p. 87 and Thomas Ross to Rebecca p. 96.
61 Ibid., p. 75, Rebecca Jones to John Pemberton.

Part III
Women Writers with Causes

6

'Afraid to be Singular': Marianne Farningham and the Role of Women, 1857–1909

Linda Wilson

In her biography of Grace Darling, first published in 1875, the writer Marianne Farningham devoted the whole of the first chapter to a discussion of the role of women. She enthused about the lives of pioneers such as Florence Nightingale and Elizabeth Fry, who were 'speakers and preachers, scientific women and teachers' and encouraged others to emulate them. Indicating the opposition which such women had encountered, she suggested that

> Many women, simply because they are not courageous enough to brave the adverse opinions of those by whom they are surrounded, lose golden opportunities of distinguishing themselves. They are afraid to be singular. But this fear is no honour to the sex. A woman should be so far free and independent as to do that which she feels to be right, no matter though the right seem to call her to heights which she had not occupied before...what does matter is, that she should gain the high praise of Him who sees not as man sees.[1]

This passage gives a clear insight into Farningham's understanding of the role of women. She believed that fear of what others might think deterred women from grasping vital opportunities. This could be overcome if they understood that pleasing God was more important than satisfying society's expectations. What 'she feels to be right', of course, was always in the context of Christian behaviour and morality. Farningham's belief in women's role in the public sphere was thus a consequence of her evangelical faith, and, for her, completely compatible with extremely conventional, even sentimental, beliefs about the home and the role of women within it. Both orthodox and unorthodox constructions of femininity co-exist within Farningham's writings, and her readers are enthusiastically urged to be good Victorian wives and daughters, as well as to take the initiative in new areas. Yet she was not aware of any inconsistency in her own attitudes to women.

Such a combination of beliefs demonstrates how hard it is to pigeonhole nineteenth-century women according to late twentieth-century or early twenty-first century categories. Farningham is interesting precisely because, while she did not move in what could be termed the feminist world, she reflected some of its attitudes.[2] The belief system she shared with her readers gave her an opening to influence the opinions, and to engage the sympathy of, the Nonconformist public with regard to the role of women, in a way that someone with an overtly feminist stance could never have done. As a journalist, Farningham was in a particularly advantageous position to contribute to such a process. She wrote for a weekly evangelical newspaper, *The Christian World*, from its launch in 1857 until shortly before her death in 1909, becoming salaried in 1867. At its peak in 1880 the circulation was around 130 000, and it reached many Nonconformist homes.[3] In addition, she edited *The Sunday School Times* from 1885, and contributed to several other magazines, as well as publishing collected editions of her weekly prose pieces, poems and serialized fiction. In addition, for several years, in the later 1870s and early 1880s, she gave a series of well-attended winter lectures. In many evangelical families, therefore, Marianne Farningham would have been a household name. Charles Spurgeon, the celebrated Baptist preacher, certainly regarded her as 'famous' and Lloyd George apparently claimed her as one of the influences on his childhood.[4] She received regular correspondence from readers, and some at least attested that she had helped to shape their lives.[5] Given this wide influence, her writings about women and women's role are of especial interest.

Farningham had particularly strong feelings about the need for single women to take control of their lives. Single herself, she valued her own independence, even though it was initially due to the straitened circumstances of her family, and encouraged a similar attitude in other women. 'Why *should* we', she wrote in 'Girlhood', a collection published in 1869, 'so many of us skilful and quick – gifted by God with power to achieve something noble and good for ourselves – why should *we* be dependent on fathers or brothers? Why not live to some purpose, benefiting ourselves, and thereby all who are dear to us?'[6] She thus demonstrated that for her, such a position was as much a matter of principle as necessity. Phillipa Levine found similar attitudes in a sample of nineteenth-century feminists, for whom working was a statement of principle as much as an economic function.[7] For Farningham, however, this attitude was also a demonstration of the belief that God had a useful purpose for everyone, if they were bold enough to embrace it. Faith featured as a motivating factor in her writing, meshed in with personal ambition. She was always eager for women, and men too, to make something of their lives.

This attitude also fits into a pattern suggested by Martha Vicinus, in *Independent Women*, that of a single woman with a 'passion for meaningful work, so often underestimated and misunderstood'.[8] Indeed, in old age Farningham wrote that her writing had been a source of great satisfaction to her: she took pleasure in the numbers who read her work,[9] and in the belief that her writing had been an encouragement to her readers in their spiritual lives.[10] She also took pleasure in her earning and spending power, commenting late in life that 'she had never known how to save money – there were so many pleasant ways of spending it'.[11] Work was a source of both material and spiritual satisfaction.

This belief in the importance of financial independence was a tenet which Farningham held consistently throughout her career, from her earliest work. In a piece entitled 'Female Employment', for instance, which was published as early as 1861, she reacts sarcastically to an anonymous writer who apparently suggested that it was lamentable that many women had no natural protectors. Surely, she argues, they can work for themselves:

> They may on the whole be vastly inferior in sense, and wisdom, and strength, yet, perhaps, if they tried *very* hard they might be able to pick out type for printing, to copy telegraphic messages, to sell quires of paper, or even skeins of silk and yards of calico. Not so well, *of course*, but well enough, though they *are* weak.[12]

These comments indicate that, in reality, she believed women the equal of men, and quite capable of earning their own living. She continued to explain that she liked to see women working in shops, and to read of Female Printing Establishments, and hoped that before long no-one will have to sing the 'Song of the Shirt' because the value of working women would have increased, and they would be paid more. It was sad, she argued, that many young people thought work was vulgar, and earning a disgrace.[13] At the end of her life, she still held a similar view of work. Her autobiography, published in 1907, was entitled 'A Working Woman's Life', indicating that in her old age, she was still constructing her identity as that of both woman and worker, and that her independence remained a matter of pride for her.

Other passages demonstrate that Farningham was aware of the gendered realities of life. In the autobiography she recorded her childhood longing to do something of significance with her life, but commented that because she was a girl, the role models were limited. She recalled that she read a monthly magazine which included a series of articles

> on men who had been poor boys, and risen to be rich and great. Every month I hoped to find the story of some poor ignorant *girl*, who, beginning life as handicapped as I, had yet been able by her own efforts and the blessing of God upon them to live a life of usefulness, if not of greatness. But I believe there was not a woman in the whole series.[14]

There is a clear personal ambition here to do something worthwhile with her life, couched in the language of usefulness, and linked to a spiritual dimension.

Looking back to her childhood Farningham indicates that she was given little encouragement or preparation for a journalistic career. She recalled her mother's consternation because as a child she preferred reading to 'the brush or the needle',[15] and her father's later worry as to whether she 'could make money by my pen'.[16] Despite this lack of support, however, she grasped all the opportunities she was given. Her education was rather sporadic, but she made the most of it. She was nine before she first went to the new British School at Eynesford, and spent only a few years there, interrupted for a while by her mother's death when she was 12.[17] Like many intelligent women in this period she was to a large extent self-educated,[18] and in old age she still regretted this lack of education.[19] The main encouragement in her own career came not from her family but from the pastor of her Baptist chapel in Eynsford, John Whittemore. He was the founder of *The Christian World*, and he gave her her first opportunities. The range of her work indicates that she always remained eager to make the most of her own ability: in fact, she was something of a workaholic.

Farningham's beliefs about women and work extended to take in married as well as single women, although there is always the proviso that the home is looked after first.[20] She rather naively assumed that this was the case in women she admired, such as Elizabeth Fry. Levine asserts that women who worked after marriage were by definition challenging the concept of separate spheres,[21] yet Farningham praised such women, while maintaining a belief in conventional domesticity. This is another confirmation of the astuteness of Caine's suggestion that categorizing nineteenth-century women by late twentieth-century categories is unhelpful.

The question of work was linked for Farningham with a belief that women needed to be strong. This, for her, was personified by Grace Darling. Girls should be like the heroine in being 'vigorously healthy, sensible, devoted, self-forgetful', she argued in Grace Darling's biography.[22] By strength, therefore, she partly meant physical health, encouraged by fresh air and exercise, but also strength of mind and purpose, a determination to contribute to the community. Girls can be 'strong in moral courage'[23] she had asserted in 1869. Women such as Darling, she claimed, 'are not the produce of ballrooms, where the air is poisoned by gases, and where women spend nights in scenes of excitement and gaiety'. To be free from 'sickly sentimentalism', girls should be partially educated in the fresh air, and learn to despise frivolities.[24] This disapproval of idleness was common amongst evangelicals, but was also expressed by many feminists, as Levine points out, including Frances Power Cobbe who later became a friend of Farningham.[25] On this point there was common ground between feminists and evangelicals.

Apart from assertions of the need to be independent, there is surprisingly little discussion of singleness in Farningham's writings. It was only broached with anything approaching serious consideration

in her autobiography. Even there her engagement was dismissed wi
frustrating brevity. Having mentioned that, like her three hous
mates, she had been engaged, she added that 'I was made to kno
that the sheltered life of a married woman was not God's will co
cerning me'. She explained that, before long, she discovered th
there were compensations, primarily in the areas of friendship an
of intellectual satisfaction.[26] While some of Levine's feminist wome
made a conscious choice and were relieved to have avoided ma
riage,[27] the implication is that Farningham was making the best
an unfortunate situation which she came to understand and apprec
ate as God's plan for her life. But she makes no generalizations whic
might apply to other single women.

Certainly, as with her feminist contemporaries, her network
friendships appeared to have been an emotional substitute for ma
riage. Marianne insisted that apart from her first weeks in Northam
ton, she was never lonely, and appears to have found it comparative
easy to make friends. After living for a while with her sister's family,
she had a house of her own which a succession of friends and rela
tives shared: her father, a cousin, a companion, and some of he
nieces.[29] Of the latter, she commented that they had 'made m
home life happy for many years'.[30] When she travelled, which sh
did to find fresh material for her journalism, for a holiday, or t
lecture, she often took a travelling companion.[31] She also mentione
many friends in different parts of the country, as well as 'a few inte
lectual friends' in Northampton.[32] Although she rarely elaborated o
these relationships, they were clearly important to her. Highlighte
by Levine as important for feminists, friendship networks wer
equally valuable to Marianne Farningham.

Unlike her beliefs in the importance of women's strength, the
financial independence or the importance of friendship, Farnin
gham's attitude to women's rights changed over the years. In earl
pieces she dismissed the topics of 'equality of the sexes' and 'women
rights', as absurdities, answering the question 'Why shouldn't we be a
independent and strong as they?' with the assertion that 'it is inex
pressibly sweeter to submit than to rule! Because, in our weakness, it
such pleasure to cling to something strong! Because, it has pleased ou
Maker thus to create us!'[33] In this early writing, her view of women
role was, despite her own experience, fixed firmly in the privat
sphere. This was the period which Davidoff and Hall have argued wa

he zenith of separate sphere ideology,[34] and Farningham seems to
ave unquestioningly shared the assumptions that were found within
much of evangelicalism and contemporary culture.[35] It is highly likely
hat these views were shared by almost all her readership.

Thus in 1861 she dismissed the question of 'woman's rights' without giving it serious consideration. Yet in her autobiography, written
nearly half a century later, she revealed a very different perspective,
epitomised by her friendship with Frances Power Cobbe.[36] She met
Cobbe through a mutual friend in Barmouth, where she rented a
cottage, and enthused about her work as a journalist when 'her clever
pen sent through the daily press articles which roused enthusiasm for
he good, and active antagonism to the wrong'. Attending a meeting
at which Cobbe was speaking, she wondered if the audience 'knew all
hat Miss Cobbe had done for our sex'.[37] She was enthusiastic about
he latter's work, including her support for the Woman's Property Act
and tertiary education for women. Clearly, consideration of the issues
had caused her to revise her first hasty judgement.

Verbally, although not in print, she explained that this was exactly
what had happened. Farningham gave a series of lectures in 1877 on
he subject of women's rights, and one of these was reported in the
Western Daily Press. The reporter recorded her account of the process.
She commented that the phrase 'women's rights' 'had grated on the
ears of multitudes and aroused in many hearts of both sexes feelings
of bitter hostility'. Although, she explained, she was not there to
advocate such rights, she admitted that she had some sympathy
with the issues:

> At first, in common with many of her own sex, she was greatly
> opposed to it, but a little calm thought had convinced her that
> they (the fair sex) had some wrongs which needed to be righted,
> and failed, for instance, to see why women, as householders,
> should not have Parliamentary, as well as municipal, votes.[38]

While even several of these packed lectures would not have ap-
proached the readership of her journalism, yet it is an example of
her views, stemming from faith and the need to right a perceived
injustice, encouraging and possibly influencing others.

Roughly ten years after these lectures, in one of her many volumes
of collected newspaper pieces, 'Homely Talks about Homely Things',

she first committed herself more definitely in print to the cause of women's suffrage, although in such a way that those opposed to it would have had little to criticize. The piece was called 'Women and the elections' and is very telling, as she was trying desperately hard to tread a middle line which would affirm some aspects of feminism while in no way threatening women's traditional role. She discussed women's differing attitudes to involvement in elections, and suggested that 'even those who have not yet been educated to the Women's Rights point of view' will regret that they can do little to help. There is more than a hint there that she considers support for suffrage a sensible outcome of intelligent thinking. She carefully, however, gave both sides of the argument. Some prefer not to be involved, wanting to be 'in the quiet home, out of reach of the turmoil and strife. We do not care for fighting, but cry, "Give peace in our time."' While this quotation carries unwelcome connotations for the modern reader, it is hard, given Farningham's stress on the need for women to be strong and take action, to believe that there is not some implicit criticism here. Those she specifically encouraged were those who are 'intensely interested in the struggle', while not involved publicly. She stressed the 'power of pleading' and urged them to train up their boys well.[39] Here, therefore, Farningham encouraged women to unashamedly use their influence in the private sphere in order that in the future, they may be involved in the public arena. She also explained the frustration that many women feel. 'It is probable', she suggested, 'that all women who are householders and owners of property will feel that either too much or too little has been given them, since they have power to vote at municipal and School Board elections, but are not yet considered worth to be trusted with votes when the contest is a Parliamentary one'.[40] From someone who had served on Northampton School Board for six years as the only woman, and who was herself a householder, her sympathies are evident, if not explicitly stated.

It is perhaps strange, therefore, that she so rarely wrote about the topic, not often attempting to influence her undoubtedly large audience on the subject. This could have been because she tended to avoid controversy, ignoring, for instance, the major theological issues of late nineteenth-century evangelicalism. Yet she supported feminist causes such as tertiary education for women, and the opportunities for women, even married women, to work as doctors; preachers;

orkers of all kinds. It is true that she was never actively engaged in ny campaigns, but she did use her influence as a journalist to promote some of the causes. Tertiary education and women doctors n particular were regarded by Levine as essentially feminist causes, nd Farningham's unequivocal support for Cobbe is thus very suggestive. The strongest assertion of support for some of these causes, however, is found in the biography of Grace Darling which was written under a pseudonym, and in her autobiography, published at the end of her career. One cannot help feeling that she was wary of alienating her readership by being too outspoken on these sensitive issues. Instead, she tried to use her influence in many subtle comments. She was thus a supporter of but not an activist in certain areas of women's rights.

Given her change of heart regarding the rights of women, it might have been expected that Farningham's writing about the home would undergo a similar development, yet that never appears to have happened. She remained clearly committed to the Victorian ideal of domesticity and feminine characteristics – not the idle, useless aspect, but self-sacrifice, devotion, mothering. On first reading Farningham's prose and poetry, however, the reader could be forgiven for thinking that the content was little more than a reiteration of the ideas popularized by Sarah Ellis in her books on *Women's Mission*. She reveals a conventional, sentimental, domestic ideology, combined with a distaste for idleness and frivolous pleasures such as ballrooms, and is eager to encourage women to live useful lives. She had a tendency to idealize both the home and its inhabitants in her writing. Thus in 1861, she described a wife's life at home as being 'the happiest and holiest' way to live,[41] while the husband should be 'the very sun and center, the light, and joy, and warmth of the little, earnest, loving, loyal band at home'.[42] Following Sarah Ellis, she believed in the power of the home and the hearth to keep men (it was usually men) from straying from the straight and narrow. She believed that in a truly Christian home, 'vice dare not lift its head'.[43] The first duty of women was to maintain that unsullied home.

Often that meant being a mother, and, like her contemporaries, Farningham regarded motherhood as a high calling. Perhaps the story which best illustrates this conventional attitude to motherhood is from a collection of articles, 'Women and their Work', published in 1906. In three episodes, she recounted and commented on the bib-

lical account of Hannah and Samuel. That she felt this wa
motherly activity is suggested by further comments following th
story of Hannah and Samuel:

> 'But every woman, whether married or not, is the better a
> sweeter and more loveable for having some motherliness in I
> nature. And if she has not quite the joy she longs for, she can ha
> something like it. The world wants mothers almost more th
> anything else.' And many women who have no children of th
> own can still say 'He maketh the barren women to rejoi⟨
> ' "Mother!" exclaimed a motherless girl to a lady who had broug
> her into the light of the Lord Jesus, and the woman's heart ⟨
> thrilled with joy.'[44]

It is extremely likely that Marianne was the one whose 'heart ⟨
thrilled with joy'. It is interesting, although not unexpected, that
this extract there is a sense of identification of the female with t
mother. For her, motherhood was an integral part of being fema
which needed to find its expression either in natural children, or
some other way with, as it were, substitute children. This acco⟨
with the concept labelled by Helsinger *et al.* as the 'Angel out of t
House' – the expression of motherly and home-based instincts
the world for the good of the world.[45]

There is some evidence that Marianne was occasionally wistful o⟨
her own lack of motherhood, hinting at a slight regret, but althou⟨
she regarded a wife's task as an honoured one, there is never a hint th
she would have liked such a role for herself. Levine similarly d
covered that lack of children could be more of an issue than the la
of a partner for unmarried women.[46] In addition, Farningham's n⟨
turing of teenage girls over many years through her girl's class becam
as has been suggested, a substitute for motherhood. Despite a sha
start, this group of girls from a variety of denominations, between t
ages of 15 and 25 became the centre of her life outside writing. Betwe⟨
1867 and 1901, when she reluctantly stopped leading the class due
increasing infirmity, she talked to the girls, opened her home to the⟨
prayed with them and encouraged them to pray for each other, a⟨
even took some on holiday.[47] When considering whether to accept t
invitation to edit the *Sunday School Times*, a major consideration ⟨
whether she would have to move to London, thus leaving the class,

well as her sister.[48] Fortunately, she was able to stay in Northampton, and so the potential conflict between valued relationships and an interesting job was not put to the test. Her autobiography hints that the career might have won: another indication that, despite the importance with which she regarded emotional ties, she saw herself primarily as a working woman.

The task of providing a home base was not confined to mothers in Farningham's writing. According to her, sisters could fulfil this function for their siblings. Thus in 'Carrie's Resolution', a story serialized in the weekly *Christian World Magazine* in 1870, there are stereotypes of the home-based pious woman and the errant male. Carrie was the sister of a man who was bringing distress to his parents, and it is her prayers and persistence which in the end achieve the aim, although with typical womanly modestly she says it was all God. It is significant that his salvation involves staying within the home: the world is far too dangerous a place for him.[49] Thus the redemption of a wandering male is brought about by a faithful woman, and the conventional gender expectations of Victorian evangelicalism are upheld.

Farningham's comments on the home remained cloyingly sentimental throughout her career. The biography of Grace Darling, for instance, in which she stated so categorically that women could be preachers and doctors, contains some classic formulations of domestic ideology. Grace is made to say that, even after going to Alnwick Castle, she loves her home the most of all: 'No indeed, it is the dearest and sweetest spot on all the earth to me, because it is home'.[50] Farningham uses this attachment as an opportunity to sermonize about the value of women loving their homes:

> Let the women of England remember...that the homes they know shall surely be bright or dark, sad or happy, as they shall make them, by their meek or gentle spirit, and unselfish devoted affection.... Women should understand that their home-life is the most important, and give to it their devotion and love.[51]

This was a constant theme in her writings, reinforced in many ways. The Grace Darling of her imagination epitomized all she believed best about women: love of home and respect for parents, strength both of character and body, self-control, and the ability to act in the face of opposition when God prompted. One suspects that in practice Farningham would not have stayed at home as docilely as Grace Darling did. Yet her answer is to see the whole of life, private or public, in terms of mission, calling, and obedience to God. When God provides an occasion or opportunity to act, women should take it, she believed, regardless of the opinions of others: otherwise, they should continue doing the work they have always done, whether paid or unpaid. It was a question of service. Thus while Farningham adhered unthinkingly to a basically patriarchal view of the family, or indeed society, like Sarah Ellis she wanted to see the influence of women spread beyond the home. Hence, for her, love of the home and the desire to be involved in the wider world beyond the home were all part of spirituality. In some situations this would involve being conventional, just doing mundane work to support oneself, but in others it might necessitate 'being singular', as for instance when Grace Darling rescued survivors, or Elizabeth Fry visited prisons.

For Farningham, support of this domestic ideology was entirely compatible with her declaration that women should not be 'afraid to be singular' in rising to the challenges of life. Part of the connection lies in the concept of service. Cobbe also portrayed work in society in terms of service, but for Farningham this was linked to obedience to God, which meant the need to be bold enough to take hold of opportunities, and to be faithful in serving, but not to be limited by other people's paradigms of suitable behaviour. The conflict for her was not between public and private but between the perceived need and other people's opinions and lack of courage which prevented women responding to that need. Hers was an integrated worldview which included subversive elements.

Levine, however, is inclined to reject the role of evangelicalism as being a liberating one. While she recognizes that it offered women a role in life and a sense of self-worth, in her eyes that identity was inextricably linked to separate spheres.[52] Davidoff and Hall record a similar attitude with regard to evangelicals.[53] It is undoubtedly true that much evangelical teaching supported and perpetuated an ideology in which women's role was first and foremost in the home. Yet it also carried within its teaching seeds that could contribute to the subversion of such divisions. While evangelicalism and separate spheres rose together, intertwined and to some extent mutually reinforcing, their linkage was not inevitable. The imperative to follow an individual call from God could, and did, lead women to actions that subverted the norms.[54] Marianne Farningham's advocacy of women's primary role as homemakers, the financial independence of single women and all women's obligation to react to needs, is an example of such a mix. Above all, she believed, women should be ready to respond to God's initiative.

Farningham regarded this as a possibility to be expected and prepared for, believing as she did that the whole variety of work, paid or unpaid, was a call from God. Women needed courage, in her view, to be faithful in an unobserved role, day after day, or to take initiative boldly regardless of public opinion.[55] The very faith that was the bulwark of respectability also had the potential to undermine convention. Thus the explanation for her mosaic of beliefs is to be found in the driving force of Marianne Farningham's life, her faith. Her fairly conventional views were tempered from the beginning by a working-class pragmatism. She believed that single woman should be financially independent, and that all women should be willing and prepared to respond to the needs they saw around them, whether that meant rowing a lifeboat, looking after a family, preaching the gospel or becoming a doctor. She hinted that she had become a 'woman's rights woman', yet never questioned the basic *status quo* of society; nor did she lose her belief in the importance and indeed the primacy of the domestic arena for women. For her, serving God was all, and the lost opportunities of many women who were trapped by convention, were not only lost in terms of earning power and self-fulfillment, but in terms of availability to serve God and humanity. No woman, she argued, 'ought to be content to pass her life in cutting holes to mend them up again; in playing a little, reading novels, and visiting. There ought to be some real tangible good done. . . . The first thing necessary, then, is to seek that religion which comes from above'.[56] It was for godly service that women, she believed, should summon up their courage, and not be 'afraid to be singular'.

Notes

1   Eva Hope, *Grace Darling* (London, 1875), p. 11
2   As Caine indicates, defining feminism is itself becoming increasingly difficult. (Barbara Caine, *English Feminism 1780–1980*, Oxford: Oxford University Press, 1997, pp. 2–4)

3 James Munson, *The Nonconformists* (London: SPCK, 1991), p. 73.
4 Marianne Farningham, *A Working Woman's Life* (London, 1907), p. 148, and *The Christian World*, March 25 1909, account of sermon at Barmouth following Marianne Farningham's death.
5 See, for instance, Farningham, *Life*, pp. 266–7.
6 Marianne Farningham, *Girlhood* (London, 1869), p. 34.
7 Phillipa Levine, *Feminist Lives in Victorian England* (Oxford: Oxford University Press, 1990) p. 53.
8 Martha Vicinus *Independent Women: Work and Community for Single Women, 1850–1920* (London: Virago, 1985) p. 1.
9 Farningham, *Life*, op. cit., pp. 277–8.
10 Farningham, *Life*, op. cit., p. 275.
11 Farningham, *Life*, op. cit., p. 284.
12 Marianne Farningham *Life Sketches* (London, 1861) p. 134. Her italics.
13 Farningham, *Life Sketches*, op. cit., p. 135. Levine also indicates that for bourgeois women, earning could be an embarrassment (Levine, *Feminist Lives*, op. cit., p. 134).
14 Marianne Farningham, *Life*, op. cit., p. 44. Her italics.
15 Farningham, *Life*, op. cit., p. 23.
16 Farningham, *Life*, op. cit., p. 144.
17 Farningham, *Life*, op. cit., pp. 26, 46.
18 Levine, *Feminist*, for instance, on p. 54.
19 Farningham, *Life*, op. cit., p. 46.
20 Hope, *Grace Darling*, op. cit., p. 5.
21 Levine *Feminist Lives*, op. cit., p. 44.
22 Hope, *Grace Darling*, op. cit., p. 13.
23 Farningham, *Girlhood*, op. cit., p. 87.
24 Hope, *Grace Darling*, op. cit., p. 14.
25 Levine, *Feminist Lives*, op. cit., p. 126.
26 Farningham, *Life*, op. cit., pp. 92–3.
27 Levine, *Feminist Lives*, op. cit., p. 46.
28 Farningham, *Life*, op. cit., p. 115.
29 Farningham, *Life*, op. cit., pp. 144; pp. 157; pp. 256.
30 Farningham, *Life*, op. cit., p. 256.
31 Farningham, *Life*, op. cit., p. 157.
32 Farningham, *Life*, op. cit., for instance Mrs. Wilshire, p. 155; unnamed friends in Devon, p. 177; Miss Kirkpatrick, p. 179; friends in Northampton, p. 172.
33 Farningham, *Life Sketches*, op. cit., pp. 6 and 29.
34 There is, of course, much discussion on this subject. See Amanda Vickery, 'Golden Age to Separate Spheres? A Review of the categories and chronology of English women's history', *Historical Journal*, vol. 36, no. 2 (1993).
35 Leonore Davidoff and Catherine Hall, *Family Fortunes: Men and Women of the English Middle Class, 1780–1850* (London: Routledge, 1987). For an exploration of the influence of separate spheres on Nonconformist

women, see Linda Wilson, *Constrained by Zeal: Female Spirituality Amongst Nonconformists* (Carlisle: Paternoster Press, 2000).

36   It is worth noting that although Farningham wrote about Cobbe, Cobbe does not appear to have written about her, an indication that the relationship was of more significance for the former than for the latter.

37   *Life*, op. cit., pp. 237–8. The meeting was the National Union of Women Workers, Birmingham, 1890.

38   *The Western Daily Press*, Tuesday, November 13, 1877.

39   Marianne Farningham, *Homely Talks about Homely Things* (London, 1886), pp. 33–6.

40   Farningham, *Homely Talks*, op. cit., p. 32. The 1869 Municipal Franchise Act gave women the right to vote in Municipal elections.

41   Farningham *Life Sketches*, op. cit., p. 5.

42   Farningham *Life Sketches*, op. cit., p. 4.

43   Farningham *Home Life*, op. cit., p. 5.

44   Marianne Farningham *Women and their Work* (London, 1906) p. 86.

45   Elizabeth K. Helsinger, Robin Lauterbach Sheets and William Veeder, *The Woman Question. Society and Literature in Britain and America 1837–83*, Vol. 1 (Chicago, IL: University of Chicago Press, 1983), pp. xiv–xv.

46   Levine, *Feminist Lives*, op. cit., p. 44.

47   Farningham, *Life*, op. cit., pp. 111–30.

48   Farningham, *Life*, op. cit., pp. 190–1.

49   *Christian World Magazine 1870*, January–June.

50   Hope, *Grace Darling*, op. cit., p. 275.

51   Hope, *Grace Darling*, op. cit., p. 279.

52   Levine, *Feminist Lives*, op. cit., p. 31.

53   Davidoff and Hall, *Family Fortunes*, op. cit., See, for example, p. 90 for the link between evangelicalism and separate spheres, p. 99 for the opportunities it gave to women.

54   For further discussion, see L Wilson, 'Constrained by Zeal: Women in mid-Nineteenth Century Nonconformist churches', *Journal of Religious History* (June 1999), pp. 185–202.

55   Hope, *Grace Darling*, op. cit., pp. 300–3.

56   Hope, *Grace Darling*, op. cit., pp. 300–3.

7
Evangelicalism and Feminism. Josephine Butler, 1828–1906[1]

Helen Mathers

Josephine Butler's campaign against the Contagious Diseases Acts was prompted by horror at the fact that male policemen and doctors were legally empowered, obliged even, to detain women thought to be prostitutes and subject them forcibly to an internal examination, in order to discover whether they had a venereal disease which might infect their male clients. This battle against the double standard, explicitly feminist in language, owed much to the support of men like James Stansfeld, James Stuart, H.J. Wilson and George Butler, but was indisputably led by one woman, Josephine Butler. The campaign forced the repeal of the Acts in 1886, but long before then Josephine's ambitions had widened, towards preventing the 'state regulation of vice' in European capitals and abolition of child prostitution at home and abroad. She never stopped campaigning from 1869 until her death in 1906.

Josephine Butler's campaigns are well known and have been expertly described, particularly in two volumes by Judith Walkowitz.[2] Her life and personality, however, have received much less attention, and the only biography is now seriously outdated.[3] This is surprising, because research material exists in quantity. Josephine Butler was a prolific writer of books, pamphlets and letters and she wrote biographies of her husband, father and sister which contain much autobiographical material. The interpretative dilemmas presented by these writings, however, are vast, since they are not only passionately feminist, but also often sentimental, melodramatic and, above all, intensely religious. Alison Milbank, writing in 1987, found that, in the climate of feminist history at that time, to write about Josephine

Butler was 'to enter a minefield' – the explosive debates about male and female sexuality, the feminist stance on prostitution and, above all, the juxtaposition of Christianity and feminism.[4] Many feminist historians at the time believed the two were incompatible and one criticized Butler for her adherence to a patriarchal Christian church.

This academic stumbling block probably served only to further obscure the interpretative complexities surrounding Butler. This chapter contends that it is impossible to understand Josephine Butler unless one accepts that, for her, Christianity and feminism were hand-in-hand. The subordination of women advocated by the Pauline epistles has understandably been seen by many feminists as reason to reject Christian teaching, but Butler herself explicitly dismissed St Paul in favour of an 'appeal to Christ and to him alone'. She argued that Christ himself had treated women as of equal importance and had liberated them:

> Search throughout the Gospel history, and observe his conduct in regard to women, and it will be found that the word liberation expresses, above all others, the act which changed the whole life and character and position of the women dealt with, and which ought to have changed the character of men's treatment of women from that time forward.[7]

This is a profound statement, truly radical in its nineteenth-century context and anticipating the developments of feminist and liberation theology in the twentieth century. It has recently been used by Eileen Yeo to emphasize, as did Milbank, that Josephine Butler drew power from being consciously prophetic.[8] Yeo believes that such statements:

> Scraped away the historical encrustations of the patriarchal church (including St Paul) and appealed to Jesus and his vision of non-gendered human value ('there is neither male nor female neither plebian nor noble but all are equal before me').[9]

Recent feminist exposition, of which Yeo's book is one example and the present volume is another, has moved beyond the dichotomies of Christianity versus feminism. Some historians, indeed, were never comfortable with them and the pioneering work of Leonore

Davidoff, Catherine Hall and Jane Rendall is acknowledged here and will be described later. There is no doubt that Josephine Butler's legacy to feminists is contradictory, combining radical talk of liberation with extreme idealism about moral purity and a capacity to victimize prostitutes almost to the point of denying their personal independence and autonomy. But the contradictions may be points of challenge to our preconceived ideas, the narrow gate through which a broader critical understanding can be reached.

While preparing the study on which this chapter is based, the buzzing voices around Josephine Butler's inheritance were deliberately excluded for a while in order to 'listen to her voice'. This voice is a revelation; sometimes inspirational, sometimes melodramatic, sometimes straining credulity, but always heart-felt. Her voice has to be considered in its entirety if a proper assessment of her life and work is to be made.

Since most previous studies of Josephine Butler have focused on her feminism, or in Barbara Caine's case her liberalism, there has been little speculation about the possible nature of her religion. The first historian to link Butler with Evangelicalism was Judith Walkowitz in 1980. The focus of Walkowitz's study was her campaign rather than her personality.[10] Nancy Boyd contributed a valuable account of her religion in her 1982 book on Josephine Butler, Octavia Hill and Florence Nightingale, but remained equivocal about defining it as Evangelical.[11] One or two other historians have used the term 'evangelical', but as a convenient label which requires no justification and yields no insight. This is an important oversight because it has led to a failure to 'place' Butler fully within a religious tradition.

One result has been that there is still no consensus among historians about Josephine Butler's religion. For example, a chapter-length study of her feminism by Barbara Caine, published in 1992, makes no reference to Evangelicalism and suggests that the religion of Josephine's family, the Greys, was 'a non-sectarian religion concerned rather with states of feeling than with particular doctrine'.[12] On the evidence of Josephine's biography of her father, the Greys were clearly Evangelical, as I have argued elsewhere.[13]

Evangelicalism transcended the traditional denominations, but was the primary belief of Methodists, Congregationalists and Baptists, as well as of a significant section of the Anglican Church, to which the Greys belonged. The family was liberal, prosperous and well connected, with lands in Northumberland, near the border with Scotland. In the early years of the nineteenth century, there were often close links between Anglican Evangelicalism and Wesleyan Methodism, which had split from the parent church in 1791. Josephine Butler's mother, Hannah Annett, could remember sitting on John Wesley's knee as a child.[14] The experiences of Josephine's father, John Grey, were just as ecumenical. Living so near the Scottish border, the Grey parents were very friendly towards Scottish Presbyterianism, and one of John's sisters vividly remembered being chided by her mother for 'speaking scornfully of Presbyterians' and thus receiving her 'first lesson in toleration'.[15] Another sister, Josephine's aunt, married a Presbyterian cousin, Henry Grey, who was one of the Evangelical leaders of the Scottish Church Disruption in 1843. Josephine Butler followed three generations of family tradition. Although remaining Anglican, she was never strongly attached to one particular church, worshipped with every kind of Protestant congregation and had friends of every type of Protestant persuasion.

Her fluid, almost casual, relationship with the established churches has proved a stumbling block for some historians, Nancy Boyd in particular, in defining her as Evangelical.[16] Josephine Butler was certainly unusual among Evangelicals in this respect, but it may be that, once again, this unconventional, dynamic woman is pushing against the boundaries of our current paradigms. There are compelling reasons for regarding her as Evangelical, not least the traditional nature of many of her beliefs. They are evident in her published writings, but more spontaneously expressed in her unpublished prayers and spiritual meditations. This, for example, is part of her 'Prayer for the last night of the year' (December 31st 1881):

We thank Thee that Thou hast called up a great army of Evangelists throughout our land, to gather in the multitudes of perishing souls. O grant to them an abundant harvest in the year upon which we are to enter. May Thy Kingdom be greatly enlarged: O! God, revive the churches ! May there be no more congregations which draw nigh to Thee with their lips only while their hearts are far from Thee. May Christ everywhere be preached in simplicity and in power, and His name be glorified by the salvation of thousands and tens of thousands of our people.[17]

Evangelicalism is defined by belief and activity rather than church-going. Four essential attributes suggested by David Bebbington in 1989 have been widely accepted.[18] They are conversionism, a belief in a conversion experience as the route to Christian faith; activism, the need to do some 'work' for Christ, especially to spread the gospel; biblicism, a belief that the bible is the authoritative source of all spiritual truth; and crucicentrism, the conviction that the fundament of Christianity is Christ's atoning death on the cross to redeem mankind. Mark Noll's 1994 analysis identifies two factors basic to Evangelicalism, 'the historic Protestant attachment to Scripture' and 'the active experience of God'. Three other factors are almost as significant; 'a bias – whether slight prejudice or massive rejection – against inherited institutions'; a flexibility about intellectual and political ideas, since ultimate reality is to be 'found in Scripture and the experience of Christ'; and a conviction 'that the gospel compelled a search for social healing as well as personal holiness'.[19]

Josephine Butler was an Evangelical by the criteria of both Bebbington and Noll. She described, in her 'Spiritual Diaries', several experiences which would be regarded by Evangelicals as 'conversion', took the bible as her guide to conduct and belief and prioritized a daily discipline of prayerful meditation and bible reading. Her profound personal spirituality was certainly 'an active experience of God' and her faith was based on crucicentrism. She longed to find some 'work' in God's service, and when she was asked to lead the women's campaign against the Contagious Diseases Acts wrote, 'this is perhaps after all the very work, the very mission, I longed for years ago, and saw coming, afar off, like a bright star'.[20] Above all, she was an individualist, at all times relying for personal guidance on her study of the bible and her understanding and experience of God.

Since Evangelicalism was a primary motivation for Josephine Butler's activities and campaigns, failure to recognize this can make her decisions and life-choices very difficult to explain. For example, in the only book-length biography, E. Moberley Bell laments the fact that Butler chose to abandon the campaign for the higher education of women in order to take up the fight against the Contagious Diseases Acts.[21] This is a failure on Moberley Bell's part to understand the power of Josephine's call, for the campaign against the Contagious Diseases Acts was a campaign against sin in one of its most corrupting forms. Identification of a sin aroused Evangelicals to fight against it particularly if, as David Bebbington argues, they 'became convinced that they were responsible as citizens for a state of affairs that necessarily entailed sin'.[22] Josephine Butler believed that the Contagious Diseases Acts were 'a deadly poison working through the wholesale, systematic, and now legalized, degradation of women'; she was battling the Anti-Christ.[23] The campaign for women's higher education was a feminist campaign; the campaign for the rights of prostitutes and against state sanction of vice was both a feminist campaign and a battle against sin. Only the latter was capable of arousing all her passions and consuming all her energies.

At the outset of the campaign, in 1869, she wrote:

> Nothing so wears me out, body and soul, as anger, fruitless anger; and this thing fills me with such an anger, and even hatred, that I fear to face it. The thought of this atrocity kills charity and hinders my prayers. But there is surely a way of being angry without sin. I pray thee, O God, to give me a deep, well-governed, and lifelong hatred of all such injustice, tyranny and cruelty; and at the same time give me that divine compassion which is willing to live and suffer long for love to souls, or to fling itself into the breach and die at once.[24]

This was the emotional commitment of the dedicated enemy of sin and nothing, neither home, children nor her frequent prolonged illnesses, diverted her from it.

Josephine Butler was 40 when she wrote those words, heralding her first appearance on the public stage. Much has already been written about the years that followed, and so much less will be said here, due to pressure of space. The resolution and courage she showed in 1869 and thereafter developed over long years of enquiry and frustration, years of political, personal and spiritual development which were crucial to the battle ahead.

Butler's hatred of injustice and tyranny began in her childhood home. Her father was a passionate supporter of the anti-slavery movement and Josephine was horrified by his accounts of brutality towards the slaves and especially the rape of female slaves by their masters. There is a direct link to her later descriptions of prostitutes as 'white slaves'. In an account written in 1900, she recalled that the stark reality of sin challenged her faith, forcing her to demand, 'Why is it thus with the creatures of Thy hand?' No person could help resolve her crisis and she withdrew to the woods and hillsides around her home:

> For hours and days and weeks in these retreats I sought the answer to my soul's trouble and the solution of its dark questionings. Looking back, it seems to me the end must have been defeat or death had not the. Saviour imparted to the child-wrestler something of the virtue of his own midnight agony in Gethsemane.[25]

This terrible struggle was, by this account, only finally resolved by her decision to take part in an 'outward and active conflict' against sin. That decision took her many years to reach, and even during the early years of her marriage she was often still in retreat from the world, praying and studying the bible, seeking a deeper understanding of God and 'the light, hope and guidance which he never denies to them who seek and ask and knock'.[26] The evidence for this period of her life is her 'Spiritual Diaries', never cited before, perhaps because they are not to be found in the main collection of her letters and pamphlets in the Fawcett Library, but among family papers in the Newcastle Archives.[27] These diaries are intense accounts of spiritual experiences, so personal that in one entry she confessed, 'I could not bear to tell this to anyone in whom there was not sympathy'. Here she describes a profound moment of insight and resolution:

> Since the New Year I have been seeking very earnestly the outpouring of the Spirit on me and my House. Today about dusk, Christ revealed Himself to my Spiritual sight in a manner which I never felt before . . . These are not words of 'enthusiasm' so called, but words of sober truth. I saw no vision nor had I any sensuous perception. It was, I think, simply the fulfilment of the promise so little believed in 'I will *manifest* myself to him'.[28]

This account describes an 'active experience of God' which Evangelicals sought but which many will never have found to the profound depth described by Josephine Butler. It could certainly be regarded as an account of conversion, although Butler did not believe in sudden, instantaneous conversion, but rather in a more gradual, Anglican version. She herself experienced several moments of divine revelation and once told a friend, 'To be converted, in the sense in which you have been converted, having turned *from* sin and *to* God with an honest purpose, is a very small part of the work of God in our souls. It is only the door leading to the true life.'[29]

She was so preoccupied with her own 'deep individual holiness' at this time, the mid-1850s, that she experienced some guilt at her lack of involvement in the world and its problems.[30] In retrospect, however, this period can be seen as an essential prelude to the obsessively intense commitment of her campaigns, the time during which she developed the psychic and spiritual strength for her work. She was aided in this by her new husband, George Butler, whom she married in 1852. He was that most unusual of Victorian husbands, a believer in the equality of husband and wife. During their engagement he wrote, 'I should think it undue presumption in me to suggest anything to you in regard to your life and duties. He who has hitherto guided your steps will continue to do so'.[31] George was the scion of a traditional Anglican family, the son of the Dean of Peterborough, and he himself was eventually ordained, although he never had a parish, preferring to exercise his ministry in two boys' schools, Cheltenham and Liverpool Colleges. In the early years of their marriage, he held the post of Oxford University Examiner and it was in Oxford that he and Josephine first 'rescued' a prostitute, the abandoned mistress of a university don.

His role in Josephine's 'mission' was fundamental; she wrote, 'he had a part in the creation of it, in the formation of the first impulses towards it. But for him I would have been much more perplexed that I was. . . . The idea of justice to women, of the equality of the sexes . . . seems to have been instinctive to him'.[32]

In the early 1860s, while living in Cheltenham, Josephine endured further agonizing self-conflict, 'years when my soul was in darkness on account of the sin, the misery, and the waste which are in the world . . . I could see no God, or such as I could see appeared to be an immoral God'.[33] The thought of 'the multitudes who seem to be created only to be lost' oppressed her, as it did Darwin, whose *The Origin of Species* must have been read by the Butlers at this time. They were also deeply distressed by the outbreak of the American Civil War in 1861, and especially by the early success of the South. A terrible tragedy occurred in August 1864 when their only daughter, Eva, a healthy and happy five-year-old, was killed accidentally and both parents were plunged into a period of intense grief and regret. Josephine emerged with her faith renewed and her mission resolved; in March 1865 she 'stood before the Lord' and on Easter Sunday wrote:

> I long to have a hundred voices, that with all of them I might pray without ceasing that Christ will come quickly, and deliver for ever the poor groaning world: the slaves from all their woes, the victims also and slaves of lust in our own land, the poor women who are driven as sheep to the slaughter, into the slave market of London; prisoners, captives and exiles. My heart is bruised and crushed every day, in going its rounds through the suffering world.[34]

Richmond, the 'capital of the slave states' had just fallen in the American Civil War. The connection between black slavery and the 'slaves of lust' was always close in her mind. In 'Sursum Corda' (1871) she specifically compared her campaign with the struggle to emancipate the slaves.

There is no reason to disagree with the general view that this period, 1865–66, was the moment when Josephine Butler found her mission, but the reason was rather more complex than the one she herself gave. It was not only her misery after Eva's death and her 'irresistible desire to go forth and find some pain keener than my own' that drove her to the women of the Bridewell in the Liverpool workhouse.[35] It was the culmination of a spiritual journey of many years' duration. After 1865 she became not only an activist but also a preacher, developing her experience into lessons for others. She wrote her first didactic pamphlets and articles and even her journal changed its personal character and became lessons for her sons to follow and copies of letters full of preaching. She had become a leader, sure both of her mission and of her message to the world.

When the Butlers lived in Oxford, Josephine was often unhappy, 'revolted' by the arrogant masculinity of the university world but silenced by the superior debating skills of the dons.[36] A letter written to Florence Nightingale by Benjamin Jowett, the Oxford Professor of Greek and a leading member of the Anglican 'Broad' Church, shows that the dons, in turn, regarded her as histrionic. Jowett did not support her work for prostitutes, 'a class of sinners whom she had better have left to themselves'.[37] In a letter to Jowett, written after leaving Oxford, Butler courageously defended her right, as a woman, to her own beliefs and an independent means of achieving them:

> I could not stake my soul's destiny upon a faith received at second-hand, or on mere probabilities... So I sought God. I spoke to Him in solitude, as to a person who could answer. I sometimes gave whole nights to prayer, because the day was not sufficiently my own.[38]

She attacks directly the criticism that women are emotional, that religion is 'rather an indulgence of the feelings with them, than anything else'. For herself, day by day, 'I am obliged to give feeling a subordinate place, and to be guided by a stern sense of right throughout a life which involves daily and hourly self-denial... and yet I am inclined to think that in the greatest things of all, we are obliged to fall back upon feeling, or on something like it'.

She concludes with the challenge:

> I never sat at the feet of any man; I never sought light or guidance even from any saint, man or woman, though I dearly loved some such whom I had known, and learned much from their example; nor on churches and creeds had I ever leaned.[39]

Because 'the things which I believed I had learnt direct from God', Josephine Butler's Christianity became self-consciously feminist. If God communicates directly with every human being, then He can communicate directly with a woman and no man has the right to dispute her perception of God.

The strongest public expression of this theology, for it merits no weaker word, came in the introduction she wrote for *Woman's Work and Woman's Culture*, published in 1869. This contained the passage quoted above (in the Introduction), in which she argues that Christ's acts towards women had been liberating. Two of her examples are 'the woman taken in adultery', who Jesus forgives, and the 'woman in the city, which was a sinner', to whom Jesus says, 'Thy faith hath saved Thee: go in peace'.[40] These were both prostitutes, generally taken to be different stories about Mary Magdalene.

Josephine Butler regarded herself as having been liberated by Christ in exactly the same way as Mary Magdalene, and identified with her:

Looking my Liberator in the face, can my friends wonder that I have taken my place, (I took it long ago) – oh! with what infinite contentment! – by the side of her, the 'woman in the city which was a sinner'.[41]

Jesus was 'her Liberator and mine'.

Josephine magisterially dismissed St Paul's claims to be the authority on women's position in the church. 'This apostle spoke for the exigencies of a given period, and from the point of view of a man born under limitations of vision and judgement, but enabled by a divine insight to apply with wisdom the essential teaching of his Master to the time and society in which he lived'.[42] Even the writers of the gospels were not exempted from the recognition that they were only human, but about them she adds an original comment:

> to bring the fullness of the reflected light of intelligent consciences to bear upon the principles announced by Christ's acts and words towards women, would need the combined thoughtfulness and wisdom of a man and a woman; and the writer is a man and not a woman, nor does he thoroughly know women.[43]

Thus she reiterated her view that the female perspective on Christ was as valid and as necessary as the male. Her ideas became popular among women philanthropists who, Prochaska has remarked, revered Christ as 'the atoning saviour of the innocent and craving heart, who treated women with the utmost respect and tenderness'.[44]

Josephine Butler looked to history as well as to the bible for models of the Christian woman she aspired to be, as her 1878 biography of Catharine of Siena shows.[45] On the face of it there is little to link a nineteenth-century Protestant woman and a fourteenth-century Roman Catholic saint, but Butler clearly empathized with a woman whose life of prayer became a career of reform and leadership in the world. God called Catharine to this work because she was a woman: 'at the present time the pride of man has become so great ... I will send to them *women*, unlearned, and by nature fragile, but filled by my grace with courage and power'.[46] She also identified with Catharine's lonely search for knowledge of her Creator: 'He whom she loved gave her neither an angel nor a man to be her director, but appeared to her himself in her little cell, and taught her all that was most needful for her to know'.[47]

By Butler's account, both Catharine and (implicitly) she herself discovered their missions by independent effort and conviction, both received God's call *as women* to adopt a leadership role and both battled, successfully, against men who denied their right to exercise this power.

Josephine Butler's writings provide one example among the growing documentary evidence of the connections between Victorian Evangelicalism and feminism. Jane Rendall's research prompted the conclusion that the Evangelical emphasis on individual conversion put women on a level with men and empowered them to assert their moral standards at home and to battle against sin.[48] Leonore Davidoff and Catherine Hall argue that religion offered the key to a world 'where women could be valued for their spiritual worth if not their material power, where a "religious career" could give meaning to women's experience and express some of their aspirations'.[49] Hempton and Hill, in a study of Evangelicalism in Ulster, conclude that, 'there is much evidence to support the view that evangelical religion was more important than feminism in enlarging women's sphere of action during the nineteenth century'.[50]

In coming to these conclusions, these historians do not deny the repressive effects of much Victorian Christian teaching on women, with its emphasis on the 'domestic sphere'. Olive Anderson, indeed, has argued that women's experiences of religion 'contributed nothing to the spread of feminist ideas'.[51] The example of Josephine Butler alone is enough to refute this statement, and even Anderson admits that there were a 'few women' who spoke out effectively against the churches' attitude to women. They were, despite official condemnation, *de facto* female preachers.

Josephine Butler believed in the 'open and acknowledged teaching of inspired women' and, when her husband was ordained, remarked: 'I felt as if I was being ordained too'.[52] She followed the biblical injunction to 'prophesy', meaning to speak openly from deep personal conviction, and had a strong argument against St Paul:

St Paul could not have disapproved of women prophesying without being guilty of a neglect of one of the most momentous of the prophetic utterances of Scripture (in the book of Joel) 'your sons and your daughters will prophesy'.[53]

Josephine Butler believed in her own prophetic role and justified her right, as a woman, to independent speech and thought, through her interpretations of the bible and her identification with historic models, such as St Catharine. Josephine Butler emphasized not only that men and women were equal before God, but that some women, like herself, were called to be leaders of both men and women. In this assertion lay a profound contribution to feminism.

Notes

1 This chapter is drawn, with the permission of the editors, from arguments developed for a more extensive paper, 'The Evangelical Spirituality of a Victorian Feminist. Josephine Butler 1818–1906', published in *Journal of Ecclesiastical History*, vol. 52, no. 2 (April 2001), pp. 282–312.

2 For the history of the campaigns, see Glen Petrie, *A Singular Iniquity: the Campaigns of Josephine Butler* (London: Viking Press, 1971), Paul McHugh, *Prostitution and Victorian Social Reform* (London: Croom Helm, 1980) and Judith Walkowitz, *Prostitution and Victorian Society: Women, Class and the State* (Cambridge: Cambridge University Press, 1980), pp. 90–147. Her own account is Josephine E. Butler, *Personal Reminiscences of a Great Crusade* (London, 1898).

3 For Butler's life and work, see Barbara Caine, *Victorian Feminists* (Oxford, 1992), pp. 150–95; Jenny Uglow, 'Josephine Butler: from Sympathy to Theory', in Dale Spender (ed.), *Feminist Theorists. Three Centuries of Women's Intellectual Traditions* (London: Women's Press, 1983), pp. 146–64; Margaret Forster, *Significant Sisters: the Grassroots of Active Feminism 1839–1939* (1984, 2nd edn London, 1986), pp. 168–202. At the time of writing this chapter, the only full-length biography was E. Moberley Bell, *Josephine Butler: Flame of Fire* (London: Constable & Co., 1962), but this has now been completely superceded by Jane Jordan, *Josephine Butler* (London: John Murray, 2001). Edited extracts from some of her autobiographical writings were published by George W. and Lucy A. Johnson as *Josephine Butler: an Autobiographical Memoir* (Bristol and London, 1913), hereinafter cited as *Autobiographical Memoir*.

4 A. Milbank, 'Josephine Butler: Christianity, feminism and social action', in J. Obelkevich, L. Roper and R. Samuel (eds), *Disciplines of Faith: Studies in Religion, Politics and Patriarchy* (London: Routledge and Kegan Paul, 1987), p. 154.

5   Introduction to Obelkevich, Roper and Samuel, ibid.; Uglow, 'Josephine Butler', p. 151.
6   Josephine E. Butler (ed.), *Woman's Work and Woman's Culture* (London, 1869), p. liii.
7   *Ibid*, p. lix.
8   Milbank, 'Josephine Butler', p. 156; Eileen Janes Yeo (ed.), *Radical Femininity: Women's Self-Representation in the Public Sphere* (Manchester: Manchester University Press, 1998), p. 137.
9   Yeo (ed.), *Radical Femininity*, op. cit.; pp. 127–48.
10 Walkowitz, *Prostitution*, op. cit., p. 115.
11 Nancy Boyd, *Three Victorian Women who Changed their World. Josephine Butler, Octavia Hill, Florence Nightingale* (London: Palgrave Macmillan, 1982). See especially p. 54.
12 Caine, *Victorian Feminists*, op. cit., p. 159.
13 Helen Mathers, 'The Evangelical Spirituality of a Victorian Feminist. Josephine Butler 1828–1906', op. cit., section 3. The biography is J.E. Butler, *Memoir of John Grey of Dilston*, 1st edn (London, 1869).
14 Ibid., pp. 25–6.
15 Ibid., p. 13.
16 Boyd, *Three Victorian Women*, op. cit., pp. 53, 54.
17 Liverpool University, MSS Butler, JB 1/4/5.
18 David Bebbington, *Evangelicalism in Modern Britain: a History from the 1730s to the 1980s* (1989, 2nd edn London and New York: Routledge, 1993), pp. 1–19. The capital 'E' for Evangelicalism derives from Bebbington's practice in this book.
19 Mark A. Noll, 'Revolution and the Rise of Evangelical Social Influence in North Atlantic Societies', in M.A. Noll, D.W. Bebbington and G.A. Rawlyk (eds), *Evangelicalism: Comparative Studies of Popular Protestantism in North America, the British Isles and beyond 1700–1900* (Oxford: Oxford University Press, 1994), pp. 129–30.
20 Sept 1869, quoted in *Autobiographical Memoir*, op. cit., p. 91.
21 Bell, *Josephine Butler*, op. cit., p. 65.
22 Bebbington, *Evangelicalism in Modern Britain*, op. cit., p. 133.
23 Quoted in *Autobiographical Memoir*, op. cit., p. 100.
24 Quoted in *Autobiographical Memoir*, op. cit., p. 91.
25 Josephine Butler (ed.), *The Storm-Bell*, no. 19 (Jan 1900).
26 Ibid.
27 A study by Anne Summers, *Female Lives, Moral States* (Newbury: Threshold Press, 2000), has been recently published which also quotes these diaries, particularly to show Butler's state of mind at the time of writing *Catharine of Siena*.
28 'Private Thoughts', Northumberland County Council, MSS Josephine Butler ZBU E3/A2. I am grateful to my student Janet Heywood for first drawing my attention to this source.
29 'Part of a letter to a person who complains of want of love in religion...', 'Private thoughts'.

30 Entries for February 1856 and Dec 8 1856, 'Private thoughts'.
31 Quoted in Josephine Butler, *Recollections of George Butler* (Bristol, 1892), pp. 57–8.
32 Ibid., p. 101.
33 Josephine Butler, *The Hour before the Dawn* (1882), p. 95. The dating of this period is clear from entries in her 'Private Thoughts' journal.
34 March 10 1865, April 18 1865, 'Private thoughts'.
35 See *Autobiographical Memoir*, pp. 58–9.
36 *Recollections of George Butler*, pp. 94–7.
37 Quote from Faber's *Life of Jowett*, in Bell, *Josephine Butler*, op. cit., p. 79.
38 Josephine Butler to B. Jowett, nd (*c.* 1865), Fawcett Lib., MSS Butler correspondence, microfiche sheet 2.
39 *Recollections of George Butler*, op. cit., pp. 98–9.
40 The Bible (Authorised version), Luke vii. 50. *Woman's Work*, op. cit., pp. lviii– lix.
41 *Autobiographical Memoir*, op. cit., p. 16.
42 *Woman's Work* op. cit., p. xlix.
43 Ibid., p. lvi.
44 F. Prochaska, *Women and Philanthropy in Nineteenth Century England* (Oxford: Clarendon Press, 1980), p. 15.
45 Josephine Butler, *Catharine of Siena*, 1878, 4th edn, 1885.
46 Ibid., p. 67.
47 *Catharine of Siena*, op. cit., p. 47. Anne Summers contributes a powerful analysis of this text and its significance to Butler, *Female Lives, Moral States*, op. cit., pp. 66–77.
48 Jane Rendall, *The Origins of Modern Feminism. Women in Britain, France and the United States 1780–1860* (Basingstoke: Macmillan, 1985), pp. 73–107.
49 Leonore Davidoff and Catherine Hall, *Family Fortunes: Men and Women of the English Middle Class 1780–1850* (London: Routledge, 1987), p. 148.
50 D. Hempton and M. Hill, *Evangelical Protestantism in Ulster Society 1740– 1890* (London: Routledge, 1992), p. 129.
51 Olive Anderson, 'Women preachers in mid-Victorian Britain: Some Reflexions on Feminism, Popular Religion and Social Change', *Historical Journal*, 12 (1969), 484.
52 *Recollections of George Butler*, op. cit., p. 105.
53 Josephine Butler, *Prophets and Prophetesses: some Thoughts for the Present Times*, London 1898, p. 5.

8
Victorian Women with Causes: Writing, Religion and Action

Suzanne Rickard

Perhaps we should blame Charles Dickens! Through his writing in the 1850s, this celebrated novelist managed to damn the endeavours of a particular type of Victorian, notably the religious and philanthropic woman – a woman with a cause.[1] Although Dickens' literary intentions may have been otherwise, one unfortunate consequence of his biting satire was that, for a time, he managed to deride the efforts of many contemporary women committed to philanthropic work and important social campaigns. Admittedly, selective benevolence bestowed by pious 'Lady Bountifuls' was usually unwelcome even in the lives of the deserving poor, but individual women involved in practical work and animated by their religious beliefs, did not deserve literary humiliation.

Ironically, the immensely popular author who wrote so caustically about 'ladies societies' in *Sketches by Boz*, and who angrily lampooned 'do-gooders' with the grotesque stereotypes characterized by 'Mrs Jellyby' and 'Mrs Pardiggle', adopted a number of social causes himself. Through his blockbuster novels, Dickens campaigned ardently against child abuse and, in association with a number of female philanthropists, provided financial and moral support for those who worked against prostitution. His partners in these endeavours were all women with causes, committed Victorian activists.

Dickens' philanthropic association with the well-known rich and charitable patron, Angela Burdett-Coutts, and their mutual interest in rescuing young women from sexual slavery, did not prevent an exacting misogynistic criticism within his disturbing novels. The misguided 'Mrs Jellyby', the over-zealous evangelist from *Bleak House*, damaged the reputation of many other religious women with causes; the portrait was indelible. Of course, Mrs Jellyby was a fictitious stereotype – while working relentlessly to collect money for missions abroad, she neglected her own children at home. She served as a powerful metaphor, but Dickens had a sharp point to make. A keen observer of humanity, Dickens elaborated the worst as well as the best qualities in all his characters; here, however, was he criticizing religion in general or its all-pervasive influence on evangelical women in particular? A woman with a cause was often regarded as a volatile or, worse still, a subversive creature.

Criticism of women with causes did not, of course, always come exclusively from male quarters. There was always controversy. While thousands of women were actively engaged in philanthropy in private and individual acts, or in more public and systematic schemes, sharp differences emerged among women. They too, applied double standards and gave voice to vociferous criticisms. While unmarried middle-class girls and women were characterized by W.R. Greg as 'redundant',[2] those ambitious to be useful outside the home were also admonished. Women who dared to step beyond accepted Victorian domestic familial roles of daughters, mothers or wives, or those who acted independently and connected philosophically and practically their feminist concerns with philanthropy, engendered feelings of ambivalence. Not unexpectedly, conservative and radical female reformers, evangelists and philanthropists differed over many questions, including women's entrance into the public sphere, on the necessity for women's suffrage, or for the need for institutional and domestic reform to achieve women's rights and equality.

Sarah Stickney Ellis, published as 'Mrs Ellis', provided warnings in her advice books in the 1840s reminding all 'restless daughters that charity began at home and that an excessive zeal for visiting the poor meant a neglect of home duties'.[3] Countering this restrictive view was Frances Power Cobbe, the Victorian feminist, philanthropist, intellectual and Deist, who argued passionately that there were limits to the obedience of daughters.[4] While she attacked the 'claustration' of women,[5] Cobbe disliked attempts by some to organize the work of women into large-scale societies.[6] She could be irritated by enthusiastic and unphilosophic 'angels of charity' and 'lady-bountifuls'. Once, frustrated, she referred scathingly to such as the well-to-do 'lady guerillas of philanthropy',[7] using the pejorative term to describe middle- and upper-class married women whose well-meaning but unfocused efforts to 'do good', intruded upon the feelings of those receiving philanthropic attentions.

Cobbe, with her extensive philanthropic networks, was well aware that amongst the minority of untrained 'guerillas' were greater numbers of highly articulate women proficient in philanthropic work and strategic in their attempts to transform an inequitable social order. In her own experience, philanthropy informed and merged with her feminist concerns as it had for other lesser-known, able women workers who fought for the woman's cause'.[8] As she also knew, there were knowledgeable, educated, often single and single-minded women (particularly important for Cobbe) who regarded philanthropy as legitimate work and tackled their causes with a mix of idealism, religious faith and professionalism. Through writing, religion and personal action, there were other women who pursued causes. They brought written information before a wide reading public and attempted not only to transform the social conscience of individuals but also to reverse the inequalities of everyday circumstance.

From the late 1850s in England, a new type of woman was beginning to clearly emerge from the shadows of men, of literary caricatures and of household obscurity. This was a woman with a social conscience and a public cause to champion. She was a woman with a new and eloquent voice – a woman in public.[9] Of course, she was not the first woman to speak out. She followed in the footsteps of the female pioneers of an earlier generation – the philanthropists, educationalists, and prison visitors of the late eighteenth and early nineteenth century who allowed their names to be associated with 'difficult' causes, including the campaigns for prison reform, education and social purity.

In terms of sensibility and consciousness, this 'new' woman (not to be confused with the so-called New Women of the 1880s and 1890s) was overwhelmingly motivated by religious faith and spirituality as well as by her 'women-centred' concerns. Often only one major social cause was close to her heart, but her religious beliefs were paramount. Her social work took her to many places and touched different and equally prominent causes championed by other women. Unless she was part of the first circle of feminists, characterized perhaps best by the Ladies Institute at Langham Place established in 1857,[10] it is likely that she would have initially rejected the description of herself as 'feminist' even when the word entered the lexicon. And whether this portrait figure would have openly supported the suffrage campaigns pursued by many later nineteenth-century feminists remains an open question. Exercising the luxury of historical hindsight, we are inclined to view such women as incipient or proto-feminists and, taken in the context of mid nineteenth-century conditions, we may recognize their feminist agency.

It is important to clarify what 'feminist' agency could mean in the context of the mid-Victorian era, and also to find ways of reconciling what many modern historians might misconstrue as an innate conservatism rather than a dawning feminism. The first measure might be a woman's personal activism and pronouncements, oral and written, connected with her public activities. Working collectively was the exception rather than the rule in the 1850s, and individual women were initially more likely to find particular niches for themselves before joining with others. Settling on definitions of Victorian feminism when considering a diverse range of feminist interests, has presented a challenging task. In retrospect, how may we accurately judge or contextualize those who had feminist interests at heart?

Feminist historians have faced this interpretive conundrum and some have argued perceptively that it has always been easier to bemoan the conservatism of mid-Victorian feminism because of the 'acceptance by [Victorian] feminists of certain prevailing ideas about the distinctive nature of womanhood'.[11] In the twentieth century, there was a reluctance or at least a delay in connecting Victorian women's religious impetus with emerging feminism. One late-conceded view has admitted that 'religion was a central element in the lives of many Victorian feminists', and that for many Victorian feminists involved in public life, 'religious questions were of central importance'.[12] Prominent women including Frances Power Cobbe and Josephine Butler have been cited as particular examples, with an acceptance that their religious beliefs 'were central to their feminist commitment and provided the framework through which they could articulate their feminist beliefs'.[13] This framework evidently also supported many less prominent Victorian women who neither left records nor published.

In attempting to establish meaningful criteria for gauging feminist agency in the context of the mid nineteenth century, historians have raised some challenging questions. For example, could a 'conservative woman' be a feminist without formally acknowledging or even conceptualizing such status? In seeking to broaden the definition of a 'true' feminist, the net has been cast widely. 'Usefulness' was one strong and prevailing ideology that has been drawn upon. For many Victorian women *'doing* rather than developing ideas' was most crucial.[14] In this light, we may be compelled to include as feminists all those women 'whose writings, declarations or actions invoked a sense of gender as a concrete political agency'.[15]

These questions and approaches may today seem overly cautious but have been employed to understand the diversity and significant nuances of difference amongst Victorian women. Feminist scholars examining individual lives and writings in great detail have produced further reflective analyses that have finally recognized the pervasive and yet positive role of religion in the development of feminism and feminist perspectives. One of the first studies to bring together a significant body of work, edited by Gail Malmgreen, celebrating religion in the lives of English women, appeared in 1986. In this collection, scholars identified religious faith as both a binding and empowering force for feminism and its precursors.[16] In another important study of independent women in mid nineteenth-century England, Martha Vicinus captured the essence and positive significance of religion when she wrote that 'underpinning all women's work was a sense of religious commitment. Single women of vastly different convictions felt consecrated in their work to the highest cause'.[17] This inclusive theory referred to broad Christian values and women animated by their own scriptural interpretation, biblical injunctions *and* the desire to ameliorate distressing social conditions.

My earlier archetypal image suggests that a Victorian woman with a cause, a feminist cause, was more often than not a woman inspired by deep religious beliefs and by a personal interpretation of women's duty of stewardship, as well as an awareness of the inequalities of gender. She may have best understood women's role as that articulated by Josephine Butler, the anti-Contagious Diseases Act crusader who believed that women were 'stewards of the manifold gifts of God...expected to dispense those gifts to others'.[18] Following strongly held beliefs, such women were able to confirm to themselves and also to interested observers and supporters that they, as women first, had a positive role to play in society. Faith in the basic tenets of

Christianity – a belief in responsibility to others and faith in the power of Christian love – this was an empowering credo. These essential understandings provided many with the impetus for action. Contrary to the stereotypical image of a 'do-gooding' charity lady – a married woman enervated by domesticity – such committed individuals were characteristically well educated, middle-ranking women, often single, independent-minded and working for a living, frequently by writing.

Despite the injunctions of writers such as the widely read Mrs Ellis,[19] whose publications actively encouraged a subservient 'suffer and be still' mentality, the mid-Victorian age produced a highly visible generation of women writers prepared to speak plainly and challenge some highly constructed social norms. Paradoxically, by using to their advantage various gendered social conventions, particularly the convention of female modesty and decorum, it became possible for committed individuals to move out of the 'proper sphere' of domestic and private life and make highly public utterances on pressing social problems. The range of social, moral and economic problems was vast and the complex chain often linking these was typically underwritten by poverty, deprivation and lack of education.

To many minds, lack of any knowledge of the Christian gospel compounded social problems and encouraged such 'evils' as prostitution,[20] and such a problem was often perceived to be intractable. Certainly this particular problem was thought to be well beyond the comprehension or power of 'respectable' women to ameliorate or change. In an ideal Victorian world, respectable women remained ignorant of vice, brothels, gaols or houses of ill-repute. Moving outside the 'proper sphere' to tackle such work was regarded by many as unfeminine behaviour. But this constricting attitude failed to discourage strong-minded if otherwise conventional women who felt compelled to take action. For many, the combination of action, united with the desire for 'usefulness' springing from notions of Christian stewardship, moral guardianship and civic duty, appealed both to religious notions and scriptural models of womanly virtue.

At this time in Britain, amongst the diverse community of women motivated by religion, there were a number of female authors who drew upon their religious convictions to inspire readers with a consciousness of the power of faith to change ideas and behaviour. Through this they hoped to hasten social legislation and, hence, improve society. These writers, while drawn to religion, did not choose a religious platform from which to preach, instead they used their books.

There were other women drawn by faith to answer their vocation by working through a religious life that, to an extent, was already a form of public life. The establishment of Anglican religious sister-hoods was regarded with deep suspicion by churchmen and others, while at the same time the number of women missionaries was growing. The deaconess movement attracted women who wished to be popular preachers,[21] and the spiritual and medical work under-taken by Mrs Ellen Ranyard's bible nurses – 'women's mission to women'[22] – was powerfully attractive to many women with faith. A form of religious feminism was exercised through various practices of female ministry when it was coupled with an insistence on a disre-gard of gender in religion. This movement was strongest in Christian sects outside the Established church and was especially strong amongst those women drawn into revivalist religious movements. Yet, while public religious activities of this kind could be related to a growing interest in women's rights within various denominations and, for some, was a distinct challenge to the prevailing gender hierarchy within religious establishments, this was restricted. The same women disowned any connection with the secular women's rights movement; their preferred cause was recognition of an emerging female ministry.[23]

Two women who successfully articulated a distinctly female vision of a more perfect world through their own practical involvement, and through writing works of popular religious fiction, were the highly successful writers Hesba Stretton (1832–1911), a Wesleyan turned Anglican, and Felicia Skene (1821–99), an Anglican High Church woman. Both embraced highly visible causes, both were social campaigners and each made powerful associations with influ-ential national institutions, including the Charity Organization Soci-ety and the London (later National) Society for the Prevention of Cruelty to Children. Writing from a religious perspective for them was not a genteel or 'hand-maidenly' task; it involved social investi-gation, personal involvement with struggling philanthropic causes and exposure to many of society's ills. Such endeavours required a careful negotiation through religious and gender hierarchies in everyday social life as well as in the harsh commercial world of publishing.

It is fair to say that amidst the diversity of Victorian feminist campaigns, the reforming activities of philanthropic and literary women have often been overlooked, or at least relegated to the background. The ways in which Stretton and Skene articulated their careers, and the ways in which they were acknowledged, reveals much about their religious and feminist commitments and women's practical involvement in social campaigns. Stretton and Skene each created a specialized and recognizable literary niche in popular religious publishing, raising simultaneously the identity of women not only as professional authors but also in the emerging forms of expert social work.

Writing was an arena of significant feminine and feminist activity and increasing professionalism, and Stretton and Skene were not alone in contributing to public discourse by raising matters of urgent social, moral and legislative concern in print. In addition, they tackled contemporary questions concerning the hierarchical church establishment and its social role, the clergy, controversies over church politics, doctrinal interpretation and matters of faith and doubt. Such topics and issues absorbed Stretton and Skene privately and emerged in their published writing. Over and above their informed and popular works of fiction aimed at different religious audiences, Stretton and Skene both produced social documentary pieces, free of sentimentality and highly critical of the *status quo*.

Hesba Stretton was one of England's most successful writers of evangelical fiction and began her writing career in Wellington, in Shropshire, where she lived with her widowed father and three older unmarried sisters. Her real name was Sarah Smith but seeking something more memorable, she contrived a pen name by combining the initials of her siblings to make 'Hesba' with the name of 'Stretton', a familiar location of her childhood.[24] The *nom-de-plume* became a publicly acclaimed name from the late 1850s onwards. Her first short fictional story was published in 1859 in *Household Words*, the popular journal published by Charles Dickens. He accepted further articles from her and these were later published in *All the Year Round*.[25] Dickens was to become one of Hesba Stretton's important literary mentors, and she one of his prized writers, and his observant skills and writing style almost certainly inspired her to write more directly about what she saw. Dickens could not have known in 1859 that Hesba Stretton was to embrace a number of philanthropic causes, but unlike his character 'Mrs Jellyby', Miss Stretton remained unmarried and herself scathing of 'do-gooders'. She confided privately in her journal that she loathed ladies charity societies, especially Dorcas sewing circles and, as she put it, 'stupid mothers' meetings'.[26] Although a religious women herself and a writer of evangelical fiction, she resented overbearing evangelical women who demanded to know the state of her soul.[27]

Inevitably, as a writer of popular evangelical fiction, Hesba Stretton has been linked with an earlier generation of women writers, particularly Hannah More, Mrs Trimmer and Mrs Sherwood whose didactic fiction and tracts were most popular and widely disseminated in the earlier decades of the nineteenth century. Hesba Stretton followed these evangelical literary precursors and, to the extent that she used her writing to appeal to the moral conscience of her readers, she was the inheritor of both a womanly tradition and a distinctive literary form. Her writing was both religious and extremely popular, but thereafter any similarities with her precursors diminished. Hesba Stretton had an agenda, an independent and possibly feminist agenda, insisting on authorial recognition, equitable remuneration for her efforts, and control over her work. She was not afraid to write explicitly about the social ills she observed and focused directly upon thorny issues such as the underlying causes of juvenile crime, prostitution, child abandonment and abuse, exploitation of workers and the subordination of women as daughters and as wives.

Recognizing Hesba Stretton's hard-hitting accuracy some critics complained, suggesting that she wrote on difficult subjects best kept from the eyes of innocent readers. One critical review of her successful three-part tale, *The King's Servants* (1873), that appeared in *The Athenaeum*, objected to Miss Stretton's reference to 'fallen girls' – 'we object strongly to this specific form of wretchedness being revealed to young creatures who ought not have their minds darkened by the shadow of such knowledge before the mind is fitted to receive it'.[28] By this time, however, Hesba Stretton's name was greatly respected and her reputation for tackling issues attracted many more admirers than detractors. But while she was so well regarded, she was not associated with any concerted campaign organized by feminists. She was not seen on the same stage as Josephine

Butler and yet she wrote about the same young girls and women whom Butler sought to protect. Stretton wrote and worked alone she was not a joiner.

Her first major success was a tale entitled *Jessica's First Prayer* published first as a serial, then a book, by the Religious Tract Society in 1866. It was a runaway bestseller. By the end of the nineteenth century it had sold millions of copies worldwide and had been translated into more than a dozen languages. The story told of 'Jessica', a young girl abandoned by her father and then by her drunken mother, who was befriended reluctantly by a curmudgeonly churchwarden. The simple plot includes a scenario of abuse and violence, neglect, the indifference of the established church to children such as Jessica, a desperate alliance with a teenage girl already involved in prostitution, and the eventual rescue of them both. This was the first of a run of successes and at the heart of all Hesba Stretton's fiction and social investigation was a deep concern for the welfare of women and children. This is what led her through years of agitation for legislative protection for children with her vital association with the London (later National) Society for the Prevention of Cruelty to Children founded finally in 1884, and the passage of the Act for the prevention of cruelty to children, known popularly as the 'Children's Charter', adopted by Parliament in 1889.

Hesba Stretton participated in other debates (including the campaign for safer working conditions for colliers, the introduction of the 'Plimsoll' line on cargo ships, and the protection of circus children and child entertainers), and she allowed her name to be used to attract public attention. Well informed through personal visits, social observation and knowledge of poverty in Manchester, Liverpool and London, by the late 1860s she wrote with obvious authority and was taken seriously by influential individuals including Florence Nightingale and Lord Shaftesbury. Her regular visits to institutions, including workhouses, refuges and orphanages, as well as close reading of contemporary Parliamentary reports and investigative newspaper articles, meant that she could publicly advocate the work of other campaigners, including Mary Carpenter, Maria Rye and Dr Barnardo who cared for and re-settled abandoned and destitute children. She campaigned for the retention of Ragged Schools after the introduction of compulsory primary schooling in 1870 under the Education Act. She publicized the educational work of Dr James Kay Shuttleworth who was a pioneer in providing humane care and instruction for 'feeble-minded' children. She lent her name and her pen to expose the need for specialist children's hospitals, to provide open missions for discharged prisoners, and she joined with others to write of women's work for children in institutions and other care schemes founded and run exclusively by women for women and children.

In her personal life, Miss Stretton worked to achieve financial independence and professional autonomy. She did not believe that holy matrimony was any salvation for women nor was it a way of achieving economic security; she considered that women in marriages were often exploited and at risk. Although she did not speak out publicly on the issue, she believed that marriage was a form of 'domestic slavery' and wrote passionately on the need for legislative protection of married women's property in two novels, *The Doctor's Dilemma*, published in 1872, and *Under the Old Roof*, published in 1882. Both fictions highlighted the loss of women's inheritances by the acts of unscrupulous husbands. On the issue of the legal protection of women and children, Hesba Stretton was at her most vocal. Protection of children was paramount to her: 'What the nation will be thirty years hence depends chiefly on what the children in the present decade are. The world makes its progress on the little feet of children. That the work of women should ever cease is impossible'. She expressed this view at a congress held in London in 1892 on women's philanthropic work for children, a powerful gathering at which eminent writers were asked for their comment. Hers was a political view, underscored by her conviction that only 'where women have their rights, childhood is happy'.[29]

Informing her writing and her life was a belief in the power of women to effect change, and with this in mind she made a continuing demand that society acknowledge the debt owed to philanthropic women. She made this without referring directly to women's religious faith – to those listening and to those further afield, this was implicit in her statement. Hesba Stretton referred to the earlier impact of Elizabeth Barrett Browning's poem 'Cry of the Children' which, she said, 'rang throughout England and found an echo in every true woman's heart' – 'the consciences of many women were then awakened and have never slumbered again'.[30] She listed the multitude of works performed by women that contributed to safeguarding children, particularly the 'gutter' children roaming

London's and other city streets. She made no particular claims for the impact of her own writing, but many others did, claiming, like Florence Nightingale, that Stretton's fictional depictions were amongst the most perceptive insights into the best and worst aspects of English domestic life.[31]

Her writing provided her with a platform, a place to speak and access to a wide audience. Hesba Stretton never claimed to be a feminist and yet her writing was underpinned by a belief in women's power as well as by faith in the essential New Testament doctrine of compassion. Her belief was in human and divine love as a guiding force. Her theological leanings were non-denominational and during her lifetime she was a self-confessed 'sermon taster'; she moved from Methodism through Congregationalism and finally adopted Anglicanism. In her politics she was declared privately to be 'thoroughly a Radical, even a Republican'.[32] She was an assertive and consciously professional writer and managed to skilfully negotiate the boundaries of propriety, commerce and gender without attracting undue criticism. Intellectually, she was an incipient feminist. In her dealings, she took a woman-centred view of the world and chose to work through her own experience and writing rather than through any feminist, political or church organization. Her feminist consciousness lay in her recognition of the need to defend and protect the rights of women and children in a world controlled by men.

Working on entirely separate causes and in a different social milieu, Felicia Mary Frances Skene was an author and an activist who often worked anonymously or at least pseudonymously. Only in late life did she use her own formidable set of initials, F.M.F. Skene, to identify herself. She began writing in the 1840s. Her travelogue, *Wayfaring Sketches Among the Greeks and Turks*[33] was well received, a serious religious dialectic, *The Divine Master*[34] went into 11 editions, and her sensational Gothic-inspired religious novel, *Use and Abuse*, was described by George Eliot as a 'wild book'.[35] One of her novels, *Hidden Depths*, published first in 1866, was regarded by many critics as too sensational for respectable libraries to circulate, a tale in which her themes included the seduction of innocent young girls, 'fallen women', penitentiaries, 'baby-farmers' and procuresses. This, coming from the pen of a High Churchwoman who had briefly contemplated joining an Anglican sisterhood, marked the author indelibly in some circles as a dangerous subversive. She was an opponent of capital punishment and campaigned vigorously against this in print. She worked for prison reform, she wrote against the English penitentiary system, she assisted women prisoners to find work after release from prison, she believed in women's rights within the church establishment and she supported women's religious sisterhoods.

Felicia Skene's practical mission was concerned ultimately with the exposure of social hypocrisy and injustices that foremostly affected women, although she well understood that injustices, particularly in the prison system, affected men as well as women. British justice failed many and the poor were usually the victims. For her, the final arbiter was not man but God. Legislation was a poor remedy for social ills, while a Christian conscience and consciousness of wrongs was most highly desired in human existence. She believed in 'God's estimate of right and wrong and the measure of his justice'[36].

Felicia Skene came from a noble Scottish family, part of the minor aristocracy. Her birthplace was France, she lived also in Scotland and resided in Greece until her early twenties with her father, James Skene of Rubislaw, and her mother, Jane, a member of the High Church family of Forbes. Her religious formation was formidable, tutored by her cousins Alexander Penrose Forbes who became Bishop of Brechin and his brother George, a Patristic scholar and parish priest who established his own church and printing press in Burntisland. Dean E.B. Ramsay prepared Felicia for confirmation and the Dean of Westminster, Arthur Stanley, conversed with her on religious questions. Adherence to the tested tenets of Christianity and the Articles of Faith set down by the Anglican Church were of utmost importance in Felicia Skene's religious development, leading her to seriously contemplate a religious life in one of the first Anglican sisterhoods established in Oxford. She resisted this course, believing that she was of more practical use in the world.

Her first view of sexual slavery was the sight of forlorn young girls and women on sale in a slave market in Constantinople. In many respects, this initial reality of such a shocking and degrading sight contributed to her later crusade against brothel keepers and pimps operating in Oxford. She later wrote about this experience in *Wayfaring Sketches*, and the powerless and humiliating position of those slave women never left her mind. During a seven-year residence in Greece, she became a fluent linguist and travelled extensively in Asia Minor, Syria and Turkey. By the time she returned to England in 1845, Felicia

Skene had observed many cultures and religions and she was greatly attracted by the Greek Orthodox faith. On her return to England she was drawn immediately into religious circles, coming first under the influence of an earnest High Church clergyman, the Rev John Lincoln Galton. She admired his devotion to a religious life and initially accepted his views unquestioningly. Later she regretted having surrendered 'too much of her religious liberty and independence' to him [37]. Securing feminine independence of mind and spirit was vitally important to her – as important as her religious faith.

It was another High Church priest who brought Felicia Skene into direct contact with social problems in Oxford. Thomas Chamberlain pioneered social work in the slum areas of Oxford and encouraged Felicia to join with him and the newly established Sisterhood of the Holy and Undivided Trinity in this work. She resisted the strong temptation to join the sisters, but she never abandoned her devotion to the Church. In Oxford, she threw herself into charitable work, including teaching at St Edward's School, nursing the poor in the parish, nursing cholera victims in 1849, working through the Oxford Penitentiary with prostitutes and also with young girls at risk sheltering in the Oxford Refuge. This heavy workload was combined with regular prison visiting at the Oxford Gaol. She also assisted Chamberlain with much of the editorial work involved in producing a religious journal, the *Churchman's Companion*. From this springboard, she developed as a writer and took great effort in developing her own recognized style of fiction in which she could address questions related to many issues, to the loss of faith, the prevalence of suicide amongst young men, capital punishment, prison reform and prisoners' rehabilitation. She became a prolific writer, contributing articles to a wide range of popular, religious and sociological journals.

Giving assistance to women who had been drawn into prostitution continued, as well as writing about the problem. This was one of Felicia Skene's 'woman-centred' activities. It took her into a realm of action that related directly to individual women and to exposing the gender inequalities – the sexual double standard – that affected all women's lives. In respect of prostitution, the so-called sin and social evil, she was less concerned with establishing what she called the 'the balance of comparative guilt' since this, she wrote, had already been established through 'a social law which protects the sin of [profligate] men in the one case, and hunts it down in another by punishing "fallen women"'[38]. She was more concerned with achieving amelioration. She tackled the problem in *Hidden Depths*, her most controversial work of fiction and also in an authoritative and detailed article entitled 'Penitentiaries and Reformatories' that received praise for its lucid arguments against the punishing regimes imposed on penitents[39]. Ironically, those critics who criticized *Hidden Depths*, suggesting that no respectable woman could know the details of houses of ill-repute and the sexual predations of men, found the accuracy and unemotional reportage of 'Penitentiaries and Reformatories' commendable. Little did they realize that the author was one and the same. Another form of double standard was in operation – the critical double standard.

Felicia Skene refused to accept the inevitable 'weakness of human nature' argument that many men advanced in relation to prostitution. One critic of *Hidden Depths* suggested that 'so long as human nature continues to be sinful, this particular sin is sure to flourish. Missionaries and midnight meetings may lop off a few branches, but the roots will still remain'[40]. This was flatly rejected by Skene, a mid nineteenth-century reformer who refused to accept this unproblematic explanation for the *status quo*. Apart from continuing the degradation of women (often involved in prostitution for economic need alone), such an argument called for a continued silent acceptance of hypocritical standards that punished women and left men free; this she would not accept, as a woman, as a religious believer and as a proto-feminist.

On another front, as a campaigner against capital punishment, Felicia Skene went against the establishment in legal and religious circles, as a public crusader and as a woman. In keeping with her moral principles and religious beliefs, she argued that no one had right to extinguish life even for the crime of murder. She called hanging and other forms of execution 'legal murder'. Apart from moral revulsion, she did not believe that capital punishment was an effective deterrent and that prejudiced judges had often been responsible for sentencing innocent men and women to the gallows, usually poor men and women. Her most powerful exposition on anti-capital punishment arguments were set out in *Scenes from a Silent World*, a factual series of articles turned later into a book published by Blackwoods[41]. In this she related the circumstances of a range of murders committed by men and by women, and she set out the mitigating circumstance as described to her. She regarded these as confessions from those with little to lose as no pardons or transmutations had been issued. In fiction, the same argument appeared in her work entitled *Through the Shadows: a Test of the Truth*[42]. Using her knowledge of testimonies given to her by condemned prisoners, she created a plot involving a murder and the execution of an innocent man.

Her statistics exposed the relationship between poverty and crime; furthermore, her work revealed that the likelihood of transmutation of the death sentence was greater for women than for men but that was simply because only women could be charged with the crime of infanticide. Abandoned women were often driven to the crime. Her campaigns started in the 1850s and ran almost until her death in 1899 when her authoritative writings on all aspects of prison reform were acknowledged by penologists, jurists and men of the cloth.

In this brief exposure, the lives and works of two women have been brought into prominence through their actions and writing. Today, adopting a more inclusive approach to all the strands of Victorian feminism, Hesba Stretton and Felicia Skene would be included in the pantheon of incipient feminists. They were women involved in pursuing and championing justice, rights and equity for women and children in a society which refused to accept the need for separate and, indeed, protective legislation.

The ways in which Stretton and Skene articulated their careers and how they were acknowledged as professionals in their writing, and in their discrete fields of knowledge and social campaigns, reveals much about their religious and feminist commitments. Appearances were deceptive. Writing with a pseudonym, guarding individual privacy jealously, working alone and writing alone, were all signs of conventional behaviour in Victorian England. Joining groups was not necessarily a yardstick against which personal commitment could be measured, although Stretton and Skene each allowed their names to be associated with organizations whose major works, in the main, assisted women and children. Like their own books, they could not necessarily be judged by their covers. They challenged stereotypes by using conventionality as a kind of shield, blurring the divide between public and private, combining the conservative and radical, employing conventional and subversive techniques to get their message across in literally millions of printed pages.

Women in public, those involved in any aspects of the Victorian women's movement, were usually motivated by a sense of personal outrage, by a desire for usefulness as well as by religious sensibilities. In the 1850s it was more difficult to combine feminine respectability with a public life, but even the most conservative of women were gradually able to break with convention with the rock of religious faith to hold fast. Rather than inhibiting feminism as its agenda focused consciousness on the need to improve women's status and rights, religion bolstered many women in their beliefs and actions. Whether they were authors, Anglican sisters of charity, bible women, members of the Women's Help Society, the Charity Organization Society, the National Society for the Prevention of Cruelty to Children, the Salvation Army or the Ladies Association for the Care of Friendless Girls, in addition to thousands of other women-centred associations, Victorian women with causes were part of a strategic and interactive 'noble army', energized by the forces of faith and feminism.

Notes

1 *Sketches by Boz* was first published in 1836, and *Bleak House* appeared in 1853.
2 This description is attributed to Frances Power Cobbe. See Pauline Nestor, *Female Friendships and Communities: Charlotte Brontë, George Eliot, Elizabeth Gaskell* (Oxford: Clarendon Press, 1985), p. 21.
3 See Patricia Hollis (ed.), *Women in Public 1850–1900: Documents of the Victorian Women's Movement*, London: George Allen & Unwin, 1979.
4 The origins of organized British feminism can be traced to the Langham Place offices of the *English Women's Journal* which provided a forum for a national exchange of ideas and information between women. Langham Place, close to the University of London, quickly became the hub of feminist campaigns in the 1860s. The *English Women's Journal* appeared first in 1858 under the leadership of Bessie Rayner Parkes and Barbara Leigh Smith. For a short history of the group, see Sheila Herstein, 'The Langham Place Circle and Feminist Periodicals of the 1860s', *Victorian Periodicals Review*, no. 1, Spring 1993, pp. 24–7.
5 Barbara Caine, *Victorian Feminists* (Oxford: Oxford University Press, 1992), p. 72.
6 Ibid., pp. 12–13.
7 Mary Maynard 'Privilege and Patriarchy: Feminist Thought in the Nineteenth-Century', in Susan Mendus and Jane Rendall (eds), *Sexuality and Subordination. Interdisciplinary Studies of Gender in the Nineteenth Century*,

London, 1989, p. 225. Cited in Phillipa Levine, *Feminist Lives in Victorian England: Private Roles and Public Commitment*, Oxford: Basil Blackwell, 1990.

8   Levine, ibid., pp. 4–5.

9   Gail Malgreen (ed.), Introduction, *Religion in the Lives of English Women 1760–1930* (London: Croom Helm, 1986).

10 Martha Vicinus, *Independent Women: Work and Community for Single Women 1850–1900* (London: Virago Press, 1985), p. 36.

11 Josephine E. Butler (ed.), *Women's Work and Women's Culture: a Series of Essays*, London, 1869, p. xxxix.

12 Ellis, Sarah, *The Wives of England: Their Relative Duties, Domestic Influence and Social Obligations*, London, 1844; Ellis, Sarah, *The Daughters of England*, London, 1845, Ellis, Sarah, *Education of the Heart: Woman's Best Work* (London, 1869).

13 For an introduction to this question, see K.S. Inglis, *The Church and the Working Classes in Victorian England*, London, 1963.

14 William Pennefether was the founder of the Training Home for Female Missionaries that later became the London Deaconness Institution. See Olive Anderson 'Women Preachers in mid-Victorian Britain: some Reflexions on Feminism, Popular Religion and Social Change', *The Historical Journal*, XII, 3 (1969), p. 468.

15 See F.K. Prochaska, 'Body and Soul: Bible Nurses and the Poor in Victorian London', *Historical Research: The Bulletin of the Institute of Historical Research*, vol. LX, 1987, pp. 336–48.

16 See Olive Anderson, loc. cit., pp. 467–84, for a useful early discussion of the ambivalent outcomes of women's challenges to prevailing gender hierarchies in religion.

17 Her sisters were named Hannah, Elizabeth, she was christened Sarah, and her eldest sister was Anne. Her surviving brother, Benjamin, her favorite sibling, emigrated to Canada in 1866. Three younger brothers died young. Sarah Smith has strong family connections with the Shropshire villages of Church Stretton and All Stretton.

18 A full bibliography of Hesba Stretton's work appears in my unpublished PhD thesis, Suzanne L.G. Rickard, 'On The Shelf: Women Writers, Publishing and Philanthropy in mid-Nineteenth Century England', Canberra: Australian National University, 1995.

19 Hesba Stretton recorded this in her journal (known as her 'Log Book') on Jan. 12, 1870. Mss 5556/1–9, Shropshire Local Studies Library, Shrewsbury, England.

20 Hesba Stretton wrote, 'Went to see the Pennefeathers [sic]: an odious woman inquired about my [religious] conversion before we had been in the house two minutes', Log Book, Jan. 12, 1870. William Pennefether was the founder of the London Deaconesses Institution, see note 13 above.

21 *The Athenaeum*, December 13, 1873. The reviewer was probably Geraldine Jewsbury, one of three powerful contemporary women reviewers, includ-

ing George Eliot for the *Westminster Review* and Eliza Lynn Linton for the *Saturday Review*.

22   Hesba Stretton, 'Women's Work for Children', in Angela Burdett Coutts (ed.), *Woman's Mission: a Series of Congress Papers on the Philanthropic Work of Women by Eminent Writers* (Sampson Low, Marston & Co., London, 1893), p. 5.

23   Ibid., p. 4.

24   Florence Nightingale to Lady Parthenope Verney (her sister), MS 1138, Nightingale Archives, Claydon House Trust, Buckinghamshire, England.

25   Hesba Stretton to Mrs Pattison, ALS, 16 April 1886, Manuscript Collection, University of London Library.

26   *Wayfaring Sketches Among the Greeks and Turks and on the Shores of the Danube, by a Seven Year's Resident in Greece* [F.M.F. Skene], London: Chapman and Hall, 1847.

27   *The Divine Master*, Joseph Masters, London, 1852 (Eleventh edition printed in 1888).

28   *Use and Abuse: a Tale* (London: Francis & John Rivington, 1849).

29   Anonymous [F.M.F. Skene], *Hidden Depths*, 2 vols. Edinburgh: Edmondston & Douglas, 1866, reprinted as *Hidden Depths: a Story of A Cruel Wrong*, London: Hodder & Stoughton, 1886, reprinted as *Hidden Depths: a Tale for the Times*, New York: Rand McNally, Chicago 1894.

30   E.C. Rickard, *Felicia Skene at Oxford: a Memoir*, London: John Murray, 1902, p. 81. For a detailed picture of Felicia Skene's life, see my account 'Felicia Skene – Sensational Maiden', unpublished thesis, loc. cit., above.

31   *Hidden Depths* op. cit. (1866), vol. 2, p. 222.

32   Anonymous [F.M.F. Skene], Penitentiaries and Reformatories, *Odds and Ends*, vol. 1, no. 6, Edinburgh: Edmonston & Douglas, 1865, pp. 3–32.

33   *Saturday Review*, vol. 21, no. 537, 10 Feb 1866, p. 181.

34   *Scenes from a Silent World; or, Prisons and their Inmates*, by Francis Scougal [F.M.F. Skene], Edinburgh and London: W. Blackwood & Sons, 1889.

35   *Through the Shadows: a Test of the Truth*, by Erskine Moir [F.M.F. Skene] (London: Elliott Stock), 1888.

9
Equal Questions: the 'Woman Question' and the 'Drink Question' in the Writings of Clara Lucas Balfour, 1808–78

Kristin G. Doern

At the heart of many key social reform movements of the nineteenth century was the evangelical notion of creating a just, moral society through *personal* Christian conversion and salvation, what Callum Brown has referred to as the 'salvation revolution'.[1] Considered within this framework, the nineteenth-century temperance movement operated within a climate of reform which was concerned as much with the possible moral and social gains to be had from converting individuals to God as with actual levels of excessive alcohol consumption.

Women temperance campaigners and their writings exhibited just this double vision, conducted within the dominant discourses of a domestic ideology which situated the family at the centre of the ideal moral, Christian society. As a result, their work has largely been considered as 'conservative' by contemporary feminist historians. I would like to suggest instead, however, that temperance women, as with many other moral reformers of the nineteenth century, manipulated this ideology to create new roles for themselves, which although not comparable with twentieth-century feminist ideas of equality, still provided an initial step towards what would become the women's movement of the latter nineteenth century. Nor is it accidental that these women chose to use the temperance issue as part of the justification for their transgression into the public sphere. Temperance for them was integrally linked to wider issues such as the 'moral' salvation of society and 'social purity'; excessive drinking was inextricably connected to poverty, unemployment, violence, crime and familial decline. Crucially, these women (some explicitly, some implicitly) recognized that the issues surrounding temperance and social reform were gendered issues. Their work was most often pursued in connection with their negotiation of nineteenth-century gender divisions and always within and through the parameters of their religious beliefs.

Discussed in the context of these issues and debates, this chapter will focus on the life of Clara Lucas Balfour (1808–78) – writer, lecturer and temperance campaigner. Brought up within the Church of England, she became a Baptist at the age of 32 and remained a lifelong, central figure in the congregation of the Baptist Chapel, Edgware, until her death. Balfour's religious conversion occurred at roughly the same time as her introduction to the still-young Temperance Movement, and this joint 'conversion' was to change her life. Through her prolific lecturing and writing career, which spanned over 40 years, Balfour not only campaigned for temperance, she also championed the cause of women, focusing on women's role in society and history in works including *The Women of Scripture* (1847), *Working Women of the Last Half Century: the Lessons of their Lives* (1854), *The Bible Patterns of a Good Woman* (1867), and *Women Worth Emulating* (1877). Previously, she has been considered almost exclusively in the light of her temperance work, but through an analysis of her social and religious motivations and beliefs, I will argue that it is possible to view Balfour's 'separate spheres feminism' as an important precursor to late nineteenth-century feminism.

Between the late 1830s and 1870s, Balfour published over 70 temperance novels, stories and collections and contributed to a number of temperance journals. She also lectured and wrote on a wide variety of topics, including biography, history and literature, as well as women's historical and contemporary role in society. At a time when women did not usually lecture, even as amateurs, she supported herself and her family with the proceeds of her professional speaking and writing engagements.

In the tributes paid to her by the temperance press at the time of her death, Balfour was hailed as one the movement's pioneers and as one of its most successful and prolific writers, and her claim to distinction still lies predominantly in this role.[2] Lilian Shiman has commented for example that Balfour was 'a writer of temperance stories who broke barriers in her actions but not in her writings'.[3] Although she acknowledges Balfour's unusual status in the mid-nineteenth century as a female public speaker and presents her as 'one of the very few women who would mount a public platform and address a mixed audience on the evils of drink',[4] Shiman does not consider her substantial polemical writing on the 'Woman Question'. As I will illustrate below, Balfour's personal life circumstances influenced her subsequent writings and activism on both temperance and gender issues.

Clara Lucas Balfour (née Lyddell) was born in 1808 and married James Balfour before her sixteenth birthday. Nothing is known about how they met, but the temperance campaigner and writer John Dunlop (later to become a close friend and colleague of the Balfours) speculated that they perhaps eloped in order for Clara to escape the drudgery and unhappiness of her life with her mother.[5] Unfortunately, her new married life was not the escape she had envisaged, for the Balfours lived, with their six children, precariously close to poverty, exacerbated by James Balfour's 'habits of intemperance' which 'became a source of great trouble' to Clara and this, combined with his 'apparently aimless drift from job to job', contributed to the harsh, poverty-stricken circumstances of the Balfours' first 13 years of marriage.[6]

A key event in their lives occurred in 1837 when the Balfours joined the still-young temperance movement. Although somewhat hesitant at the notion of 'total abstinence', which she felt was extreme, Clara signed the pledge a week after her husband, on October 16 1837.[7] Writing 30 years after their 'conversion' to temperance, Balfour's tract, *Our 'Old October': Being a True Sketch of a Temperance Meeting in the Earliest Days of the Temperance Reformation* (1868), recounts how she decided to attend a temperance meeting at a Bible Christians' Chapel one stormy night and listened to various testimonies from members of the small, bedraggled group of women gathered in the Chapel. Eventually, she was persuaded to join those who had already testified and sign the pledge herself. *Our Old October* ends with a tribute to the importance of individual testimony and conversion:

> The whirlwind, the fire, the rending of the rocks of prejudice, which is the work of genius and oratory, I can admire and honour;

but, for me, the remote, obscure nook, and the 'still, small voice', had a power they have not lost through one- and-thirty years of wandering to and fro amid all the clamours of a noisy world.[8]

Throughout her lecturing and writing career, Balfour was at pains to convince others – especially women – that the 'still, small voice' had great potential and was just as vital as the 'work of genius and oratory'. 'Consciousness-raising' among women did not have to wait until the late twentieth century. This small, bedraggled temperance meeting perhaps marked Balfour's first experience of female solidarity.

While the change in her husband's 'habits' must have been a great relief to Balfour, their financial circumstances were not initially improved. They were still struggling when Dunlop first met them in 1840, an event memorable enough for him to comment on at length:

> The children directed me up a dark stair...at the platform at the top, was a young woman about 30 years of age, on her hands & knees, with a tub of hot water near her, engaged in washing the floor....She ushered me into what was Dining Room, & kitchen both...When I got time & light to look around, I perceived that a great space of the walls was covered with shelves, & well filled with Books: it was like a regular student's library: the volumes were well arranged, the folios and quartos at the bottom. These still she kept safe amid the wreck of their affairs.[9]

Somehow, despite the trials of the early years of her marriage, Balfour had collected her own library; she had found both the means and the time to continue her own self-education and even to begin a serious writing career.[10] In May 1841, Dunlop arranged for Balfour to co-edit the *Temperance Journal* with Jabez Burns and for her to have a £25 salary.[11] Although her husband's work as an agent for Dunlop was not highly paid, together with her salary from the *Temperance Journal*, and whatever other income was generated through her writing, the Balfours were earning enough to be able to move to 'better accommodation' in Lisson Grove, near Edgware Road by June 1841.[12]

At the same time as this change in their fortunes, Balfour's first major temperance volume was published. *The Garland of Water*

Flowers, a Collection of Poems and Tales (1841) conformed to the distinctive patterns of temperance didactic writing, and is reminiscent of the structure and content of Hannah More's *Cheap Repository Tracts*. One of Balfour's tales, published in this collection for example, contains a stereotypical portrayal of the 'drunken husband' of many temperance narratives, although in this case there was probably an autobiographical element involved.[13] 'The Reclaimed' tells the story of a young woman named Kate Morely who, against the better judgement of her wise aunt, marries William Horton, a charming, but roguish young man. William drinks the family into poverty and shame and finally, 'in a spirit of ungovernable vengeance', strikes Kate to the ground 'with a violence that apparently deprived her of sense and life'. In the end, William, having almost drunk himself to death over remorse at his violence towards his wife, is rescued by an old man who 'was of a now numerous and much ridiculed class who strove to apply a *practical remedy* to a *practical evil*'. The message in 'The Reclaimed' is unequivocal:

> William never, for a moment, forgot to be grateful to the great CAUSE which had found him in his degradation and led him back to that good path from which he had so wildly wandered. TEMPERANCE and diligence deserved and obtained success.... Every moment of William Horton's leisure was employed in spreading the principles to which he was so deeply indebted, *'for'* as he frequently remarked, *'if I was saved let no one* DARE DESPAIR!'[14]

As with the Balfours themselves, for Kate and William, redemption and reconciliation could only come through conversion to a true faith *and* to temperance.

Not content simply to leave it up to men, her poem, 'The Claims of Temperance on Woman', contained Balfour's first encouragement to women to convert to the temperance cause, making explicit what was to be her life-long conviction in the integral relationship between religion, temperance and domestic harmony. The publication of her first collection of temperance writings coincided with Balfour's first foray into public lecturing and it would appear that Dunlop was again instrumental in helping her take the next step in her public career. At the age of 33, with four children between the ages of six and fourteen, Balfour's career as a professional, touring lecturer was finally underway. Following Dunlop's advice, she quickly expanded from the subject of temperance to broader lectures on literature, history, biography, and, most notably, the topic of women.[15]

By the end of the 1840s, Balfour had become the 'key female lecturer on topics about women within the Mechanics' and Literary Institutes Movement' and her lectures on women included titles such as 'Female Influence', 'The Influence of Women on Society', 'The Influence and Education of Women', 'Remarkable Women', 'Obligations of English Literature to Female Writers', 'Historical Women of England and France' and 'Women of Scripture'.[16] It is significant that the ideas and issues presented publicly in these lectures were also discussed in private between Balfour and her own circle of feminist friends, almost a decade before the advent of the Langham Place Circle. Dunlop wrote that on September 23 1846 he had 'drank tea at Mrs. Balfour's with Mrs. Anne Knight the Quaker, advocate of Woman's Rights & Mr. Hugo Reid. Talked about political claims of the fair sex, their oppression, education – also suffrage'.[17]

For Balfour, the real obstacle facing women was society's unwillingness to recognize their 'moral responsibilities', their 'high mental capability', and their 'perfect equality of spiritual privileges and eternal destiny with men'[18] and she vigorously challenged this in her writing. Her first book, *Moral Heroism; or, the Trials and Triumphs of the Great and Good* (1846), set out her feminist manifesto for the first time; this despite its 'separate spheres' orthodoxy, claimed that women were paramount to a nation's prosperity and its moral elevation:

> No station in life is more important and arduous than that of a wife and a mother. The happiness and the virtue of society depend mainly on the wise and faithful fulfilment of those relationships. A nation is truly prosperous, not merely by its wealth, its commerce, its political enactments, and relations, but by its social purity and moral elevation; and these depend on a 'Well ordered home, man's chief, best good, below'.[19]

The difficulty of portraying instances of moral heroism in women did not 'arise from scarcity, but [was] rather the difficulty of wise selection from a mighty mass of material', she argued, pointing to women in the bible as a rich source of such heroism, before going on to focus on Lady Rachel Russell and the intrepid prison reformer Elizabeth Fry as two other outstanding examples.[20] Thus, even in a text devoted largely to celebrating the moral heroism of men, Balfour's future commitment to championing women as the guardians and saviours of the nation's moral fabric was clearly evident.

From this point on, the relationship between women's social role, individual moral and religious salvation, and the transformation of society at large, were at the centre of all of Balfour's work. Her first treatise devoted entirely to the 'Woman Question' considered these issues in terms of the representation of *Women of Scripture* (1847), in which she searched the bible for 'a record of woman's endowments, their privileges, and their responsibilities' as a humanizing force within society.[21] This analysis made it clear to her that whereas the bible recognized woman's 'moral responsibility' and 'high mental capability', the 'more polished nations of antiquity' seemed to have 'formed a low estimate of the female character, and regulated their social institutions, in conformity to that low estimate'.[22] This had resulted in a multitude of injustices being perpetrated against women. Echoing arguments already used by both Mary Wollstonecraft and Hannah More over 40 years earlier, Balfour believed that these resulted in the enslavement not just of women, but of all:

It is an immutable and instructive fact in morals, that every act of injustice perpetrated by one human being against another, oper-ates as unfavourably on the injurer as on the injured. Thus the social system of the most intellectual nation of heathen antiquity, by sanctioning the tyranny of man, and compelling the slavery of woman, deteriorates the character of both.[23]

Balfour's positive depiction of female biblical imagery in which women were 'not help-less, not inadequate, and therefore not infer-ior' was nonetheless grounded in traditional notions of woman as 'wife', 'mother', 'healer', and 'comforter'. She categorically denied, however, that the 'character of woman' was in any way 'feeble' and ended her introduction to *Women of Scripture* by commenting that the Scriptures 'undoubtedly inculcate subordination as the duty of woman, but inferiority is no where either expressed or implied'.[24] For Balfour, it was women's place in 'the maternal office, to teach virtue, to train the mind for usefulness here, and immortality hereafter' and, she concluded, 'who shall say her office is inferior?'[25] Castigating men for their self-serving elevation of their own 'public' duties above women's responsibilities within the family, then, Balfour sought to distinguish between subordination and inferiority by professionalizing and elevating women's maternal 'office'.

Before ordinary women would be able to believe themselves capable of reforming the nation, Balfour was convinced that they needed to learn about the lives and work of past women reformers, and much of her writing on the 'Woman Question' thus often takes the form of collective female biographies that celebrate the exploits of such women. Because of this, her work has been criticized for conforming to the 'woman worthies' genre of pre-twentieth-century women's history.[26] However, as Sybil Oldfield has recently challenged, if the collective biographies of 'notable' women are taken seriously within the record, it is possible to suggest that women have not been so completely 'hidden from history' in the ways that conventional feminist historiography has so often argued. In books such as Balfour's *Women of Scripture* (1847), *Working Women of the Last Half Century: the Lessons of Their Lives* (1854) and *Women Worth Emulating* (1877), young women could – and did – learn about 'remarkable, mould-breaking women who were not content to live out their lives unquestioning, mute and confined either to the paternal or marital home'.[27]

Uniquely amongst her contemporaries, Balfour insisted that Mary Wollstonecraft should be considered as one of these foremothers alongside more 'acceptable' women like Hannah More. In her *Sketches of English Literature, from the fourteenth to the present century* (1852), Balfour argued that Wollstonecraft was an 'influential female name whose claims have neither been candidly considered nor honestly admitted by her own sex'.[28] Summing up the negative impact of the combination of Wollstonecraft's radical views on women's rights and her own 'scandalous' personal circumstances, Balfour concluded that 'when she died, in some respects a martyr to her mistaken theories, the general belief was she had injured rather than advanced the interests of woman'. In spite of the conventional condemnation of both Wollstonecraft's person and her ideas, Balfour went on to suggest that 'gradually amid the mist of prejudice this truth loomed distinctly forth, that woman was not all she might be, and that society was not as just to her as it ought to be'.[29] With this awareness seeping into general consciousness, 'woman's duties, privileges, rights, character and capabilities' began to be investigated. Anticipating the view of Wollstonecraft as the 'mother' of feminism, Balfour believed that, however problematic and controversial a personality, it was still Wollstonecraft who had asked the first questions about women which precipitated the whole nineteenth-century 'Woman Question' debate.[30]

However, for Balfour, the 'Woman Question' formed only a part of a larger debate over the urgent need for moral and social reform. As we have seen, Balfour's involvement with this larger debate was precipitated by her confrontation with her husband's excessive drinking and their joint conversion to temperance and active religion. Although both the 'Woman Question' and the 'Drink Question' played equal parts in much of her work, in her fictional writing, Balfour's driving motivation was to bring the plight of the 'miserable inebriate' to the attention of society in order to further the cause of temperance.

Balfour's prolific temperance writing may have been unique for the period in terms of quantity, but her style was not. Her first temperance novel anticipated the conventional pattern of temperance fiction epitomized by Mrs Henry Wood's *Danesbury House* (1860), in which all the characters 'succeed or fail in life precisely in proportion to their indulgence in alcoholic liquors'.[31] *Confessions of a Decanter* (1862) is a classic example of Balfour's mid-nineteenth-century temperance fiction, an example which epitomizes the worst in this genre while at the same time presenting a humorous and imaginative account of the 'evils of drink'. The narrator is the decanter and the tale begins with its purchase by a young, newly married couple. The husband is a Lieutenant in the Navy and due to his frequent absences from home takes his young bride to live with his widowed father, Squire Rubicand. The housekeeper, Mrs Specious, 'who drinks out of a black bottle and then chews on lemon before joining the company', does not want a new mistress and offers to get the 'pale' looking bride 'a restorative', an 'elegant cordial of [Mrs Specious'] own making – a sovereign remedy against low spirits, languor and fatigue'.[32] The temptation works, and the young Mrs Rubicand asks for the cordial to be kept in the decanter in her room.

Over time, her use of the cordial increases until she and her young baby are dependent on it. When Lieutenant Rubicand returns home he is shocked at the change in his young wife, but does not discover the cause. The baby's wet nurse, a total abstainer, requests permission to take the child home with her to care for and much to the nurse's surprise, the Captain agrees to let her take the child. When rumours begin to circulate that the Captain's visits to the nurse's cottage are not just to see his child, his wife believes them, and drinking the entire contents of a bottle of brandy, goes to the nurse's cottage to repossess her child. On her way home she slips by the riverbank and falls into the river with the baby. The child is drowned, Mrs Rubicand is saved by the nurse, but loses her sanity and is finally institutionalized by her husband.

In this particular melodramatic tale, all the women who drink meet with stereotypically terrible ends. The only salvation in this case ironically comes for the decanter itself which eventually finds its way to a chapel where it holds water for use in temperance meetings! For Balfour, the 'consequences arising from female intemperance [were] undoubtedly far more awful than in any other case' because if 'the mother falls into that vice . . . the poison of her example contaminates all around: a disordered home, a neglected family, must be the inevitable results'.[33] Her belief that it was much more 'difficult to reclaim' the intemperate woman was shared by many contemporary temperance campaigners and the purpose of temperance fiction such as *Confessions of a Decanter* was not necessarily to turn confirmed female drunkards away from the bottle, but rather to stop other women from ever drinking in the first place.

For many mid-nineteenth-century temperance converts and campaigners, only 'total abstinence' was the 'practical remedy to a practical evil'[34] provided it was combined with a real commitment to Christianity. Defending the principle of total abstinence against a barrage of disbelief and ridicule from unconverted critics was a significant proportion of temperance campaigners' work. Charles Dickens, for example, mocked the notion that drunkenness could only be alleviated by the 'whole hog or nothing but' approach to social reform, publishing his 'Whole Hogs' article in 1851. 'It has been discovered', he wrote, 'that mankind at large can only be regenerated by a Tee-total Society, or by a Peace Society, or by always dining on Vegetables'.[35]

'Whole Hogs' made a mockery of the 'practical remedy', which for Balfour's family had proved very successful, and Clara Balfour responded to Dickens with righteous indignation. Speaking from both her and her husband's observations after 15 years of temperance campaigning in 'Stopping Half Way' (1852), Balfour tackled head on the charge of 'extremism' by challenging 'any half-hog philosopher or humorist' to:

> please tell his readers what good work has ever been done in this world of ours by reformers, who stopped half way in their reforms? ...Onward! onward! leave the half-hearted and the half-witted to stop half way, and employ themselves in a careful dissection and mastication of the favourite 'half-hog.'[36]

Experience had taught Balfour that nothing was 'worse than the half-and-half system'.[37] At no point in her life did she waver from her adherence to the path of total abstinence. More than this, she was convinced that only committed activism could defeat intemperance, and that the best activists for the temperance cause were women.

From the early 1840s on Balfour had attempted to convince her female audiences that they too could utilize their innate womanly capabilities and strengths for much needed social reform.[38] Her first explicit call to women had been in *Women and the Temperance Reformation* (1849) in which she declared:

> Few persons in the present day will dispute the assertion, that women are the most influential moral teachers of society....every discovery in morals that scientific investigation and conclusive experiment have proved to be calculated to advance the cause of human improvement, depends on the candid attention and co-operation of women; since on them is laid the solemn responsibility of increasing human happiness, by promoting human virtue.[39]

In spite of the fact that women had always participated in 'great numbers' in 'religious and benevolent societies', however, the temperance movement had not 'met with so great an amount of patronage and co-operation from the gentler sex as might reasonably be expected'.[40] Balfour's tract outlined what women could do for the temperance cause privately and publicly, concluding with a rallying cry for women to do all that lay within their sphere of influence:

> Women of England! Let it no longer be said that you are indifferent to a principle that dries the tears of suffering wives, relieves the

miseries of neglected childhood, reclaims the degraded, preserves the sober, removes poverty, and by preparing the mind for the reception of religious truth, elevates man to his true dignity as a child of God and an heir of a blissful immortality.[41]

Balfour's mission to increase the numbers of women working for temperance continued throughout her life. In the 1860s and early 1870s she frequently spoke at various 'Ladies' Conventions' to facilitate the establishment of women's temperance societies.[42] Having been instrumental in the creation of the British Women's Temperance Association (the BWTA, founded in 1876), Balfour was elected its president in May 1877. Because of their initial involvement in the women's temperance movement and the BWTA, large numbers of women became involved in the wider nineteenth-century struggle for women's emancipation in general and the suffrage movement in particular.

Balfour's presidency of the BWTA was unfortunately short-lived, as in 1877 she was already seriously ill with cancer. She died in Croydon on July 3 1878. Her son-in-law, Dawson Burns, later wrote that 'it is doubtful whether, among the galaxy of Temperance women, any other single star has emitted so much light, for so long a period, and over so wide a surface as did Mrs. Balfour'.[43] To her contemporaries, Balfour had been a pioneering figure in the nineteenth-century temperance movement.

Recognition of Balfour's importance in terms of the history of women's contribution to the temperance cause is borne out by the tribute paid to her by the *Englishwoman's Review* shortly after her death, her inclusion in so many late nineteenth-century temperance histories, and her lengthy entry in the original *Dictionary of National Biography*.[44] Now, however, she is relegated to brief inclusions in lists of conservative temperance women who perpetuated Victorian domestic ideology and seldom is her non-temperance work even considered. A rare example is June Purvis' *Hard Lessons: the Lives and Education of Working-Class Women in Nineteenth Century England* (1989) which mentions Balfour in terms of her influence on the working-class audiences at lectures for the Mechanics' Institutes, although again the conservative elements of Balfour's life and work are overemphasized.[45]

While Balfour's appeal to Institute organizers may very well have owed something to her endorsement of 'appropriate', 'middle-class ideas' as Purvis suggests, she was, in the very act of sustaining a career as a paid, professional lecturer, simultaneously contradicting many of those same ideas associated with 'appropriate womanly behaviour'. Furthermore, she was the living embodiment of the benefits of adhering to a combination of 'self-improvement', personal religion and temperance in order to achieve the 'happy home life' that for Balfour, among many others, lay at the heart of improving women's lives. Her categorically stated beliefs and life work quite clearly fit within a more radical feminist agenda than has previously been contemplated, for Balfour never wavered from her explicit adherence to the essential equality of men and women, both in society, but especially within religion, the bible, and in the eyes of God. She sought to emancipate women from unfair, gender-based subordination, while celebrating both their uniqueness, their proven capabilities and their potential. From the young girl bartering her year of needlework for a few months education, to the young wife and mother scrubbing the floor outside her amazing 'library kitchen', to the itinerant Adult Education lecturer, Balfour emerged as an authoritative voice who, 'fighting the world and winning',[46] justified women's claims for material, intellectual and spiritual dignity *and* equality with men. She supported her convictions by claiming scriptural authority and on citing examples of the achievements of exemplary feminist foremothers.

Balfour's religiosity and her almost exclusive association with temperance have made her an unfashionable figure, resulting in her absence from secular histories of the nineteenth-century women's movement. To date, her place in history has been confined to that of a leisured, philanthropic, middle-class temperance lady. In reality, Clara Balfour embodied the spirit of the 'salvation revolution' which called her to self-contemplation and conversion, to congregational participation, and to evangelical action in society at large.[47] As an active participant in the 'Victorian pursuit of moral progress' Balfour found not just spiritual salvation, but economic – and perhaps intellectual and social – salvation as well.[48] Through her own personal conversion to the temperance cause and to active, evangelical religion, Clara Lucas Balfour spent her life arguing that this salvation was the inalienable right of all – men *and* women.

Notes

1   Callum G. Brown, *The Death of Christian Britain: Understanding Secularisation 1800–2000* (London: Routledge, 2001), pp. 36–9.
2   See for example 'Mrs. Clara Lucas Balfour', *The Temperance Record*, July 11th 1878 and 'Mrs. Clara Lucas Balfour', *Englishwoman's Review* LXIII (1878). See also Peter T. Winskill, *The Comprehensive History of the Rise and Progress of the Temperance Reformation from the Earliest Period to September, 1881* (London: 1881); Dawson Burns, *Temperance History. A Consecutive Narrative of the Rise, Development, and Extensions of the Temperance Reform*, 2 vols (London: National Temperance Publication Depot, 1889–91). See also Norman Longmate, *The Waterdrinkers: a History of Temperance* (London: Hamish Hamilton, 1968) p. 127; Brian Harrison, *Drink and the Victorians: the Temperance Question in England 1815–1872*, 1994 (ed.) (Keele: Keele University Press, 1971) pp. 159, 162; Brian Harrison, *Dictionary of British Temperance Biography, Society for the Study of Labour History Bulletin Supplement: Aids to Research* (London: Society for the Study of Labour History, 1973) pp. 5–6.
3   Lilian Shiman, 'Changes Are Dangerous: Women and Temperance in Victorian England', in *Religion in the Lives of English Women, 1760–1930* Gail Malmgreen (ed.) (London: Croom Helm, 1986), p. 197. See also Lilian Shiman, *Crusade against Drink in Victorian England* (London: Macmillan, 1988), pp. 143, 182 and *Women and Leadership in Nineteenth-Century England* (London: Macmillan, 1992), pp. 82, 112–13, 127, 155–6; Margaret Barrow, 'Temperate Feminists: the British Women's Temperance Association 1870–1914' (PhD thesis, University of Manchester, 1999), pp. 63, 71, 266.
4   Shiman, 'Changes Are Dangerous', op. cit., p. 197.
5   John Dunlop, *Autobiography of John Dunlop* (London: Spottiswoode, Ballantyne & Co. Ltd, 1932), pp. 173–4. For biographical details on Balfour, see Kristin G. Doern, 'Temperance and Feminism in England, c.1790–1890: Women's Weapons – Prayer, Pen & Platform' (University of Sussex, 2001). See also Cecil Burns, *Memorial Leaves. A Selection from the Papers of Cecil Burns (Mrs. Dawson Burnes) With a Biographical Sketch* (London: Ideal Publishing Union, 1898); Dawson Burns, *The Late Mrs. Clara Lucas Balfour: a Memorial Discourse Preached by the Rev. D. Burns, with the Address in Paddington Cemetery, Delivered Rev. J.W. Todd* (London: S.W. Partridge & Co., 1878); Janet Cunliffe-Jones, 'Clara Lucas Balfour 1808–1878: Lecturer, Writer and Pioneer of Women's Studies' (Masters of Education, University of Liverpool, 1988) and Balfour's entry in the *Dictionary of National Biography*.
6   Cunliffe-Jones, 'Clara Lucas Balfour'. p. 16. See also Peter T. Winskill, *The Temperance Movement and Its Workers*, 2 vols (London: Blackie, 1892). p. 202 (vol. II). John Dunlop later recounted that Balfour's husband was 'aware of his fault; & to please his anxious partner used, on bad occasions, to come home intoxicated, with a hymn book he had bought for her: by & by she had a great number of these'. Dunlop, *Autobiography of John Dunlop*. p. 153.

7 Cunliffe-Jones, 'Clara Lucas Balfour', pp. 19–21. See also Balfour's *DNB* entry as well as Jabez Inwards, *Memorials of Temperance Workers: Containing Brief Sketches of Nearly One Hundred Deceased and Worthy Labourers* (London: S.W. Partridge & Co., 1879). pp. 18; Winskill, *The Temperance Movement and Its Workers*, p. 202 (vol. II).

8 Clara Lucas Balfour, *Our 'Old October': Being a True Sketch of a Temperance Meeting in the Earliest Days of the Temperance Reformation* (London: W. Tweedie, 1868). pp. 6, 14. Because Balfour's conversion to temperance occurred in the Bible Christians' Chapel, she has most often been referred to as a Bible Christian herself, when in fact she was originally christened into the Church of England in 1818 before eventually becoming a Baptist in 1847.

9 Dunlop, *Autobiography of John Dunlop*, op. cit., pp. 153–4.

10 In 1838 Balfour had published 'The Triumph of Teetotalism over Quackery', a Response to an Attack on Teetotalism by a Chelsea Doctor, followed in 1839 by 'King Alcohol's Walk', a temperance poem. Neither of these works appear to have survived.

11 Dunlop, *Autobiography of John Dunlop*. p. 170. This appears not to have Balfour's first experience of working on a journal. According to Caroline Fox, at some point during the 1830s she had found work 'correcting the press' for the *London and Westminster Review*, and had corrected Thomas Carlyle's 'Mirabeau' (January 1837). See Catherine Fox, *Memories of Old Friends; Being Extracts from the Journals and Letters of Caroline Fox*, Horace N. Pym (ed.), 2nd edn, 2 vols (London: Smith, Elder & Co, 1882), pp. 147–9 (vol. II). Jabez Burns (1805–1876), Balfour's co-editor on the *Temperance Journal*, was a temperance writer and campaigner, and from 1835 pastor of the Church Street Baptist Chapel, Edgware Road where Balfour was converted to Baptism.

12 Cunliffe-Jones, 'Clara Lucas Balfour', op. cit., p. 26; Dunlop, *Autobiography of John Dunlop*, op. cit., p. 178.

13 See also Clara Lucas Balfour, 'The Drunkard's Wife', in *The Garland of Water Flowers, a Collection of Poems and* Tales (London: Temperance Depot, 1841).

14 Balfour, 'The Reclaimed', in *The Garland of Water Flowers*, ibid.

15 Dunlop, *Autobiography of John Dunlop*, op. cit., p. 208.

16 June Purvis, *Hard Lessons: the Lives and Education of Working-Class Women in Nineteenth Century England* (Cambridge: Polity Press, 1989), p. 153. See also Cunliffe-Jones, 'Clara Lucas Balfour', Appendix.

17 Dunlop, *Autobiography of John Dunlop*, op. cit., pp. 276–7.

18 Clara Lucas Balfour, *Women of Scripture* (London: Houlston and Stoneman, 1847), p. 2.

19 Clara Lucas Balfour, *Moral Heroism; or, the Trials and Triumphs of the Great and Good* (London: Houlston and Stoneman, 1846), pp. 14–16.

20 Balfour, *Moral Heroism*, op. cit., pp. 18–20.

21 Balfour, *Women of Scripture*, op. cit., Preface to the 2nd edn, pp. iii–iv.

22 Balfour, *Women of Scripture*, op. cit., p. 2.

23 Balfour, *Women of Scripture*, op. cit., pp. 2–4. See Mary Wollstonecraft, 'A Vindication of the Rights of Woman', in *The Vindications: the Rights of Men. The Rights of Women* (1792) and Hannah More, *Strictures on the Modern System of Female Education*. For recent analysis, see Moira Ferguson, 'Mary Wollstonecraft and the Problematic of Slavery', in *Mary Wollstone-craft and 200 Years of Feminisms*, Eileen Janes Yeo (ed.) (London: Rivers Oram Press, 1997); Kathryn Gleadle, *The Early Feminists: Radical Unitarians and the Emergence of the Women's Rights Movement, 1831–51*, 1998 (ed.) (London: Macmillan, 1995). pp. 82–8; Jane Rendall, 'The Citizenship of Women and the Reform Act of 1867', in *Defining the Victorian Nation: Class, Race, Gender and the Reform Act of 1867*, Catherine Hall, Keith McClelland, and Jane Rendall (eds) (Cambridge: Cambridge University Press, 2000), pp. 123–4.

24 Balfour, *Women of Scripture*, op. cit., p. 4.

25 Balfour, *Women of Scripture*, op. cit., p. 4.

26 June Purvis (ed.), *Women's History: Britain 1850–1945, an Introduction* (London: University College London Press, 1995), pp. 1–5.

27 Sybil Oldfield, *Collective Biography of Women, 1550–1900: a Select Annotated Bibliography* (London: Mansell, 1999), Preface.

28 Clara Lucas Balfour, *Sketches of English Literature, from the Fourteenth to the Present Century* (London: Longman, Brown, Green and Longmans, 1852), p. 305.

29 Balfour, *Sketches of English Literature*, op. cit., p. 306.

30 Balfour, *Sketches of English Literature*, op. cit., pp. 305–7.

31 Aruthur Shadwell, *Drink, Temperance and Legislation*, 2nd edn (London: Longmans, Green & Co., 1903), p. 97. For a more positive review of *Danesbury House*, see 'Books of the Month', *English Woman's Journal* (1863).

32 Clara Lucas Balfour, *Confessions of a Decanter* (London: S.W. Partridge & Co., 1862).

33 Clara Lucas Balfour, *Women and the Temperance Reformation* (London: 1849), p. 59.

34 Balfour, 'The Reclaimed', op. cit., p. 132.

35 Charles Dickens, 'Whole Hogs', *Household Words* (1851).

36 Clara Lucas Balfour, 'Stopping Half Way', in *The Temperance Offering: Consisting of Essays, Tales, and Poetry by Eminent Temperance Writers*, J.S. Buckinham (eds) (London: London Temperance League, 1852), pp. 34–6.

37 Balfour, 'Stopping Half Way', op. cit., p. 36.

38 Balfour, 'The Claims of Temperance on Woman', in *The Garland of Water Flowers*, op. cit.

39 Balfour, *Women and the Temperance Reformation*, op. cit., pp. 5–6.

40 Balfour, *Women and the Temperance Reformation*, op. cit., pp. 5–6.

41 Balfour, *Women and the Temperance Reformation*, op. cit., p. 69.

42 Clara Lucas Balfour, *Woman's Work in the Temperance Reformation: Being Papers Prepared for a Ladies' Conference Held in London, May 26th 1868 (Published for the National Temperance League)* (London: W. Tweedie,

1868). See also Burns, *Temperance History*, op. cit., pp. 13, 97, 122 (vol. II); Cunliffe-Jones, 'Clara Lucas Balfour', op. cit., p. 45.

43 Burns, *Temperance History*, p. 337 (vol. II). Dawson Burns also preached and subsequently published Balfour's 'Memorial Discourse'. See Burns, *The Late Mrs. Clara Lucas Balfour* cited earlier.

44 'Mrs. Clara Lucas Balfour', *Englishwoman's Review* LXIII (1878): p. 322. See also Winskill, *The Comprehensive History of the Rise and Progress of the Temperance Reformation* and *The Temperance Movement and Its Workers*; Burns, *Temperance History*; Inwards, *Memorials of Temperance Workers*, op. cit.

45 Purvis, *Hard Lessons*, op. cit., pp. 153–4.

46 Undated letter from Balfour to her son John, cited in Cunliffe-Jones, 'Clara Lucas Balfour', p. 15.

47 Brown, *Death of Christian Britain*, op. cit., pp. 36–9.

48 Brian Harrison, 'A Genealogy of Reform in Modern Britain', in *Anti-Slavery, Religion and Reform: Essays in Memory of Roger Anstey*, C. Bolt and S. Drocher (eds) (Folkstone: Dawson, 1980), p. 123.

Part IV

Independent Women Missionaries

10

Ministering Angels, not Ministers: Women's Involvement in the Foreign Missionary Movement, c. 1860–1910

Judith Rowbotham

In origin, the modern foreign missionary in Britain was a male enterprise. However, by the early years of the twentieth century not only were women established as missionaries in their own right, but also formed (when missionary wives were taken into account), the bulk of the British movement's personnel. In addition, and despite an amount of hostile rhetoric, women had taken on some roles within the central organization of most of the major societies, having long been key figures in most localities in the organization of publicity and fund-raising. Overall, it could be said, therefore, that British women involved in the foreign missionary movement had raised their public profile markedly within a movement which constituted one of the most significant developments for modern British Protestant Christianity. This raises a number of questions, most crucially those relating to the extent to which the numbers of women involved in all these various aspects of the running of the foreign missionary movement had affected attitudes towards women's capacity and competence. Had a recognition of this so worked as to have given women a level of influence in the religious organizations which reflected something more appropriate to their numbers? How far could or did the example provided by such missionary women aid in campaigns to establish women formally as part of the organizational structures of, for instance, the Church of England?

The initial missionary vision was of a rapid global conversion exercise undertaken by British men from a wide range of Protestant denominations and a fairly wide class range. This does not mean that women were totally excluded from this vision. They were from the start admitted to have some part to play, as adjuncts and supporters. The need to raise missionary finance in Britain itself entailed an early involvement of women in fund-raising, through rapidly-expanding (yet informal) networks of female associations and working parties.[1] In addition, on the missionary frontline, the male missionary with his wife in the background was a familiar image. But, as the missionary lists of the various societies indicate, such wives – for all their work – were not seen as independent figures. Up to the mid-century, their names are largely absent: their presence often indicated only by an asterisk or similar device by the name of the husband, to indicate that the individual was married: 'In the earlier days of the modern mission, the missionary's wife was so completely identified with her husband that people seemed indisposed to regard her work as worthy of individual comment. She was her husband's helper: that sufficed'.[2]

A brief glance at the presentation of early missionary women indicates the scale of the change by the end of the century, but also of the continuing constraints on women's full participation on equal terms. Mary Moffat, wife of the African pioneering missionary Robert Moffat, or Mary Williams, the wife of the Polynesian missionary martyr John Williams, were seen as useful exemplars, being identified as long-suffering, energetic and self-sacrificing. Their initial fame was not so much for the work they undoubtedly did on their own accounts to further the missionary enterprise, as for the ways in which they could be shown to have submerged themselves and their needs into their husbands' agendas. Even where their work was later admitted as missionary in character, it continued to be characterized as intrinsically feminine.[3] On the whole, it was agreed by the various missionary societies that, despite the extra expense involved in the support of a family, a married missionary was more valuable than a single missionary, and also that married missionaries were better looked after and, short of martyrdom, stayed healthier and lived longer than single missionaries, who stereotypically were so dedicated that they could not be expected to remember to look after their own bodily needs.[4]

This is not to say that women themselves saw marriage as the only passport into foreign missions. A steady trickle of single women enquired about independent missionary service in the foreign field from as early as 1815, when the Church Missionary Society (CMS) had no home-grown male volunteers but were having to rely on imports from Germany to send out to the foreign field. However, with rare exceptions, such British women were turned away by the missionary societies, regardless of denomination. In the period up to 1870, approximately 100 women, most of them of advanced spinster years or widows, did establish themselves in some way with work which came to be classified as missionary labour. Yet the missionary title was not generally accorded to these workers who generally laboured in association with schools and training. Characteristic, though, of the female personnel of such organizations, was the reality that the majority usually had some familial links to their particular foreign field or to missionary work, and were either widowed or sufficiently advanced in years to be considered beyond marriage. Thus there was Mrs Bowen Thompson, widow of a former Bishop of Jerusalem, who intrepidly waded into the 1860 civil war in Mount Lebanon and established the British Syrian Schools, and the indomitably unmarried Miss Bliss of the London Missionary Society (LMS), who established schools for that society in Madagascar.[5]

The reasons given for the masculine lack of enthusiasm for independent female involvement in the mission field varied, and included Bishop Wilson's comment: 'I object on principle to single ladies coming out unprotected to so distant a place with a climate so unfriendly, and with the almost certainty of their marrying within a month of their arrival'.[6] In summary, though, the rejection of independent women's usefulness in the mission field was a reflection of wider attitudes which took as a given a female inability to make any substantial, genuinely independent contribution to society. In the popularly accepted view, woman was acceptable as helpmeet and coadjutor, but not as equal partner on equal footing, and the single woman with no prospect of marriage was widely seen as a problem requiring 'solutions'. The shock of mid-century census figures revealing the significant surplus of women over men in the British population, making the anecdotal actual, undoubtedly helped to shift individual attitudes. It did not change the fundamental social belief that it was unnatural for women to remain unmarried, since it deprived them of their divinely-ordained sphere of usefulness to the community as wives and mothers. However, this pool of maritally redundant British womanhood became part of public perception at the same time as did an uncomfortable reality for those involved in foreign missions.

As part of the half-centenary celebrations of the Missionary Society, a number of assessments of the work of the first 50 years of the movement were undertaken, and the conclusions reached made uncomfortable reading. There were undoubted successes, but India in particular seemed largely impervious to the efforts of missionaries from all the denominations involved. Yet much of the rhetoric surrounding and justifying the missionary enterprise had invoked the concept that a Divine Providence had carefully marked out Britain for success on a global scale during the nineteenth century – how else could the acquisition of so huge an empire by so small a state be explained?[7] And, how, short of condemning either their competence or their faith and purity or saying the whole enterprise was mistaken, could missionaries and missionary societies account for this 'failure', especially within the bounds of its own territorial empire? The response of the majority of commentators was to lay the blame mainly on heathen women who, it was claimed, actively stood in the way of conversion.[8] What was at work was the well-known influence of women over men and their families generally in emotional and moral matters – but in such cases, employed for evil ends. Commentators pointed out that missionary success was at its slightest in terms of numbers of conversions in those lands where the vast majority of women were secluded and inaccessible to male missionary teaching. Having spent years turning women away, the various missionary societies became convinced during the 1860s, if reluctantly, that the advice of numbers of their male workers in the field was sound: the only way forward was to call on women to work with heathen women. As that prominent Methodist missionary commentator, Reverend William Arthur, put it: 'It soon also became obvious that the work was too vast to be left wholly to the wives of Missionaries. Some must be found who would take woman's cause as woman's mission, and who, wedding that cause, should make it their life-work'.[9] In other words, missionary wives were too useful an asset to be encouraged to put missionary work first, even though many had, still did and would continue, to 'assist' their husbands' labours.

The answer was to turn to Britain's 'unappropriated blessings'. The various denominations and their publicists began to launch appeals for women who 'for the luxury of doing good, will endure hardness willingly'.[10] Slightly to the astonishment, even the alarm, of the missionary societies, considerable numbers of women volunteered. Taken aback by the initial numbers coming forward, the position adopted from the first by all the long-established societies was that while there was a need, the need was for 'workers of the right kind' – in other words, 'ladies of some education, culture and refinement'.[11] While some determined women like Mary Slessor of Calabar did overcome a humble working class background, through a particularly overt and respectable piety allied to determined efforts at self-education, and manage to get themselves accepted for service in the field, such were to remain exceptional in the period up to the First World War.[12] One useful way of weeding out the 'undesirables' was to insist, as most societies did, that the women accepted as missionary probationers already had a substantial track-record of work in home missions. For one thing, work amongst the 'home heathen' was seen as good practical preparation for the rigours of work in the field. But there was a more subtle factor in this reasoning. There was no desire to send out lady missionaries who would not be prepared to accept male supervision and direction. Few Anglican clergymen or Nonconformist ministers, it was believed, were prepared to employ women in their home missions who would not make good missionaries in this sense. The euphemism used for what was desired was that of 'true women, full of love, gentleness and sympathy'. What this actually meant was women characterized by 'humility' and 'willingness to take the lowest place'.[13] Men were, perforce, willing to accept women as workers in the mission field – but not as equal co-workers. Women had to remember that though they might be, as befitted women, ministering angels, they were not ministers. Thus, it was essential that any preparation the women undertook for the mission field was not such that missionary ladies would be encouraged to think their work more significant than it was. As Edward Storrow emphasized, women's agency was only successful in the last half of the century because of the 'success of prior mission work. Had not the latter told powerfully on the opinions and sentiments of men, women certainly could not have been reached as they are now'.[14]

As each missionary society began to train its female volunteers for independent service in the field, a number of training institutions began to spring up (and these also included the wives and fiancées of their male recruits in their sessions to add to their effectiveness). Along with the practicalities of language training, all such societies included in their range of useful courses training in housekeeping, singing and bookkeeping, along with industrial training as part of preparation for practical mission work. In other words, the training was not so much theological as practical, with the emphasis firmly on honing their natural womanly talents and on their acquired domestic skills, so as to fit them to be adjuncts but not rivals to male missionaries. In the field, they would have been fitted to serve as educators, trainers, nurses and, generally, as accompanists to male missionary preaching and conversion labours, but not to work independently. To cite the LMS's list of qualifications, women missionaries were required to have talents which would enable them to know 'how best and most effectively to convey new thoughts and ideas to the minds of those to whom they are strange', and that 'Almost every useful womanly art or accomplishment is likely to prove of value in foreign mission work', but the chief feminine art was 'the art of *teaching*' which left the actual preaching and formal conversion to men.[15]

However, once independent lady missionaries had been accepted by the major missionary societies as part of their army in the field, the relations between women and these societies took on a new dimension as the women involved sought to reconcile their sense of personal identity and their religious beliefs with the established agendas and perspectives of the societies. For profoundly practical reasons, rather than ideological conviction, the established societies had accepted the need for women recruits to work in the mission field, just as they had long relied on women's contributions as fundraisers and organizers of mission events in Britain. But what the societies and the officials had not bargained for was the impact that lady missionaries, and their supporters in Britain, would seek to have – on policy and practice. Independent female missionaries, encouraged by their home supporters, were increasingly determined to move to a position where they could establish their own agendas and move away from the constraints originally imposed and subsequently sustained (at least in the rhetoric of the missionary commentators). Despite the deferential comments regularly made in the directions of male susceptibilities, women were rapidly successful in carving out considerable degrees of independence, as reports home and the memoirs of such missionary women and the development of not just separate women's committees in the mainstream societies, but also of independent women's missionary societies, underline. While this may seem more feminine than feminist, the wider implications of women's successes in this field had a dramatic effect on recognition of women's capacities, certainly in the secular arena.

The rapidity of women's impact on the shape of the British foreign missionary movement can be explained partly by their undoubted enthusiasm for the service offered to them. Women themselves were conscious of the demographic imbalance between the sexes, and accepted that many of them were unlikely to marry. Dissatisfaction with such a prospect meant that numbers looked for an alternative to the traditional patterns. But the employment opportunities in Britain itself for respectable women in the 1860s and 1870s were restricted, and even when they opened up more in the 1880s and 1890s, were still limited by the boundaries of respectable conventionalities. In purely pragmatic terms, employment as a lady missionary gave hope of a greater degree of independence within the work, and of a more exciting lifestyle than remaining in the confines of respectable domesticity or employment at home. But while such motivations were undoubtedly present to a degree in the thoughts of many of those who volunteered for the foreign field, the genuine convictions held by most, if not all, who actually went out as lady missionaries – that they were involved in a great and necessary religious crusade – cannot be ignored. Nor can the romance.

In the propaganda poured forth by the various societies, much of it aimed at women, missionary work was surrounded with a romantic glamour. A certain glamour and hint of improved importance surrounded even the early reports of women's experience in the mission field: 'the wives of the Missionaries were generally regarded as oracles of wisdom, especially by the native females; and their counsels and example were employed by Divine Providence to elevate them from their degradation'.[16] There were also the patriotic overtones that were added to the appeals for lady missionaries, with comments such as 'The only really adequate final cause for the retention of India lies in our determination to win her to the feet of Christ, as one of the brightest jewels in His crown'. The 'last solution' to 'the great Indian problem, strange as it may seem lies in the contribution made by England's educated daughters'.[17] For women it thus appeared one of the few exciting and romantic things in which they could indulge perfectly acceptably, because the characterization of the process of offering oneself for the missionary field was presumed to involve self-sacrifice, not self-indulgence. The lady missionary was yielding up the comforts and securities of home to venture herself in a holy cause and risk disease, dirt, the sight of degradation and a host of other things considered to be anathema to her feminine nature – how could it be aught but sacrifice?[18] This lure was also intensified by the fact that missionary heroics received considerable publicity. So participation in the mission field would not automatically be the silent, hidden variety of self-sacrifice that domestic duty was likely to entail for all but the exceptional Florence Nightingale or Sister Dora. Another major selling point of missionary recruiting material was the very 'ordinariness' of the women and girls who volunteered, making it seem more accessible.

As already suggested, the particular impact of these messages related to the very considerable female audience for them that existed in Britain by the time independent women missionaries arrived in the field, because women were so firmly established at the core of the domestic fund-raising efforts of the various missionary societies. Women took on the bulk of organizing foreign missionary 'events' locally, from bazaars and their associated working parties to missionary lectures, concerts and recitations. From very early on, the stimulus to do this work was extremely personal for the majority of the women so involved, because they were the target of the less official reporting home from the mission field. The societies received regular reports, particularly from the male personnel, for national (or even international) dissemination, but missionary wives in particular wrote personally to family and friends, to old parishioners and to other contacts. These letters and memoirs, read aloud to a wide circle or circulated via copies through the post, acted to inform their recipients of the daily doings in the field, and, through this, to appeal for cash and goods for very specific objectives, notably for educating local women and children in the rudiments of 'proper' household management and in early lessons in piety and bible reading. The effect of this kind of targeted appeal on British women at home was huge, as Anne Hellier has underlined. While 'From the first days of the Missionary Society women had been enthusiastic and faithful collectors', it was such pioneer missionary wives who were the real founders of the home-based organized feminine efforts to sustain the movement, using the message sent home that 'everywhere' was there 'work that only women could do'. The missionary wives who 'tackled it' and exhorted the help of an increasing band of sympathizers in Britain for comprehensible and intimate projects where they could hope to receive news of real results, made the whole exercise seem real through this 'personal touch'.[19]

Home-based women also took an increasing interest in the production of information about the mission field intended to have a substantial popular appeal and so to keep interest in foreign missions alive. The arrival of independent women missionaries ensured that there was an intensified interest in women's work in the field, manifesting itself through a demand for more literature on the subject. A survey of the missionary literature produced by both religious and commercial publishers shows a marked expansion not only in titles dealing with women's work, but also in those written by women. This expansion in women's writing on missionary topics was not confined to that aimed at a female or child audience, but also comprised that aimed at a less educated, more working class general market. Certain names, such as that of Emma Raymond Pitman, became well-known as purveyors of both tales of women's missionary work and the more populist type of general missionary tract. As a result, the female perspective came to have an increasing effect on popular British understandings of the scope, nature and intent of missionary labour. Yet this is disguised by the frequent employment of men, often those famed for association in some way with foreign missions, to write an introduction 'legitimizing' their writings and their judgements, as in the case of Mary Leslie's writings on zenana mission work (see below), which was 'introduced' and explained by that famous Indian missionary figure, Edward Storrow.[20]

Generally, it has remained easy, certainly if relying primarily on the official records of missionary societies, to downplay the work actually undertaken by women. It is true, for instance, that the majority of their labours, especially in India, related more to their work as 'civilizing agents' rather than as 'evangelists'. However, as has also been pointed out, 'the adoption of such a strategy was forced on women missionaries as a means of establishing sustained contact with an illiterate and often secluded clientele', especially if they sought to succeed where male missionaries had failed.[21] The English Presbyterian Mission, for example, accepted the foundation of their 'official' auxiliary in the shape of the Women's Missionary Association (WMA) in 1878 as a result of the 'growing feeling that some such association was necessary in order to develop the work among the women and girls of China'. Since missionary wives 'could not always spare the time' for this 'important work', it became clear to the society's home organization that 'full-time women missionaries were required'. This in turn led to consideration of the need for 'some form of women's organization in the home Church was highly desirable', so long as it was not too independent.[22] Thus it was 'not without significance that the office of President was filled by the wife of the Convenor of the Foreign Missions Committee' – and 'those who have succeeded Mrs. Hugh Mathieson in the President's chair have always been distinguished' by their loyalty to, and 'recognized the value of co-operation' with, the main committee.[23] This subsidiary role was further emphasized by the comment that it was not until 1893 that the WMA had public meetings for women alone, and that between 1878 and then, 'our Association had to depend on the men of the church to conduct these Public Meetings, and to plead her cause, and right nobly they did her part'.[24] The Society for the Propagation of the Gospel (SPG) set up its Ladies Association in 1866, with a list of objectives that firmly underlined its intentions that its lady workers would be auxiliaries only. Thus their educational responsibilities loomed large, with a reminder that the Association was also responsible for keeping up an interest in Britain in the general work of the SPG.[25]

Some independent ladies missionary societies did spring up – notably the Church of England Zenana Missionary Society (CEZMS), founded in 1880 – but they were careful to preserve an official front of dependence on, or association with, both the overall hierarchy and the mainstream missionary societies for their particular denomination. While some, such as the CEZMS, became more assertive in their actual policy over subsequent years, they still preferred to avoid challenging the dominance of these established male-dominated societies in terms of their official relations with government (metropolitan or colonial) or with the relevant religious authority structures. As Irene Barnes wrote, 'It has been from the first a great desire of this Society that its work should be its one advertisement. Little is said of it in the newspapers. Quiet, unobtrusive, simple and to a large extent, what may be called underground labor, has characterized our mission from the first'.[26] Often they utilized men in positions of appropriate

authority to present their work and ambitions, to give greater legitim-
acy for their society, following the pattern already established by
women writers on missionary topics, as when Thomas Valpy French,
the former Bishop of Lahore, fronted a series of appeals for the
CEZMS.[27] Historians seeking to uncover the history of this society
still need to turn to official CMS histories to get much of their information, because the CEZMS was so careful to avoid trampling un-
necessarily on male susceptibilities and preconceptions about what
was appropriate work for women in the mission field.

Yet the growing consciousness of the importance of their efforts did
encourage individual women missionaries to assert themselves more
strongly from the late 1870s on, with genuine impact on women's
missionary agendas at home. Reports home showed very plainly to
both men and women involved in the societies that lady missionaries
had their own ideas about the direction of missionary work, and the
locations in which it needed to be established. Furthermore, especially
as their work expanded, they were apparently successful in their enterprises, with increases in numbers of 'heathens' contacted and
brought significantly within the missionary ambit, thus raising considerable expectation of subsequent conversions. This was not met
with universal pleasure. In the eyes of many males, women were
initiating too many of these expansions without submitting to male
guidance and supervision. For instance, once let into the missionary
field, women refused to accept being restricted to posts of minimal
danger and maximum masculine supervision. As Band commented,
'WMA agents were to cause the Council frequent headaches by their
independent action and reluctance to submit to male jurisdiction',
and they were far from alone in that.[28] It was the reports home from
lady missionaries, and from missionary wives emboldened by their
independent sisters, that convinced the CEZMS, for instance, to
expand their work to China from 1882, in the face of considerable
male hostility to women missionaries adventuring themselves independently in such a dangerous location.[29] Despite continuing worries
over the safety of their missionary agents expressed by male authority
in a number of ways, the numbers of CEZMS missionaries in China
increased steadily, and then, in 1895, they acquired their first martyrs,
in the shape of the four missionaries murdered at Fuh-Kien, alongside
several CMS workers, including Reverend Robert Stewart and his wife.
The most important impact of this incident, and the subsequent

martyrdoms of British missionaries during the Boxer Rebellion in China, was that it forced a public and official acceptance of the equal value of women's work in the mission field, in terms of its achievements and impact. It also underlined (since the lady missionaries were presumed to be 'ordinary' and not 'exceptional' women), that women had a potential for competence in a number of areas which was being fulfilled in the mission field, but not yet at home.[30] There was also a demand from women for a higher profile within the home-based official organizations of the missionary societies, and within the hierarchies of the various denominations.

It was certainly believed by supporters of women missionaries that the development of separate societies and committees was an entirely positive development, and, as shown above, it certainly gave the lady missionaries a considerable degree of practical independence in their daily work. Yet, despite the numbers in the field, and the genuine belief of a number of men, including William Arthur, Sir William Hill and Gordon Northcote, that the success of the missionary crusade depended on women's involvement as dedicated missionaries, it can be argued that the experience of women, both in independent societies and when dealing with the mainstream societies, was as a result of this emphasis on women's work being directed towards women, and not more generally towards the 'heathen masses' like the men, made it more difficult for them to participate in the movement on equal terms. As Brian Stanley has pointed out, for instance, 'The formation of the Baptist Zenana Mission created welcome opportunities for missionary service for Baptist women, but, if anything, made it even harder for single women to secure a recognized autonomous role within the BMS itself'. Into the twentieth century, the BMS 'remained a predominantly male society, staffed and controlled almost entirely by men'.[31]

In other words, despite the greater visibility granted to them, women's remit was either directed firmly at women's work within the mission field, or at 'helping' the male heads.[32] Women, despite their undoubted dedication to this religious cause, remained lay workers in the missionary enterprise – reflecting the wider debate in the British Christian denominations about the 'right' of women to claim any formal role that was marked as apart by some form of ordination. There were the Anglican sisterhoods, though these remained a cause of great controversy both within the Church of England and outside, but what else was possible, both to satisfy the feeling of women that their work for religious causes deserved some such acknowledgement, and to keep women from another 'preposterous' proposition – that of a form of ordination that placed some women at least on a genuinely equal basis with men in areas of work such as the mission field? From the 1860s, a debate was sparked off amongst theologians as to the precise nature of women's place in the hierarchy of religious institutions in the light of these developments, if only for the eminently practical reason of establishing proper missionary authority structures: 'We must have some organization ... you cannot place down a solitary woman here and there, bound by no rules. ... Some sort of subordination is indispensable'.[33] 'Subsidiarity' was generally held to be the key to understanding the place to which women's undoubtedly necessary contributions entitled them, while not setting them up as a rival to male religious authority. There was much revisiting of the prominent women of the early Christian Church, as part of such discussions, and much thought about the authority that any of them held. John Ludlow argued in 1865 that:

> The early church from the apostle's own times, set the seal upon the ministering functions of women, by the appointment of a Female Diaconate, strictly excluded from the priestly functions of public teaching and worship, but nearly coequal with the male diaconate as respects the exercise of active charity.[34]

Such debates were widely shared with women, as indicated by the series of articles on 'The Women Workers of the Bible' which appeared in *India's Women* during 1882, but there was no substantial shift in attitude towards their right to authority. When discussing Phoebe [Romans xvi], for instance, Reverend Sampson was typical in agreeing that modern zenana workers were 'our sisters' in the Church, but what more? He described Phoebe as a 'servant' of the church in Cenchrea, adding that 'The word "servant" may also be rendered "deaconess"', but that 'the term is not necessarily official'.[35]

In 1861, the Bishop of London had actually commissioned (but *not* ordained) the first modern deaconess in the Church of England, but such women were to evangelize, and not preach – a clear distinction being made thereby between the essentially masculine work of preaching and certifying conversion, and the preparatory *teaching* work comprising evangelization, spreading the good news, which entailed the involvement of women formally or informally dedicated to the service of the Lord as a full-time occupation or career.[36] Other deaconesses followed, mainly in association with the home work of the Mildmay Mission, but some were consecrated for work in foreign missions, such as Ellen Goreh of the SPG. But there were two distinguishing factors of such women. First, the deaconess (while not a member of a sisterhood) was supposed to consider herself as consecrated and set apart from the normal feminine agenda with marriage and motherhood always a possibility. She might not have taken formal vows, but the social pressure within the Anglican church on this was considerable. Second, the work of the deaconess was intended to be philanthropic and ancillary to that of the ordained clergy, and not supplementary to it.[37] This was a position which, despite the growing prominence of women missionaries and missionary wives and the growing evidence of their ability to make successful independent choices in their labours, remained unchanged into the twentieth century.

Women's high profile work in foreign missions underlined their potential competence. In a number of secular areas this was referred to when women made bids to expand their career opportunities.[38] But this was not capitalized on within the religious denominations, enabling women to challenge men to consider them as potential equals within their hierarchies, and nowhere was this more apparent than in the Church of England, which through its various missionary organizations provided the bulk of British female personnel in the field. There was a feeling that missionary work was set apart, and not a useful model for the normal domestic situation in Britain. The rhetoric associated with foreign missions established the concept that this was a 'crusade', a 'war' against the legions of Satan who were fighting eviction from heathen lands. This 'emergency' allowed women to perform extraordinary work which forced them to step (to some extent) outside their normal constraints, especially where there was a scarcity of the higher (that is, male) 'officers' in this Christian army.[39] Despite the existence of the Salvation Army, and attempts of the Church of England, for example, to parallel some of its successful aspects through the Church Army, the mainstream rhetoric associated with home missions became, in the last 20 years of the century, far less military in its rhetoric and much more 'welfare' orientated, especially for its women workers. It is thus a paradox that by fighting hard and successfully to open up the foreign mission field to 'career' religious women, women themselves made it more difficult to win parity of esteem and equal rights of consecration or dedication in Britain itself. Women remained ministering angels and not ministers in the shorter term, despite the high profile efforts of missionaries from Charlotte Tucker (ALOE) to Mary Slessor – but in the longer term, these women, who undoubtedly considered themselves consecrated if not ordained, acted as a powerful agency in the feminine, if not yet feminist, advancement of the women's cause in organized religion in Britain.

Notes

1 Rev. J.E. Sampson, *Parochial Associations in Aid of the CMS: a Paper Read at the Conference of Association Secretaries of the Church Mission House*, CMS (London, 1873), pp. 5–6.
2 Rev. Augustus Buckland, *Women in the Mission Field, Pioneers and Martyrs* (London: Isbister and Co. Ltd, 1895), p. 69.
3 Judith Rowbotham, ' "Soldiers of Christ"? Images of Female Missionaries in late Nineteenth-Century Britain: Issues of Heroism and Martyrdom', *Gender and History*, 12, 1 (April 2000), 96–7.
4 CMS Archives, University of Birmingham, G/AZ1/1: Regulations, 1833, Clause II x, Marriage.
5 Emma Raymond Pitman, *Heroines of the Mission Field* (London: Cassell, Petter and Gilpin, 1888).
6 See E. Stock, *History of the Church Missionary Society*, CMS, London, 2 vols, 1, 316; Mrs. Winter, *On Woman's Work in India*. Read by Rev. R.R. Winter of the Delhi Mission on June 27 1878, at the Missionary Conference on the occasion of the 177th Anniversary of the Society for the Propagation of the Gospel (London, 1878), p. 2.
7 See Judith Rowbotham, ' "Hear an Indian Sister's Plea": Reporting the Work of Nineteenth Century British Female Missionaries', *Women's Studies International Forum*, 21 (1998), p. 248.
8 Ibid., p. 244.
9 Rev. William Arthur, *Women's Work in India* (London: T. Woolmer, 1882), p. 11.
10 H.L., *Hindu Women: with Glimpses into their Life and Zenanas* (London: Nisbet, 1882), p. 138.
11 *What are the Qualifications Needed for a Lady Missionary?* (London: John Snow and Co., 1895), p. 1.
12 See W.L. Livingstone, *Mary Slessor of Calabar* (London: Partridge and Co., 1916).
13 *Qualifications*, op. cit., p. 5.

14 Rev. E. Storrow, 'The London Missionary Society during the Victorian Age', *Chronicle of the London Missionary Society* (1887), p. 200.

15 Ibid., p. 6.

16 Jemima Thompson, *Memoirs of British Female Missionaries*, London: W. Smith, 1851), p. 166.

17 Rev. T.A. Gurney, Introduction, Irene Barnes, *Behind the Pardah. The Story of CEZMS Work in India* (London: Marshall Bros, 1897), pp. iii–iv.

18 Rowbotham, 'Indian Sister', op. cit., p. 00

19 Anna Hellier, *Workers Together, the Story of the Women's Auxiliary of the Wesleyan Methodist Missionary Society* (London: Cargate Press, 1931), pp. 9–10.

20 Rev. E. Storrow, Introduction, in Mary E. Leslie, *The Dawn of Light: a Story of the Zenana Mission* (London: John Snow and Co., 1868).

21 Torben Christensen and William R. Hutchison, *Missionary Ideologies in the Imperialist Era* (Aarhuis: Farlaget Aros 1983), pp. 6, 9; Leslie A Flemming (ed.), *Women's Work for Women. Missionaries and Social Change in Asia* (Boulder, CA: Westview Press, 1989), p. 10.

22 Edward Band, *Working His Purpose Out. The History of the English Presbyterian Mission 1847–1947* (London: Presbyterian Church of England Publishing Office, 1948), p. 576.

23 *Jubilee History of the Women's Missionary Association 1878–1928* (Women's Missionary Association of the Presbyterian Church of England), London: Presbyterian Church of England Publishing Office, 1928, pp. 2–3.

24 Ibid., p. 4.

25 Deborah Kirkwood, 'Protestant Missionary Women: Wives and Spinsters', in Fiona Bowie, Deborah Kirkwood and Shirley Ardener (eds), *Women and Missions: Past and Present. Anthropological and Historical Perceptions* (Oxford: Berg, 1993).

26 Barnes, *Behind the Pardah*, op. cit., p. 10.

27 Thomas Valpy French, *Missionary Addresses* (London: Hazell, Watson & Viney Ltd).

28 Band, *Working His Purpose Out*, op. cit., p. 110; Rowbotham, 'Soldiers', pp. 99–100.

29 Irene H. Barnes, *Behind the Great Wall. The Story of the C.E.Z.M.S. Work and Workers in China* (London: Marshall Bros, 1898), p. 2.

30 For a fuller discussion of the implications of this episode, see Rowbotham, 'Soldiers', pp. 100–3; see also Barnes, *Great Wall*, op. cit., pp. 142–51 for the narrative.

31 Brian Stanley, *The History of the Baptist Missionary Society, 1792–1992*, (Edinburgh: T. & T. Clark, 1992), p. 232.

32 Ibid., pp. 214–16.

33 James Erasmus Philips, *Vicar of Warminster, Woman's Work in Foreign Missions. A Paper Read at the Church Congress held at Bristol, October 11, 1864* (London: Rivingtons, 1865), pp. 9–10.

34 John Ludlow, *Woman's Work in the Church. Historical Notes on Deaconesses and Sisterhoods* (London: Alexander Strahan, 1865), p. 244.

35 Rev. J.E. Sampson, 'The Women Workers of the Bible: VI: Phoebe', *India's Women* (1882), 2, p. 2.
36 See Brian Heeney, *The Women's Movement in the Church of England, 1850–1930* (Oxford: Clarendon Press, 1988), pp. 67–70 particularly.
37 Ibid., pp. 69–71; Isabella Gilmore, 'Deaconesses: Their Qualifications and Status', *Pan-Anglican Papers* (London: SPCK, 1908), pp. 1–3.
38 Rowbotham, 'Soldiers', op. cit., pp. 101–3.
39 Ibid., pp. 102–3.

11
Medical Missions and the History of Feminism: Emmeline Stuart of the CMS Persia Mission[1]

Guli Francis-Dehqani

The purpose of this chapter is to investigate, by means of biography, the role played by female missionary medical practitioners within the Victorian women's movement. Specific details from the life of Dr Emmeline Stuart[2] of the Church Missionary Society (CMS), working in Persia (or Iran)[3] between 1897 and 1934 are used to highlight matters of relevance both in the life of the Persia Mission and the wider nineteenth and early twentieth-century missionary movement.

The chapter considers briefly the role of medicine within mission strategy, outlining something of the strains and stresses placed on medical missionaries generally, while highlighting in particular the effects on women such as Stuart and the colleagues who worked alongside her. An analysis of Stuart's attitude towards indigenous Persian women and the religion of Islam is also included, with reference to the wider historical feminist movement. Ultimately, Stuart is presented as a woman of her time, conforming to the behaviour expected of her within the Victorian worldview, yet as one whose unusual position as a female medical practitioner also afforded opportunities for subversion.

Strictly speaking, Emmeline Stuart's career in Iran (1897–1934) was not confined within the Victorian period. However, in its formative years, from the 1870s onwards, the Persia Mission was shaped and influenced by many Victorian nuances which continued to affect British life well into the twentieth century.[4] Thus, symbolically, if not literally, this chapter falls within the ethos of the present volume.

A significant shift is discernible in the approach of the CMS during the course of the nineteenth century. From an emphasis on *salvation* as a preparatory means for civilization in the first part of the century, there was a gradual move towards an increased commitment to *service* in the latter years. This subtle change brought into mission rhetoric a new vocabulary, embracing concern for the temporal as well as the spiritual needs of humanity. The missiological shift is depicted by a growing tension between 'pure evangelism' as a mission philosophy, and the practical reality of missionaries striving to ameliorate physical needs.

While the strain between theory and practice was apparent in the lives of most missionaries, it reached its pinnacle in the work of medical practitioners such as Dr Emmeline Stuart. Whereas educational endeavours provided a relatively convenient bridge between evangelism and social improvement, medical skills caused a much greater tension.[5] The demand for medical care never ceased and time taken out for evangelism required much stricter regulating of attention to physical needs. The tension between missionary theory and practice became increasingly explicit as religious requirements on one hand, and professional incentives on the other, placed tremendous demands on the time and emotions of medical missionary women.

By the late-Victorian period, the two components commonly held to be the most vital within missionary methods were 'women's work because it wins the home, and medical work because it wins the heart'.[6] Medical women, therefore, became unrivalled amongst their colleagues as agents of mission, and the appeal for female doctors was soon ringing out across the missionary world.[7] This did not, however, represent a radical rethinking of the Victorian gender ideology with its accepted segregation of male/female spheres of work. Rather, it was a calling directed specifically towards single women free of family responsibilities who, far from forsaking their true place in society, could extend their 'natural' aptitude for maternal instincts and domesticity into the public realm. In other words, it was a vocation based upon, and justified by, an inherently feminine disposition towards service and self-sacrifice. This predilection for giving of oneself to others was exemplified most potently in physical motherhood, yet its 'natural' predominance extended to womankind generally, providing a justification for the public role of single women. This meant ideologically and practically, women – particularly medical women whose lives were a symbol of self-giving – carried the greater part of the burden of the service ideal to which the missionary cause was increasingly committed.[8] Indeed, the success of this missionary strategy relied on a philosophy endorsing traditional sexual roles. For it recognized women as respondents to a feminized vocation entirely within bounds of ideological acceptability, not trespassing on the masculine domain but acting in a complementary way alongside it.

At first glance, then, this understanding of female involvement within medical missions appears to offer little by way of a positive reinscribing of women's role and agency. However, for many religious women at the turn of the century, the emphasis on feminine self-giving did not represent a difficulty. Indeed, it was the model of service that motivated many missionary women into action and should therefore be regarded as an important strand in the history of feminism. In 1913, Ruth Rouse, an apologist for the women's movement within the missionary cause, wrote a defence of both based on an apparent affinity between their primary characteristics and purposes.[9]

Most notably, Rouse wrote of feminism's commitment to 'striving for opportunity to serve the community'.[10] The women's movement, she argued, was marked by a desire for liberation, not just for its own sake, but for freedom to serve others. 'To the question "To what end?"', Rouse wrote, 'the women's movement answers clearly and universally "To the end of service."'[11] Thus for Rouse, feminism's quest for female emancipation was validated *only* as an incentive to dedicate one's life to the service of others.

This view of feminism, which defined liberation in terms of female service and sacrifice, depicts a kind of female kenosis at the very heart of the struggle for freedom. Clearly, Rouse's views were based on the separate spheres philosophy and the complementary roles ascribed to women and men. Ultimately, her intention was to consolidate feminism with the missionary incentive, thus approving the role of women within missions. Acknowledging the particular strand from within which she wrote does not undermine the significance of her views, but rather clarifies the contrasts and tensions evident within the multifarious history of feminism.

The rhetoric of service offered female doctors myriad opportunities on the mission field at a time when the medical profession in Britain was hostile towards them. Medical training for women remained the exception during the nineteenth century and qualified female doctors found it almost impossible to practise their skills. Unsurprisingly, a significant proportion of British women doctors were attracted to the mission field.[12] Abroad, they not only had the scope to exercise their medical vocation, but many found that 'medicine acted as a special case, justifying roles which might otherwise have been seen as unwomanly and disruptive to society'.[13] Thus, the feminine service ideal, as well as Rouse's promotion of it, became a means of subversion whereby women appeared to conform to gender norms while, in fact, extending hitherto restricted boundaries.

Their unique position as women *and* doctors guaranteed female medical missionaries a distinguished place within the mission scheme. Involved in what were considered two of the most acute areas of activity, they could be confident about their role. Engaged in combat with disease and sin they became icons of the missionary movement, representing the noblest calling for Christian womanhood. Women doctors symbolized the perfect fusion of mission theory and practice in their obedience to spread the good news and alleviate suffering. Yet the potent imagery of women doctors as better able than any other missionaries to gain entrance into 'the most inaccessible stronghold of heathenism, the home',[14] did nothing to desist the growing strain of unreasonable and extreme expectations.

Moreover, the unrivalled power women doctors were consigned in their ability to forward the cause of Christian mission, proved unrealistically optimistic, at least if judged by the number of Persian converts. CMS displayed great confidence regarding its work in Iran throughout the 37 years during which Stuart was there. By 1926, *The Call from the Moslem World* claimed no Anglican sphere in Islamic lands was as promising as Persia and much of the alleged success was credited to the work of medical missionaries.[15] However, while medicine did succeed in enticing Persians towards the mission establishments, Iran was in reality far from the responsive soil missionary apologists claimed it to be. Though CMS hospitals and dispensaries were crowded with glad recipients of western medicine, gratitude rarely led to conversions and the number of converts remained few.[16]

Meanwhile, assurance in their methods drove the missionaries towards ambitious plans for Iran which, in turn, continued offering religious women in Britain significant opportunities. In 1900, Emmeline Stuart sent an impassioned appeal to the student missionary conference in London, urging them to 'let a voice from Persia plead with the medical students today'.[17] Her entreaty, based on the familiar discourse of service and duty, was an invitation to women to extend the scope of their medical skills. She called upon her Christian sisters to seize upon fresh possibilities, leave behind imposed restrictions at home and awaken to the dawn of new opportunity away from social strictures imposed by western gender norms:

> In face of the great need out here will you decide to stay at home, where the professional ranks are already over full? Here there is abundant room and scope for your energies.... Where, I ask you to ask yourselves, will your lives most count for Christ?[18]

Stuart's appeal contains much that justified the social and individual commitment of women within the Victorian missionary programme. For it shows how the involvement of female medical practitioners was dependent upon a duality that ensured their participation remained socially and ideologically acceptable, while at the same time representing a new venture for women. Stuart's own life and career also provide a pertinent example of the subversion underlying the feminine ideal of service.

Born in Edinburgh in 1866, Emmeline Stuart became one of the earliest women to train as a doctor at a British university. She graduated from Glasgow University in 1895 before beginning her career as a medical missionary with CMS at the age of 30. Arriving in Iran in 1897, she spent the following 37 years there, first in Julfa and later in Isfahan and Shiraz, before retiring in 1934. Her life and work represent a period of great transition within the mission environment. Responsible for setting up the women's medical mission in Iran, she witnessed great changes as the mission increased the number of its institutions and refined its methods of medical care in response to modern technological improvements. A commitment to better conditions for Iranian women drove her to work tirelessly for the health and welfare of her patients, as well as in her struggle to improve the position of women missionaries. Through her professional skills and her strength of personality, Stuart became a distinct and valuable figure within the Persia mission.

Because of the great value placed on women doctors within late-Victorian mission ideology, Stuart and other female medical practitioners were secure in the knowledge that they were much needed by

CMS. This gave them greater freedom to extend the boundaries of female involvement with less risk of exclusion from the mission schema. Yet dual pressures emanating from the religious and medical side of their work caused these women immense physical and emotional stress.

Like the majority of her colleagues, Stuart expressed the conviction that medicine was subservient to evangelism, yet she frequently regretted the tension inherent in this situation. In 1898 she wrote in one of her annual letters to CMS headquarters in London:

> A medical missionary could never hope to undertake all the evangelistic work rendered possible by the existence of a Medical Mission. ... The openings are so numerous that it would take several lay helpers to follow them up to any sufficient extent ... when the need for medical visits is over, who is to follow up the openings thus gained, and continue visiting and teaching the people?[19]

Stuart was clear that in practice medical missionaries should not be compromised in their healthcare work and suggested instead a clearer division of labour in which 'non-medical people' might be used more profitably for 'direct evangelistic work'.[20] This elevation of the corporeal needs of indigenous people as being of equal importance to their spiritual welfare prompted some opposition from male colleagues within the Persia mission.

Resistance to what was regarded as an apparently 'secular' view of mission was frequently allied to the shifting emphasis of gender roles within the mission station. The arrival of a woman doctor represented a significant change in the hierarchical status of missionaries. Non-medical men in particular, who felt threatened by the relatively high position of authority granted to a medically trained woman, argued that the hazards of elevating medical work were ultimately damaging to the missionary aim. One clergyman named Blackett, writing with reference to Stuart commented, 'valuable as medical work is, it is after all – from a missionary point of view – only a means to an end. We may secure the "means" but miss the "end" '.[21] Already intimidated by the presence of a woman doctor with considerable authority, criticisms such as this reflect an underlying fear that there would be a total reversal of the established gender hierarchy if Stuart were given even greater scope. For those who felt threatened, the best way of trying to maintain some control over her was to stress that her work was carried out under the religious authority of the mission with its evangelistic aims.

Helen Callaway has commented on a similar threat posed to male medicine in the empire through the establishment of the nursing profession, though this was soon controlled through the development of a gendered philosophy which identified nursing with feminine characteristics and successfully located it in a subsidiary position.[22] Female doctors, however, were more problematic, presenting a real threat to medical and non-medical colleagues through a potential subversion of the 'natural' order of male superiority. Stuart's arrival in Iran was a turning point in the Persia mission's history, for it symbolized the beginning of an ideological struggle between men's *perceived* notion of a woman's position in the station and the *reality* of a female doctor's presence. In charge of every aspect of women's medical work, Stuart's responsibilities took her into spheres once the unchallenged preserve of men. Her professional status, combined with her confident personality, strength and single-mindedness, had an inevitably destabilizing impact upon the gendered hierarchy of the mission, ushering in the start of a new era.

During CMS's early years in Persia from 1875 onwards, the missionaries were unanimous in their desire for a female medically trained colleague. Once Stuart's arrival became imminent, however, many of the staff were concerned about the ramifications it would have upon the life and politics of the mission station. This unease expressed itself through a divergence of opinion concerning the location of the new women's hospital that Stuart was to oversee. A number of missionaries were anxious about Stuart's relationship with senior male doctors and other experienced colleagues. In particular there was concern about whether she was to work under the authority of Dr Donald Carr, who was responsible for medical work amongst Persian men, or whether she was to be an equal and independent colleague, accountable for all areas of women's medicine. There was additional anxiety about the affect of her seniority on the veteran missionary Mary Bird who, though medically unqualified, had worked in Iran since 1891 and been responsible for many important innovations.[23]

A proposal was mooted to send Stuart to a different location by building the women's hospital in some other part of the country, thus minimizing the potential awkwardness of the internal dynamics amongst senior missionaries by placing considerable geographical distance between them. Removed from the immediate concerns of local missionary politics, however, CMS authorities in London disregarded the nervous propositions from Persia and instructed Stuart to take independent charge of women's medical work in Julfa, where the original Persia mission was based.[24] The ramifications of this decision were played out during the ensuing years as Stuart and her colleagues learned to live alongside each other.

Despite continued criticisms of her by male colleagues, many of whom felt threatened by her presence, Stuart was a strong, confident, stubborn and capable character, unafraid of voicing her own opinions and acting upon them whatever the consequences. This combined with her skill as a physician, rendering her a respected member of the mission team in which she came to enjoy considerable influence. However, while her unusual standing afforded her greater freedoms, her language and behaviour remained largely within bounds dictated by conventional Victorian norms. Stuart epitomized the evangelical strand of nineteenth-century feminism, ultimately regarding her senior medical role as a direct extension of women's domestic and nurturing predilections.

Yet conformity to this model of feminized Christian subservience, as well as Emmeline's typical divergence from it, can be witnessed in the following example. In 1899, Philippa Braine-Hartnell (also a CMS missionary in Iran), tentatively presented CMS with a proposal that her colleague Annie Stirling should stay in Julfa where she was needed for evangelistic work at the dispensary, rather than move to a different station. Concerned about female decorum – which meant women seldom made their opinions directly known, and mission protocol – which required that such suggestions be presented to CMS headquarters through local committees and senior missionaries, Braine-Hartnell's style is apologetic and embarrassed:

> you will pardon my pointing out that just this year there will be rather a block in Yezd...and in the mean time Julfa is short of workers....If I may just leave this suggestion in your hands, I hope you will forgive me if I am out of order in making any suggestion at all.[25]

Contrast this with a similar occasion several years later when Stuart makes a suggestion regarding the location of Annie Stirling's work.

Unlike Braine-Hartnell, Stuart presents her case with no prevarication or humility, confident that it is a worthwhile and sensible option:

> I ascertained from [Miss Stirling] that if [the CMS committee] thought good on her return from furlough next Spring she would be quite willing to come to us. I do not know what [the committee] would say to such a suggestion, but I do not think it is unreasonable on my part.[26]

Always in an ideologically inferior position by distinction of her sex, Stuart's rebellious style did not extend to any form of direct authority over male colleagues. Nevertheless, her position as a female doctor meant she could afford to push the boundaries of acceptability a little further than others. The above example is just one of several occasions in which Stuart stands out in the surviving CMS archives as the only woman missionary amongst her contemporaries able and willing to make known her views without the need to couch them in apologetic terms or religious rhetoric.

In charge of every aspect of the women's medical mission in Persia, Stuart's experiences were beyond anything she could have imagined. In Britain, religiously motivated activities, including philanthropic and evangelistic work, were always carried out under the strict authority of a clergyman. On the mission field, however, women like Stuart even encroached upon the realm of ordained ministers, as senior medical women missionaries both cared for their staff physically, and supervised and guided their daily activities.

Andrew Walls has argued that the increasingly acceptable prerogative of all mission doctors (male and female), to pastor their flock in this way contributed to a blurring of boundaries once so clearly defined, not only between the sexes, but between lay and ordained missionaries.[27] This added impetus to changes within the Anglican church, both abroad and in England, where there was growing lay and female participation during the latter part of the nineteenth and early twentieth centuries. Thus, Stuart's role, while conformist in some ways, was also subversive as together with other women missionary doctors of the period, she contributed to the overall democratization of the Church of England.[28]

Emmeline Stuart was, like most of her colleagues in Iran, middle-class, well educated and financially secure. She exhibited many attitudes and assumptions typical of her privileged background, particularly concerning culture, ethnicity and religion. Regarding east and west as profoundly different, she was steeped in an orientalist understanding of the 'other' as essentially 'inferior', which led her inevitably to a negative depiction of the Islamic faith. In common with prevalent orientalist attitudes in evangelical Britain at the time of empire, Stuart understood herself to be from a race privileged due to its Christian heritage, and called to help bring others to that same faith so that their position in this world and the next would also improve.

Over the years, Stuart aired her views on Islam through various publications for CMS journals. In one article, she reflected on the role of religion in relation to the social position of Persian women. It is a stinging attack on Islam as causing 'the degradation of all we understand by the word "womanhood"'.[29] Basing her argument on two factors in particular, Stuart interpreted the problem as a product of religious rather than cultural heritage. First, she discusses the social condition of women resulting from polygamy, divorce and child-marriages, maintaining that these make 'home, as we understand it . . . an unknown quantity to the Moslems'.[30] Secondly, the scandal of women's poor social status is blamed on Islam's refusal to permit them an education, inevitably leading to ignorance, 'invariably accompanied by gross superstition'.[31] The article concludes that Islam and civilization are incompatible, and that ultimately 'one must flee before the face of the other'.[32]

Such a display of cultural and religious superiority, together with the strength of language employed to denounce Islam, are easily dismissed as typical imperialist attitudes at the turn of the century. Yet, viewed contextually, Stuart's views were based upon a genuine desire to help her Islamic 'sisters'.

Maxime Rodinson writes of the dangers inherent in 'distorted orientalism' which, rather than demonizing the East and Islam as 'other', simply does an ideological about-face and practically sanctifies them by refusing ever to be critical.[33] Given the tendency towards distorted orientalism in much of our contemporary culture, it is important to look deeper and question whether Stuart's evaluations did not have some arguable basis. Missionaries should not be regarded as entirely reliable sources for they were culturally biased, selective in the material they communicated, and motivated by a desire to Christianize. Nevertheless, they enjoyed considerable contact with all types of Persian people and their familiarity with the lives of women, in particular, made them unique amongst most Victorian westerners abroad.

While religious imperialism was certainly a factor in her writings, growing concern for the universal suffering of womankind also provided a powerful motivation. Indeed, several of the issues she wrote about (such as divorce, polygamy and child marriages) are today still part of international debates regarding the oppression of women globally. Her oversight was in succumbing to cultural naïvety, by presenting her own Christian theology, *a priori*, as the solution to the ills of Persian society, thus failing to understand that Iran's problems had other equally important non-religious explanations. The socioeconomic and cultural reasons underlying Iranian female oppression (such as expectations of their place within family or society, as well as financial and legal restraints on their rights as human beings) in fact made the problem a cross-religious phenomenon with diverse manifestations in different countries and societies. In each situation – East or West, Iran or Britain – religion could worsen women's circumstances by confining them within the parameters of particular theological and gender codes of behaviour.

There is, of course, considerable irony in Stuart's inability to comprehend the complexities underlying the subject so important to her. Her aspiration that Iranian women should one day enjoy 'the perfect freedom of English women'[34]rings somewhat hollow, when at the same time, she and her female colleagues were struggling for basic voting rights on the Persia Mission Conference.[35]

Nevertheless, her advocacy for the improvement of women's plight is, for two reasons in particular, worth considering within the historical development of feminism. First, by arguing that a nation could make no real progress until it allowed women a rightful place, Stuart was encouraging Persian women, whom she regarded as '*full* of possibilities', to achieve their potential in the quest for a better life.[36] Having attained for herself considerable freedom from the gendered constraints of Victorian Britain, Emmeline was eager for all women to enjoy the rights that were theirs by virtue of being human. Similarly, by defining a nation's progress in terms of its treatment of women, Stuart prioritizes the female condition and experience as being of paramount political and moral significance. This aspect of her rhetoric should not be interpreted as a form of cultural imperialism, but as a desire for cross-cultural co-operation and mutuality – for women to unite in their efforts towards a better future and the establishment of a universal notion of justice.

Secondly, as suggested by Sarah Potter, Stuart's critique of Iranian women can be interpreted as a condemnation not just of Persian society but of the social condition of women in England. Potter admits that criticism of eastern women's plight by missionaries who simultaneously advocated the advantages of western womanhood appears extremely hypocritical. However, she believes that missionary women developed a 'zenana ideology' to explain the degradation of oriental women specifically and then applied it to raise consciousness about the plight of women generally.[37] In other words, they were launching a double-edged offensive against male privilege in both eastern and western contexts.

Repudiation of the wrongs they witnessed abroad was far easier for missionary women to articulate than explicit criticism of their own situation. They bore no personal responsibility for it, nor did they suffer the extent of its consequences. Their apparently straightforward reproach, however, became a means by which 'evils at home [were] being attacked in the guise of evils abroad'.[38] While appearing complacent on the surface, its success as a cause for mobilizing action suggests it contained an issue with which women in Britain wanted to contend. Therefore, largely by means of this ideology, 'feminism progressed further in the missions than it did in the church at home', ultimately contributing to the overall advance of the women's movement.[39]

In this chapter I have argued that medical missions were an important component in the history of British feminist development, according new possibilities to women at the turn of the century, encouraging them to fulfil their potential while also helping prepare the ground for new innovations by later female activists. By means of religious language which stressed vocation and a maternalism extending far beyond literal motherhood, women found increasing opportunities for moving into new and unknown territories. Initially their activities were contained within the limits of a safe ideology. However, the practical reality was consistently stretched until the very ideology itself was forced to recede.

Emmeline Stuart, as a doctor and a woman, played a significant part within this wider picture. She was undoubtedly hampered by the strictures of Victorian discourse and her shortfalls characterize her as a woman of her time shaped by the tenets of empire. The opportunities her position accorded her were often countered by efforts to contain her within acceptable ideological bounds. Therefore, her activities were mostly carried out within the context of Victorian gender norms, based on the feminized Christian ideal of service. However, from a historical perspective she may be regarded as a subversive presence, abiding by the rules where necessary, while all the time pushing at the boundaries, creating more space for the amelioration of missionary women's future. Her contributions clearly highlight significant advances in developing opportunities for British women, justifying the contention that the efforts of CMS women in Iran represented an influential strand within the historical development of feminism.

Notes

1   This chapter is a modified version of one section from Gulnar Francis-Dehqani 'Religious Feminism in an Age of Empire, CMS Women Missionaries in Iran, 1869–1934', PhD Thesis, University of Bristol, (1999), pp. 180–218; also published under the same title by CCSRG, University of Bristol (2000).
2   Further biographical details concerning Emmeline Stuart are provided later in this chapter. For greater detail see also, Gulnar Francis-Dehqani, op. cit. (2000), pp. 148ff.
3   The word Persia is linguistically related to Fars, a region in the south-east of Iran, whose language – Persian – is dominant. In the Persian language, the country has always been known as Iran – derived from the ancient Persian meaning 'land of the Aryans' and signifying the early migrations of the Indo-Aryan people to the region. However, outside its boarders it was commonly known as Persia until, in 1935, Reza Shah ordered that the rest of the world should use the name Iran also. During Stuart's time Persia was used to describe the country, however, throughout this chapter the terms Iran and Persia, Iranian and Persian, will be used interchangeably.
4   Writing as late as 1970, Max Warren commented on the long-term survival of Victorian influences, and questioned 'whether we are not still in many respects Victorians?' See his 'The Church Militant Abroad: Victorian Missionaries' in Anthony Symondson (ed.), *The Victorian Crisis of Faith* (London: SPCK), p. 58.
5   Protestant and Reformed missions had from the earliest days been pioneers in the field of education. Locals frequently sought after western education

and missionaries were always keen for an opportunity to deliver it. For the centrality of the bible in these particular Christian traditions meant literacy was essential for would-be converts. As a result, church and school often stood alongside each other on the mission compound as a visible symbol of the missionary aim.

6   Martyn Clarke (1905), in Fitzgerald, 'A "Peculiar and Exceptional Measure": The Call for Women Medical Missionaries for India in the Later Nineteenth Century', in Robert Bickers and Rosemary Seton (eds), *Missionary Encounters: Sources and Issues*. (Surrey: Curzon Press, 1996), p. 174. Throughout this section I have drawn extensively on Fitzgerald's chapter written with specific relevance to India.

7   In Iran alone, during the latter part of the nineteenth century, there are many letters in the CMS archives in which general appeals for medical missionaries are interspersed with specific calls for female doctors. See, for example, G2/PE/O 1890: 134 and Tisdall – G2/PE/O 1893: 75.

8   See also Sarah Potter (1974), 'The Social Origins and Recruitment of English Protestant Missionaries in the Nineteenth Century', PhD thesis, University of London, p. 220.

9   Ruth Rouse, 'The Ideal of Womanhood as a Factor in Missionary Work', *International Review of Missions*, 2: 5 (January, 1913), pp. 148–64.

10   Ibid., p. 153.

11   Ibid.

12   In Iran alone, of the 78 single women missionaries sent out by CMS between 1891–1934, sixteen were doctors. For further details see, Francis-Dehqani, op. cit. (2000), Appendices IV–VII, pp. 225–34.

13   Sara Tucker 'Opportunities for Women: The Development of Professional Women's Medicine in Canton, China, 1879–1901', *Women's Studies International Forum*, vol. 13, no. 4, (1990), p. 357.

14   Report of the Ecumenical Conference on Foreign Missions, 1900, quoted in Fitzgerald, op. cit., p. 176.

15   See Gordon Hewitt, *The Problem of Success: A History of the Church Missionary Society, 1910–1942* (London: CMS, 1971), p. 388.

16   The Anglican Church in Iran, which began as a result of the work of CMS in that country, has always been small numerically and remains so today. For more information on the Persian church see Robin Waterfield, *Christians in Persia* (London: George, Allen and Unwin, 1973), p. 147 ff.; Gordon Hewitt op. cit., pp 375–402; and Hassan Dehqani-Tafti *The Hard Awakening*, (London: Triangle, SPCK, 1981).

17   Students and the Missionary Problem. Addresses Delivered at the International Student Missionary Conference, London (1900). London: SVMU, p 512.

18   Ibid., p. 513.

19   Emmeline Stuart, Annual Letters (1898), p 21.

20   Ibid.

21   Blackett – G2/PE/O 1899: 3.

22 Helen Callaway, *Gender, Culture and Empire* (Urbana, IL: University of Illinois Press, 1987), p. 98.

23 For more details about the work of Mary Bird in Iran see Francis-Dehqani, op. cit., pp. 84–113.

24 Several administrative and hierarchical levels operated within CMS. Some of these were based locally through committees and individuals working on the mission stations abroad. However, ultimate authority over major decisions and the way in which work was carried out lay with the Parent Committee, based at CMS head-quarters in London. For more details regarding CMS decision making bodies and the effect of these structures upon women see Francis-Dehqani, op. cit., pp 49–51, 163–8.

25 G2/PE/O 1899: 107.

26 G2/PE/O 1906: 77.

27 Andrew Walls, *The Missionary Movement in Christian History: Studies in the Transmission of Faith*, (Edinburgh: T and T Clark, 1996), p. 219.

28 For more information on the gradual democratization of the Church of England during the late-nineteenth and early-twentieth centuries see, Brian Heeney, 'The Beginnings of Church Feminism: Women and the Councils of the Church of England 1897–1919', *The Journal of Ecclesiastical History*, vol. 33, no.1 (January 1982), pp. 89–109; and also Brian Heeney, *The Women's Movement in the Church of England 1850–1930*, (Oxford: Clarendon Press, 1988).

29 'The Social Condition of Women in Muslim Lands', *Church Missionary Review* (1909), August, p. 458.

30 Ibid., p. 459.

31 Ibid., p. 462.

32 Ibid., p. 463.

33 Maxime Rodinson, *Europe and the Mystique of Islam* (Seattle and London: University of Washington Press, 1991), pp. 78, 106, 127.

34 Stuart, op. cit., p. 463.

35 For details of women's struggle for voting rights in the Persia Mission, see Francis-Dehqani, op. cit., pp. 209–15.

36 Stuart, op. cit., pp. 463–4.

37 Potter, op. cit., p. 226.

38 Ibid.

39 Ibid.

.

12
Opportunities for Baptist Women and the 'Problem' of the Baptist Zenana Mission, 1867–1913

Laura Lauer

In 1896, 30 years after the publication of Marianne Lewis's influential call to action – *A Plea for Zenanas* – the Baptist Zenana Mission (BZM) was operating in 25 mission stations, had 52 missionaries *in situ*, employed 200 Bible-women and school teachers, ran 80 schools catering for 3000 children, reached 400 villages on its itinerating tours, and regularly visited 1200 zenanas. Its disposable income was just over £11,500.[1] Perhaps in comparison to larger societies – or even its brother society, the Baptist Missionary Society (BMS) – the totals are not particularly impressive. Certainly complaints were heard that the BZM's presence in India was small in comparison with that of the BMS. Isabel Angus, the BZM's 'Indian' Secretary, in urging the BZM to itinerate more often, pointed out that although there were three BZM stations where there were no BMS workers, there were 20 BMS stations without the benefit of the BZM.[2] While supporters of the BZM prayed for more candidates, money, and 'openings' for their work and were impatient to expand its scope, it is also true that the BZM and organizations like it were a comparatively new but nonetheless important development in British foreign missions. The second half of the nineteenth century had witnessed the emergence of missionary careers for women in a way that had not been envisaged, indeed could not have been contemplated, when the BMS was formed in 1792. The nineteenth century witnessed, if not a sea-change in attitudes towards women's abilities, then an unprecedented willingness to employ single women abroad as agents in a 'woman to woman' mission.

However, the place and significance of the Baptist Zenana Mission as a part of nineteenth-century Baptist life has been questioned by two eminent Baptist historians. John Briggs, author of *The English Baptists of the Nineteenth Century*, claims that the BZM was a relatively unimportant organization which did little to advance the cause of women within the denomination. Brian Stanley, the historian of the Baptist Missionary Society, argues that the existence of the BZM actually restricted opportunities for women in the denomination. At the heart of their analysis is a conviction that the BZM's independence and woman-centred rhetoric limited its appeal and effectiveness. This chapter argues that Baptists in general were unwilling to recognize women's authority in church matters. In the face of limited roles for women in the denomination, zenana missionaries were able to carve out a space for themselves and their work in India and to achieve a measure of independence largely denied to Baptist women in their home churches and could hence be considered a significant force for women's authority within the denomination. This independence was fostered by the conditions present in Indian society and by contemporary understanding of women's influence. Like male missionaries, the workers of the BZM grappled with the issues of culture, caste and conversion, but their answers to these problems reflected the separatist nature of their mission and the languages of domesticity available to them. Separation is the key theme of this chapter: the BZM remained a separate organization from the BMS until 1913 (despite attempts by the BMS to bring the BZM under its control), Baptists continued to subscribe to a notion of women's separate and special abilities, and the BZM's most powerful argument for its own existence was the separation of the zenana, which missionaries argued robbed women of their most basic rights and condemned them to a life of ignorance and folly. Domestic conditions in India, and missionary understanding of those conditions, opened a space around which Baptist women could organize and claim a level of expertise. This in turn allowed for a separate women's organization to flourish within the Baptist polity, an organization which relied on a separatist rhetoric for its survival; a rhetoric grounded in a particular understanding of the needs of Indian society.

The many ministries of Baptist women have received scant historical attention. Indeed, Baptists seem to have lagged somewhat behind other denominations in their construction of organizations and opportunities for women – it was only in 1890 that the London Baptist Association opened a small deaconess home; a project taken over by the Baptist Union in 1919. A national organization of local women's guilds, the Baptist Women's League, was formed in 1908.[3] For the most part, Baptist women worked very much within their own churches, in relatively small-scale activities about which historians know very little owing to the paucity of local studies. But a national organization that could claim denominational attention was lacking.

The accepted outline of the 'feminine dimension in Baptist life', as John Briggs puts it, is that following their involvement in the radical sects, there was a marked decrease in women's preaching and participation in church government in the eighteenth century; instead, women worked in education (small, private ventures or as teachers in Sunday schools) or as hymn-writers as proper outlets for their spirituality.[4] Briggs argues that the formation of an organization like the Zenana Mission and other developments in women's work for the church 'did not explicitly challenge either the social convention that respectable women played no public role in mixed society, or Christian teaching that women should be silent in the church'.[5] Instead, he argues, the engine for change in the nineteenth century was the second evangelical awakening of the 1860s and the crop of articulate women preachers attached to it, women like Phoebe Palmer and Catherine Booth. Such a development sent eminent Baptists, Joseph Angus, President of Regent's Park College, and William Landels, pastor of Regent's Park chapel, back to their bibles for a re-examination of the scriptural precepts surrounding women's preaching.

Angus, in his *Christian Churches* (1862), argued that deacons could be of either sex and that the bible did allow a public ministry for women.[6] Landels eventually came to the conclusion that the biblical office of deaconess could be seen as analogous to women's ministry in the nineteenth century.[7] But what sort of work was permissible? Here it is helpful to distinguish between the terms 'deacon' and 'deaconess'. A deaconess was simply a worker (sometimes paid) for the church, with no voting privileges. Deacons assisted a minister in governing the congregation. The scholarship of Angus and Landels may have reminded Baptists that the deaconess had a respectable biblical pedigree, but did not guarantee her acceptance. In the case of the local community (and we have to remember here that in Baptist churches, it is the local congregations not the central body that is powerful), there appears to have been widespread unwillingness to regard the work of women in the church as anything other than auxiliary.[8]

In their study of middle-class piety and society, Davidoff and Hall have shown how women came to be excluded from matters of church government as women's piety came to be more narrowly defined. Among Baptists, the numbers of women deacons plummeted in the early nineteenth century.[9] In the government of the chapel, in which all were held to be spiritual equals, women were excluded from voting. There is some evidence to suggest that women deacons, who vanished from Baptist chapels in the early nineteenth-century, had begun to reappear by the end of the century, although numbers were still very small.[10] In the church studied by Clyde Binfield, Queen's Road, Coventry, women deacons had been mooted since the 1880s. In 1917, it was seriously suggested that women be appointed to the chapel diaconate; none were.[11] Briggs suggests that the 'size of the church fellowship and the availability of men to hold office' influenced whether or not a congregation might have women deacons.[12] Certainly the large London church of Bloomsbury refused to admit women to its eldership.[13] While the second evangelical awakening may have proved that capable women preachers did exist, it did not open positions of chapel authority to ordinary Baptist women.

If positions of authority were lacking within the churches, and it seems clear that they were, the missionary field seemed destined to overturn the *status quo* as the urgency of the missionary cause was widely publicized. Among Baptists, interest in the women of India was fostered by the publication of *A Plea for Zenanas* (1866). Its author, Marianne Lewis, was acquainted with other early efforts to evangelize the women of India.[14] She and another missionary's wife, Elizabeth Sale, had attempted a similar work in the areas surrounding their husbands' mission stations. What Marianne Lewis proposed in her pamphlet (and zealously promoted during her furlough in England) was that Baptists should emulate societies already at work and employ 'ladies' full time to visit, educate, and evangelize the women of India's zenanas. Traditionally, high-caste Hindu and Muslim women occupied a 'women's' part of the house (the zenana), with multiple restrictions and customs dictating movement outside of it. Even among lower castes, the desire to project a genteel exterior led to women being kept out of sight whenever possible. The Baptist Missionary Society (and later the BZM) operated primarily in north and north-eastern areas of the Indian subcontinent (the present-day states of Bengal, Bihar, Uttar Pradesh, Rajasthan, Punjab) where the zenana tradition was still strong.[15] As a result of Mrs Lewis's campaign, a committee of women, many of whom were related to men active in the BMS, resolved to form itself into the 'Ladies Association for the Support of Zenana Work and Bible Women in India, in Connection with the Baptist Missionary Society'. From its formation in 1867 until 1920, the BZM sent about 200 women to India and just under 50 women to China.

The BZM came into being to fulfil *one* purpose – to convert the women of India to Christianity. Later, China would be added as another field of endeavour but the overriding intention, whatever the mission 'field', was the evangelization of 'native' women by Christian workers. Initially, this goal was pursued through zenana visiting, that is, paying repeated calls on individual women or small groups of women within their own homes. Schools soon followed, although the visitation of zenanas continued to be an important part of the mission (as illustrated by the 1896 figure of 1200 zenanas visited) and it remained the privilege of the BZM agent. Certainly zenana missionaries were expected to be the cream of the candidates offering for service. When Gertrude Fletcher offered her services to the BMS in 1882, one of her referees wrote:

> In Miss Fletcher you have an exceptionally fine girl – and you will not misunderstand me when I say that she is too good for Africa. . . . here you have a girl of accomplishments that would give her a position anywhere and if I understood Mr Thomson you wanted someone to teach a few children the rudiments of education. Such a one can be more easily found than one capable of doing higher work. I know that Africa needs *our best men* but I am not quite informed enough to decide about the wisdom of putting our best women to teach a few children the alphabet. I am decidedly of opinion that Miss Fletcher ought to go to India.[16]

Here was recognition that the Indian field, with its cloistered women, required the best the Baptist Union could offer.

The Baptist Zenana Mission, from its inception, constructed itself as a unique organization fitted to meet a unique need. In order to properly understand the way that the BZ validated missionary careers for women, it is necessary to examine the way the society viewed its clientele – the unevangelized women of India. If there had been no special need that only women could fill, the mission probably would never have been formed as existing missionary provisions would be deemed to be sufficient; the General Committee of the BMS was averse to sending single women as missionaries.[17] Conditions in India proved conducive to a woman-only mission, with the seclusion of the zenana, rather than the complexity of the caste system, heading the list of women's disabilities for the job.

From the earliest accounts, missionaries remarked on the absence of women from public gatherings and in 'social life' in general. Marianne Lewis reported in her *Plea* that it was the height of bad manners to even ask a prominent Hindu about his wife, let alone invite her to tea at the mission compound. Practically invisible and inaccessible to BMS missionaries, Indian women entered mission accounts as victims of suttee (the immolation of a widow on her husband's funeral pyre), child marriage (with betrothals occurring in infancy and girls leaving their natal home before puberty), and the 'general prejudice' against widows.[18]

Metaphorically, these disabilities were represented by the physical space of the zenana, seen by women missionaries as a travesty of a wholesome domestic environment. Any visit by a missionary to a zenana inevitably included a description of the room itself: the women 'inmates' clustered together, sometimes playing with trinkets; the dirt, despite the fine clothes and jewels worn by the women; the cramped nature of the women's apartments, often in sharp contrast to the size of the house; and most importantly the lack of light which was due to small, high windows to prevent the women being viewed by men other than their male relatives. Here were women literally and figuratively in darkness. The darkness of Indian women's souls was manifested by the darkness of their surroundings and in their mental lassitude. The opposite of this 'heathen darkness' was Christian 'light' or 'brightness', which would allow women to fully develop as religious and social beings. In a meeting held in support of zenana missions in the Welsh Baptist Union:

> Mrs. Charles Rees, of Abercarn, the minister's wife, presided, and in a brief but able address struck a fitting keynote to the proceedings when she spoke of the chief characteristics of the Christian

religion as being the gift to womanhood of the power of self-discovery and of the development of capabilities and powers hitherto unsuspected.[19]

By missionary standards, women in zenanas were being kept from self-discovery and were squandering their considerable powers, bringing their society down instead of raising it.

Zenana missionaries measured the achievements of the other societies in terms of the status of women. Christian societies headed the list, as Christianity was seen to be the guarantor of women's privileged position. Mrs Scott, touring Baptist stations in India was aghast:

> I was prepared for the utterly insignificant position of women from a social point of view; but, in spite of my previous knowledge, I was profoundly impressed by their absolute nonentity in religion. . . . At home in Protestant Britain, and still more in all Roman Catholic countries, we are accustomed to see women taking even more than their share in the public services of religion. . . . it means that, by both these systems [Hinduism and Islam], woman is denied an equal standing before God.[20]

In characterizing Indian society as unjust in its organization (and thus unfair in its treatment of women), the BZM was operating within an accepted imperial stereotype in which the Oriental Other was seen as materially different from and in opposition to the English norm. Sometimes this otherness was expressed as an essential femininity of Oriental cultures. The Rev. James Smith of Delhi wrote:

> Mohammed, in making polygamy, female degradation, and domestic slavery vital parts of his religious, social, and political creed, more than counteracted the good effects of the one truth that lay at the foundation of all his early successes. Nay, more, he thus planted the seeds of destruction in the wonderful system he inaugurated. Mohammedism must eventually succumb to the luxurious and enervating influence of the Zenana. So long as the people have to fight for their position, the effects are modified; but no sooner are they thrown on their own resources for existence and pleasure than they become absorbed in the luxuries of the harem; the deterioration of bravery and administrative power

rapidly follows, and the end is a second childhood, rendering them an easy prey to every enemy.[21]

A warning, should it need to be repeated, of the dangers of women's influence going awry.

Yet it was not only the physical and cultural separation of women which prompted BZM attention. Over the years, the Zenana mission honed a rhetoric not only of separation but of the centrality of women to Indian culture, and, thus, to the success of any movement to convert the nation to Christianity. They defined non-Christian women as the problem, and then presented themselves as the solution. In so doing, they drew on ideas of sisterhood, the rich high Victorian tradition of 'woman's mission' and placed it within an imperial context.

In the seminal *A Plea for Zenanas*, Mrs Lewis warned:

> Neglected and despised as women have been in India, and still are, yet there, as everywhere else they exert a powerful influence; and the writer has ceased to wonder at the insurmountable barriers they have too often opposed to the reception of Christianity, as she has witnessed the fond affection subsisting [sic] between the Hindoo mother and her sons.[22]

This fascinating portrait which she draws of Indian women, as both central to and downtrodden by a non-Christian society, contrasting power and powerlessness, became the hallmark of BZM thinking on the subject. Women – of whatever caste – were the fountain of all civilized society, and if India was to be made Christian, women had to receive the benefits of Christianity for one crucial reason – a Christian woman equalled a Christian home, which would then result in the conversion of a woman's husband and children.[23] The Zenana mission concentrated on women as mothers and homemakers, an occupation which they assumed transcended caste divisions. This heavily domesticated construction could have far-reaching and even unforeseen effects. Jane Haggis has shown that, for the workers of the London Missionary Society at Travancore, South India, the process of making good mothers of Indian women actually gave some measure of power to the Bible-women employed by the mission, blurring the distinction between the category of 'mother' and that of 'worker'.[24]

The BZM operated within a similar mental world, casting Indian women as pitiable, but mouldable into Christian motherhood. They appropriated the languages of domesticity and family responsibility and mixed it with discourses about the privileged status of Christian women to create a powerful argument for a legitimate, separate, womanly vocation within the Baptist denomination.

However, this rhetoric did not extend to its non-western workers; the BZM was always careful to claim for its own missionaries 'expert' status; in its printed accounts, Bible-women are allocated the role of loyal assistant, grateful for conversion, but the junior partner in evangelization. BZM discourse remained firmly centred on the agency of the English missionary and her dealings with recalcitrant zenana pupils or curious villagers. This focus on women and on women's agency is in contrast to the policy of the BMS in, say, China, where senior missionary Timothy Richard set out to convert imperial administrators and intellectuals who could institute change from above. Of course, by positing the family, and thus women, as the central unit of society and vehicle for social renewal, the Zenana mission made few waves in the consciousness of the denomination. John Tosh has labelled the period from the 1830s to the 1880s the 'heyday of moral motherhood', one in which women's influence over children's moral and emotional development was at its height.[25] Baptist ministers had already heavily theorized women's influence over children and cast her as the preserver of the moral tone of the home so it was no great ideological leap for them to apply a separate spheres doctrine to other cultures. The Rev. E. Medley gives a good indication of the ways in which zenana ideology harmonized with the denomination's view of women as a whole. He told the 1892 Zenana Breakfast Meeting:

> The supreme place which woman holds in the economy of this world is hers of divine right, and whilst men in their blind selfishness may seek to alter all that and take the diadem from her brow, they cannot wholly depose her. Still, a women's hand is on the springs of a nation's life, and to seek her elevation and redemption is to move along lines indicated . . . by God.[26]

These arguments proved powerful within the denomination because they echoed Baptist and indeed Christian norms on the role of women. The conditions of India were presented as standing in stark opposition to English norms and morees, hence the urgent need for the reform of the zenanas. Even after the BZM branched out into founding schools and open-air itinerating tours, the 'prison' of the zenana came to signify the perceived plight of Indian women in general – illiterate, with limited horizons, and cut off from the inheritance Christianity promised to women.[27]

What emerges from examining BZM narratives about zenana women is that it is narrative with an explicit purpose. Mary Kingsley voiced her distrust of missionary literature on the grounds that it was all calculated to raise funds.[28] Historians cannot rely on BZM narratives to present anything other than facets of India which were favourable to their position. Indeed, we might expect this; Mary Kingsley was correct – mission literature was important for fundraising purposes and to keep up the morale of the workers at home. But there were deeper implications. For fund-raising efforts to be successful, missionaries had to tap a common set of ideas about 'natives' and 'the Empire', concepts which they were also shaping. Members of the BZM appealed to their denomination and to the wider missionary world in terms of shared reference with regard to India.[29] In claiming the women of India as their special prerogative, zenana missionaries accepted the reality of British rule in India and, indeed, inequalities between men and women in Britain in return for the privilege of service and sacrifice; for instance, BZM publications are silent on the continued existence of the Communicable Diseases Acts in British cantonments.[30] By emphasizing the 'prison' of the zenana and the liberating power of Christian mother- and wifehood, BZM missionaries discursively imprisoned themselves and became effectively unable to criticize gender inequalities in British society.[31] Their optimism of the elevating influence of British and Christian rule on the peoples of India was part of a wider view of the benefit of empire, shared by contemporary feminists and colonial administrators.[32] But it was also a view which when coupled with the BZM's formula for social change – the Christian wife and mother – made any kind of identification with feminist politics impossible. Did such a view hamper women's opportunities within the wider Baptist denomination, as has been suggested by Briggs and Stanley?

As a mission by women to women, the BZM was a product of contemporary notions of women's nature, which placed her expertise in the realm of the sympathetic or emotional. The Zenana mission's appeal for the 'raising of womanhood' was also couched in biblical terms which were very much in line with thinking about 'woman's mission' and theological justifications of the nature of women. The bible abounded with examples of women whose tenderness, sympathy and sacrifice could be held up as examples – Dorcas, the women of Samaria, and Mary, mother of Jesus. Zenana missionaries strengthened their case based on the physical separation of women with the ideological buttress of a distinct women's nature which only other women could fully understand.[33] Mrs Coleman, President of the Nottingham Auxiliary of the BZM, stated it plainly, 'no woman can pass heedlessly by any individual *sister*-woman in sorrow or distress when it is in her power to render aid'.[34] In the case of the BZM, the sisterly aid rendered was to give Indian women knowledge of God, the bible and their souls.

Not only was it alien to a women's nature to refuse assistance to her heathen sisters, it was manifestly her Christian duty to see that all women received the benefit of Christianity. As 'LMR' wrote:

> It is impossible to educate the men in the highest sense, nor to raise the moral and social standard effectually, while women are debarred from sharing equal advantages. As soon as Indian women are trained and fitted to take their proper position in domestic and social life, we cannot doubt that a mighty change will take place.[35]

The mighty change was to liberate Indian women with the knowledge of their own salvation and spiritual equality, knowledge missionaries argued was denied them by Hinduism and Islam. At the turn of the twentieth century, this belief still had strong roots. When sending a donation to the BZM, the girls of a Yorkshire Sunday school wrote,

> You see that we, being young women living in this Christian country, enjoy many more privileges and freedom than our sisters in India; and we shall feel thankful if our 'little effort' [the proceeds of a concert totalling £13 10s.] can be so used by our Heavenly Father as to be the means of helping to lead to Christ some of those sisters who are bound by the fetters of Hindooism.[36]

Having constructed an image of their 'Indian Sisters'[37] as ignorant, superstitious and downtrodden, the BZM then proposed the remedy for the ills of 'heathen' society – Christianity – and the agents for its improvement – women missionaries, their fortunate western sisters. The Zenana mission, when giving thanks for their status as Christian women, also laid claim to pursue the evangelization of their less-favoured, although influential, sisters. Isabel Angus proclaimed that BZM missionaries were 'free to serve' – constrained by Christian freedom to render Christian service. Seen in the context of feminist imperial thought, itself influenced by evangelical values, Baptist women could be seen to be staking a claim to denominational citizenship by asserting their duty to evangelize non-Christian women.[38] This claim was based on conventional ideologies of women's nature and behaviour and of sisterly sympathy. By employing these discourses, members of the BZM constructed a space within the Baptist denomination in which women were the key actors in the conversion of Indian women and an important factor in throwing down the Christian gauntlet to Indian cultural practices while at the same time acting as the guardians of Christian family values.

Just what were the missionaries attempting to convert the women of India to? Christianity, certainly. But there was also a sense, already alluded to, that it was a purified home life that would give evidence of true conversion and would set Indian society on the road to advancement. Bertha Thorn, reflecting on the work in Delhi, commented, 'Every girl is not capable of receiving a high education, but if she has a deep and true sense of her duty as a Christian wife and mother she is a shining light that none can disregard'.[39] At the BZM's flagship school, Entally, it was noted that 'if our girls at Entally turn out undomesticated and "above their station" it cannot be the fault of their education, which seems based first of all on "the ministry of women"'.[40] Isabel Angus, reporting on the state of the BZM's schools, reminded her readers of the importance of educating women to Christian principles: 'to watch the raw material put into these schools and the product of a few years' training is to realize the debt which the Christian community owes them in the elevation and education of the whole mass'.[41] It seems more than ironic that the task of schooling Indian women to the role of Christian wife and mother fell upon the shoulders of women both unmarried and childless, but it illustrates the pervasiveness of the concept and its extraordinary cultural power.

The BZM, as a highly publicized vehicle for women's work within the denomination, has been criticized by Baptist historians for failing to enlarge opportunities for women within the denomination as a whole.[42] Both Brian Stanley and John Briggs have argued that the employment of single women as missionaries by the BZM ultimately circumscribed the contribution other single women could make to the wider missionary effort of the BMS.[43] Yet Stanley also admits that the General Committee of the BMS was unwilling to sponsor the work of single women. Of the two sent to the Cameroons in 1879–80, both were admitted on the strength of their family connections. One was the daughter of BMS missionary, Alfred Saker, and the other the elder sister of the three Comber brothers serving with the Mission.[44] Baptist Zenana missionaries, in claiming independence from the BMS, were able to pursue their work from 'woman to woman' without the direct superintendence of male missionaries. The few women sent out by the BMS found their authority circumscribed by male station superintendents and committees. Could such a state of affairs be the fault of the woman-to-woman mission ethos of the BZM?

Such a judgement seems unduly harsh, considering the attention Baptists as a whole paid to sex-specific authority and service. I have argued that individual Baptist congregations were unwilling to recognize women's ministerial abilities, despite the fact that two eminent Baptist ministers offered biblical justification for their ministry. Across the denomination, women's call to service was steered into 'appropriate' activities. That work for the BZM was accepted as appropriate is a testament to the power both of the imperial ideal in English culture and to the strength of the BZM's separatist rhetoric. The success of women preachers during the revival of the 1860s seems to have made little difference in terms of denominational opportunities for women. In this context, the BZM served as a positive force, giving women who felt a spiritual vocation the opportunity to live it out, while still remaining within their denomination. Stanley and Briggs seem to be arguing that the BZM was the originator of Baptist ideas of separate women's service, consigning women to 'women only' ventures. Such a process predated the foundation of the BZM by at least half a century, when women began to find the diaconate barred to them. The BZM was important in opening a new outlet for Baptist women, as well as for claiming public space and time and money for women's work but it used, rather than created, separatist discourses.

English women, allowed access to the zenana due to their sex, became key providers of information and interpretation about Indian culture, making them a crucial part of the colonial process of subjugation and subjectification.[45] It also gave them the status of workers with specific and valuable knowledge about the Indian family and Indian social customs, knowledge which the home churches rewarded by inviting missionaries to speak at chapel meetings and by holding readings of their letters home.[46] The four elements most used when describing women living in a zenana characterized them as: mysterious and exotic (with inevitable erotic overtones), filthy and ignorant (the conflation of 'darkness' and dirt), degraded and downtrodden by Indian society, or central to the spiritual and moral life of the nation.[47] Invariably, some combination of the four was utilized by women, whether travel writers, memsahibs, or missionary agents. As seen above, the BZM defined its field of work in terms of the ignorance of zenana 'inmates' (who lacked basic literacy to read the Scriptures), the degraded social state of women (their seclusion was termed a 'prison'), and their centrality to the 'soul of India' (which required a home-life transformed by Christianity).

Such an understanding of India's culture and of the elements which required changing permitted the existence of an independent self-governing women's missionary organization which selected, trained, and financed its own missionaries. The condition of the women of India, whose voices are largely silenced in BZM narratives, provided an unparalleled opportunity for Baptist women to enter into high-status evangelistic work, work which despite the second evangelical awakening was denied them in Baptist churches in England. In bringing light into the zenana, BZM missionaries may have actually forced the home churches to reconsider what their women were capable of, rather than limiting women's involvement.

Notes

1 *Missionary Herald*, 1 May 1896, pp. 296–7.
2 *The Herald*, March 1914, p. 32.
3 J.H.Y. Briggs, *The English Baptists of the Nineteenth Century*
4 John Briggs, 'She-Preachers, Widows, and Other Women. The Feminine Dimension in Baptist Life since 1600', *Baptist Quarterly*, XXXI (7), July 1986, pp. 337–352. His section on 'Women' in *English Baptists of the*

Nineteenth Century is substantially the same as this brief article, showing how little work has been done on the subject.

5 John Briggs, 'She-Preachers, Widows and Other Women', op. cit., p. 344.

6 Ibid., p. 345. Angus based his analysis on 1 Corinthians 11:5, read with Acts 2:17 and 21:9; the verses from Corinthians relate to the covering of heads, while those from Acts are about the pouring out of the Spirit and the prophecy of Philip's daughters.

7 Olive Anderson, 'Women Preachers in Mid-Victorian Britain: Some Reflexions on Feminism, Popular Religion and Social Change', *Historical Journal* XII (3), 1969, p. 481.

8 Some twenty years after her own ordination, Violet Hedger, the first women to study for the ministry at Regent's Park College, reflected on the lack of both local and institutional support in the Baptist community. V. Hedger, 'Some Experiences of a Woman Minister', *Baptist Quarterly*, X (1940–1), p. 250.

9 Davidoff and Hall, *Family Fortunes* (London: Hutchinson, 1987), p. 137.

10 Ibid.; J.H.Y. Briggs, *English Baptists*, op. cit., pp. 286–7.

11 Clyde Binfield, *Pastors and People: the Biography of a Baptist Church, Queen's Road, Coventry*, (Coventry: Queen's Road Baptist Church, 1984), p. 165.

12 Briggs, *English Baptists*, op. cit., p. 287.

13 Ibid.

14 Brian Stanley, *The History of the Baptist Missionary Society 1792–1992*, (Edinburgh: T and T Clark, 1992), p. 229.

15 Janaki Nair, 'Uncovering the Zenana: Visions of Indian Womanhood in Englishwomen's Writings, 1813–1940', *Journal of Women's History*, vol. 2, no. 1 (Spring 1990), p. 11.

16 Angus Library, Regent's Park College, CP/008, Fletcher papers.

17 Stanley, op. cit., p. 232.

18 This picture, disseminated by missionaries, was influential in shaping ideas about India and Indian women. See Jennifer Morawiecki, ' "The Peculiar Mission of Christian Womanhood": the Selection and Preparation of Women Missionaries of the Church of England Zenana Missionary Society 1880–1920', Ph.D. thesis, Sussex University, 1998, Chapter 2; Leslie A. Flemming, 'A New Humanity, American Missionaries' ideal for women in North India, 1870–1930', pp. 194–5; Barbara N. Ramusack, 'Cultural Missionaries, Maternal Imperialists, Feminist Allies. British Women Activists in India, 1865–1945', both in Nupur Chaudhuri and Margaret Strobel (eds), *Western Women and Imperialism: Complicity and Resistance* (Bloomington: Indiana University Press, 1992).

19 *Baptist Zenana Mission Magazine*, September 1905, pp. 141–2.

20 *Baptist Zenana Mission Magazine*, February 1905, p. 118.

21 *Missionary Herald*, 1 October 1883, p. 343.

22 Mrs C.B. Lewis, *A Plea for Zenanas*, n.p., n.d. [1866], p. 7.

23 The Rev. Herbert Anderson labelled the home in India 'a citadel of false creeds'. *Baptist Zenana Mission Magazine*, June 1906, p. 122.

24 Jane Haggis, '"Good wives and mothers" or "dedicated workers"? Contradictions of domesticity in the "mission of sisterhood", Travancore, South India,' in Kalpana Ram and Margaret Jolly, (eds), *Maternities and Modernities: Colonial and Postcolonial Experiences in Asia and the Pacific* (Cambridge: Cambridge University Press, 1998), pp. 81–113.

25 John Tosh, 'Authority and Nurture in Middle-Class Fatherhood: the Case of Early and Mid-Victorian England,' *Gender and History*, 8 (1), 1996, pp. 48–64.

26 *Our Indian Sisters*, July 1892, p. 173.

27 Nair, op. cit., p. 11.

28 Stanley, op. cit., p.118.

29 For the centrality of Empire to 'home' culture, see Antoinette Burton, 'Rules of Thumb: British History and "imperial culture" in nineteenth- and twentieth-century Britain', *Women's History Review* 3 (4), 1994, pp. 483–500.

30 Officially repealed in India in 1888, Cantonments were exempt from Parliamentary interference, and commanding officers were left to decide.

31 Mervat Hatem, 'Through Each Other's Eyes: the Impact on the Colonial Encounter of the Images of Egyptian, Levantine-Egyptian, and European Women, 1862–1920', in Chaudhuri and Strobel, op. cit., analyses this issue in a slightly different context. See Flemming, 'A New Humanity', op. cit., p. 192; Susan Thorne, 'Missionary-Imperial Feminism', in Mary Taylor Huber and Nancy C. Lutkehaus (eds), *Gendered Missions: Women and Men in Missionary Discourse and Practice* (Ann Arbor: University of Michigan Press, 1999), p. 45.

32 Antoinette Burton, *Burdens of History*, op. cit. Morawiecki argues that the existence of Empire made the experience of British missionaries qualitatively different from that of American missionaries, Morawiecki, 'The Peculiar Mission of Christian Womenhood', p. 63.

33 Jeffrey Cox, 'Independent English Women in Delhi and Lahore, 1860–1947', in Richard T. Helmstadter and R.W. Davis, *Religion and Irreligion in Victorian Society: Essays in Honor of R.K. Webb*, (London and New York: Routledge, 1992), p. 170.

34 *Missionary Herald*, 1 April, 1897, p. 190.

35 *Missionary Herald*, 1 October, 1896. This article, 'The Work We Are Called to Do' originally appeared circa 1883–84, but the BZM reprinted it, stating its relevance to the current situation.

36 *Missionary Herald*, April 1901, p. 159.

37 Before the addition of China to the BZM's scope of activity, the society's magazine was entitled *Our Indian Sisters*.

38 Burton, *Burdens of History* op. cit.

39 *Missionary Herald*, August 1902, p. 385.

40 *Missionary Herald*, April 1913, p. 114.

41 *Missionary Herald*, December 1901, p. 580.

42 John Briggs, 'She-Preachers, Widows and Other Women', op. cit., p. 344.

43 Brian Stanley, op. cit., p. 232; John Briggs, *English Baptists of the Nineteenth Century*, op. cit., p. 283.

44 Ibid.

45 Nair, op. cit., pp. 8, 11.

46 The letters of BZM missionary Katharine Franklin were read out at Queen's Road, Coventry, cf. Binfield, op. cit., p. 147.

47 Nair, op. cit., p. 17; Marni L. Stanley, 'The Imperial Mission: Women Travellers and the Propaganda of Empire', D.Phil thesis, Oxford University, 1990; Cox, op. cit., p. 170. See also the collection of essays edited by Leslie Flemming, *Women's Work for Women: Missionaries and Social Change in Asia*, (Boulder, CO, San Francisco and London: Westview Press, 1989), pp. 38, 40, 118–121.

Index

231